The Spider Rock Treasure

A Texas Mystery of Lost Spanish Gold

Steve Wilson

EAKIN PRESS Austin, Texas

For Linda, Christopher, Kimberly, and Kathryn

FIRST EDITION

Published in the United States of America
By Eakin Press
A Division of Sunbelt Media, Inc.
P.O. Drawer 90159 Austin, Texas 78709-0159
email: sales@eakinpress.com
website: www.eakinpress.com

1 2 3 4 5 6 7 8 9
1-57168-776-9

Library of Congress Cataloging-in-Publication Data

Wilson, Steve, 1943-
The Spider Rock treasure: a Texas mystery of lost Spanish gold / Steve Wilson.– 1st ed.
p. cm.
Includes bibliographical references and index.
ISBN 1-57168-776-9
1. Treasure-trove–Texas–Brazos River Valley. 2. Gold–Texas–Brazos River Valley–History. 3. Spaniards–Texas–Brazos River Valley–History. 4. Adventure and adventures–Texas–Brazos River Valley–Biography. 5. Brazos River Valley (Tex.)–Antiquities. 6. Texas, West–Antiquities. 7. Brazos River Valley (Tex.)–History. 8. Brazos River Valley (Tex.)–Biography. I. Title
F392.B842 W55 2003
976.4–dc21 2002156750

Contents

Introduction

The Spider Rock treasure is not my creation. I can take credit only for chronicling what surely must be the most bizarre quest for lost Spanish gold ever pursued. The participants are all real. The stories are their own, or are the recollections of those who knew them. The strange stone maps were all unearthed after a long entombment. A few of the curious Spanish artifacts yet survive, testimonial to the quest and to the seekers who found them. The stories and memories are very much a part of the history and lore of West Texas today.

J. Frank Dobie's classic *Coronado's Children* first put me on the trail of the Spider Rock and its enrapturing web of mystery. My own quest for that story has spanned more than four decades. The search has taken me over a wide expanse of plains, canyons, and rivers, always in search of a clue, detail, place, or name, often dim in an oldster's memory or long forgotten.

My own search began in the small West Texas town of Haskell one summer day in 1960. There I was directed to Dock Henderson, who lived nearby. It would be three years more before I met Dock, who himself had become trapped in the spider web forty years earlier. The hours have been many and memorable that we have sat smoking, sipping black coffee, reflecting on his long quest, his many years of reconstructing the original search, and his own triumphs of finding clues that others had missed. Many were the times that Dock and his gracious wife, Ethel, and I sat in the shade of a scrub cedar or mesquite to eat our lunch far back in the cedar brakes, close by the banks of the Salt Fork or Double Mountain Fork of the Brazos.

I first reported the Spider Rock story while writing a weekly series in 1963 for the *Wichita Falls Times*. Soon those stories were enlarged into magazine articles, and, as I had hoped might happen, stirred many memories of the turn-of-the-century quest for the Spider Rock, or its sister stones unearthed in the early years of the twentieth century.

My own quest has been only to attempt to unravel some of the two or three hundred-year-old Spanish mystery, to reconstruct as much as possible the dramatic quest over that ancient trail. In that pursuit, perhaps I have left more questions unanswered than I have answered. But after all, this is a chronicle about treasure that has eluded seekers for more than a century, treasure that has defied twentieth-century knowledge. The final chapter cannot be written until that ancient treasure is found, until its mystery is unraveled, until the Spider Rock reveals its cunning story.

I thank all those whose stories fill these pages (and many more whose names are not here), who gladly shared with me their memories of Dave Arnold and his search, or the stories of those who followed in his footsteps. Of course, without the painstaking and detailed reconstructions by Verne Sems and Dock Henderson over many years, none of this story would have been possible. Duane Hale, who freely shared his knowledge and whose company made the research trail memorable and rewarding, found Charles Terrell, who in turn provided historical perspective on much of the story, filling many gaps in the part his father and brother played.

Dr. Duane Hale, who began his thesis thirty years ago on much of this subject, continues his work to record and preserve both the lore and history of the Big Country. Abilene Christian University librarian Allen J. McDaniel Jr., a keen observer, has steeped himself in possible scientific explanations of this West Texas enigma. Johnny Terrell, who inherited the mysterious third stone map, has ensured that it will be preserved for all to enjoy. Each has assisted in many ways.

Mary Speakman helped with her genealogical expertise. Vance Tiede is responsible for obtaining Dr. E. Michael Gerli's translation of the sheepherder's letter. Dr. Gerli pinpointed the dialect of the Spanish-Portuguese wording. Dr. Clevy L. Strout provided yet another interesting translation of the document. Military historians Gillett Griswold and Dale Durham were eager to help. Raymond Watkins kindly provided the location maps.

Staff of various archives and libraries assisted with research, including the Federal Archives and Records Center, Fort Worth; Fort Worth Public Library; University of Texas at Arlington Library; Brownwood Public Library; Texas State Library, Austin; Center for American History, University of Texas, Austin; Hardin-Simmons University Library, Abilene; Abilene Public Library; Centennial Memorial Library, Eastland; and the Hamilton County Genealogy Society Library and Research Center, Hamilton.

Finally, none of this would have been possible without the understanding and assistance of my wife, Linda, who on more than one occasion worked beside me, researching or copying, in various courthouses, archives, and libraries.

1

The Mysterious Dave Arnold and His Sheepskin Map

A portly stranger clad in overalls and work boots and riding an iron-gray horse appeared in the sleepy West Texas town of Haskell one spring day in 1902. He came with a purpose and story so incredible that when he disappeared little more than a decade later, the mystery would entrance and enrapture all those with whom he had shared his secrets. That enigma, as captivating today as it was almost a century ago, has caused men to murder for its secrets, to abandon family and job alike in pursuit of its clues, and has left an ancient Spanish puzzle over a wide expanse of the West Texas landscape that defies the imagination and determination of everyone who seeks to unravel it.

The sod-street village of Haskell would never be quite the same after the stranger's arrival. In his late fifties and heavy-set, he sported a full head of sandy blond hair, had a ruddy complexion, was clean shaven, and stood perhaps five feet seven in his work boots. He was almost never seen wearing anything other than overalls. He carried saddlebags with a few personal effects and a large sheepskin map that never left his sight. Some years earlier he had lived in Mexico. His name was David M. Arnold, and his piercing blue eyes would be felt by all who came to know him.

Dave Arnold tied his mount outside the Terrell drug store at the southwest corner of the public square across from the Haskell County Courthouse. Somehow he had learned that the proprietor, forty-seven-year-old Dr. Caleb Lafon Terrell, druggist, jeweler, and optician, had some years before come by information that Arnold now sought. Dr. Terrell's son, nineteen-year-old Caleb Frederick, "Cabe," assisted his father as watchmaker, jeweler, and optician. Arnold's appearance that day would alter the course of each of their lives.

The strange meeting between Arnold and the Terrells, and many more that followed, were always had in secrecy, so much so that even seventy-five years later no member of the Terrell family could recall more than a few details about Arnold and his complete disappearance seven years later. But everything about Arnold reeked of mystery. He must have had his own reasons for his secrecy and for revealing so little about himself.

Those who knew him remember that he almost never spoke of his past or his personal

Dr. Caleb Lafon Terrell in 1896. (Courtesy Louise Terrell)

life. He had lived part of his life in Mexico, although his home in 1902 was a farm near San Angelo. He once spoke of being in the Confederacy and may have been involved in mining. He often amused children with his ventriloquism. He did not smoke, drink, or curse. He was soft-spoken and slow to anger. He has been described by one who knew him as both "secretive and a gentleman at all times."[1]

In 1905 Arnold would tell the family he was living with that he was seventy-two years old. If he kept to that story, he must have told the Terrells he was sixty-nine; however, the federal census of 1900 had him at fifty-five. He had come from Water Valley, where his wife owned a 320-acre farm on the North Concho River about twenty miles northwest of San Angelo in Tom Green County.

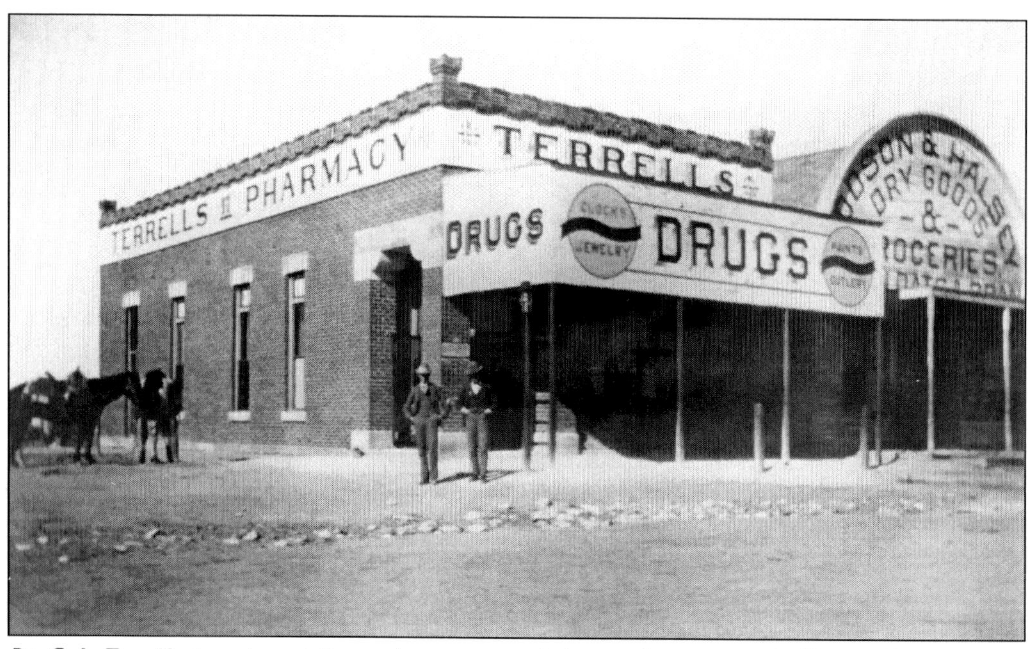

Dr. C. L. Terrell's drug store at the southwest corner of the courthouse square in Haskell, Texas, as it appeared near the turn of the century. (Courtesy Louise Terrell)

Interior view of the Terrell drug store, perhaps in early 1909. Dr. C. L. Terrell stands at center with his daughter Frankie and son Cabe. (Courtesy Louise Terrell)

While Arnold spoke little about his family or personal life, the 1900 census and various legal records reveal many facts. He was born in Missouri in July 1845. He married his wife, Martha, who was four years younger, in 1866, when she was sixteen. At the turn of the century they had been married thirty-four years. Of their five children, three were living, two at home. His oldest daughter, Mary Maude, married on January 14, 1900; another daughter, Minnie Lee, married when twenty-seven on June 1, 1902. Arnold's son, Nathan, was twenty-four that year.[2]

For his occupation, Arnold was listed as a day laborer. No one knows when he moved to Texas, but in 1897 he was living near Evant in southwestern Hamilton County in the central part of the state. In September of that year his wife, Martha, purchased the 320-acre farm near Water Valley from Martin S. and Ella Davis, longtime Texas residents who farmed land on the Lampasas River near Evant. Martha Arnold paid $2,500 for the tract of land on the North Concho River, known as Survey No. 271 in District No. 11, patented to William Lane on October 11, 1855. The Davises witnessed the sale at Evant on September 2.[3]

While living in Mexico, Arnold came into possession of his sheepskin map, perhaps as much as three feet long, laden with an enigmatic network of drawings and symbols unlike anything he had ever seen. It was a veritable waybill to an ancient treasure of the Spanish conquistadors, he was sure. That sheepskin had now brought him to Haskell and into the lives of the Terrell family.

No one knew with certainty just how Arnold came to procure the map he guarded so dearly. Several stories have been told to explain how he gained its possession. Which one may be true, if any, cannot now be determined, and Arnold himself may have told conflicting accounts depending on who was listening. One version is that he befriended an elderly brother and sister in Mexico. Somehow their home caught on fire, and Arnold saved the map without telling its owners. Another story says he killed the owner of the map, an old man with a pegleg.

Arnold once revealed that all he knew about the sheepskin—and how to interpret its cryptic symbols and numbers—was passed on to him by the former custodian. Few men ever glimpsed the sheepskin, with its curious and faint markings. One who did, however, and who perhaps knew the map as well as Arnold, was Dr. Terrell; it was Terrell's knowledge that caused the two men's paths to cross. It may be assumed that Arnold had good reason to enlist the aid of the doctor, but no one alive today knows just what his knowledge was. A tale handed down in the family might provide the key, however.

The incident occurred sometime before the turn of the century, when the Terrells still lived in Fort Worth. Dr. Terrell did not normally make house calls or practice medicine as a profession, but when someone came to him for treatment, he did not turn them away.

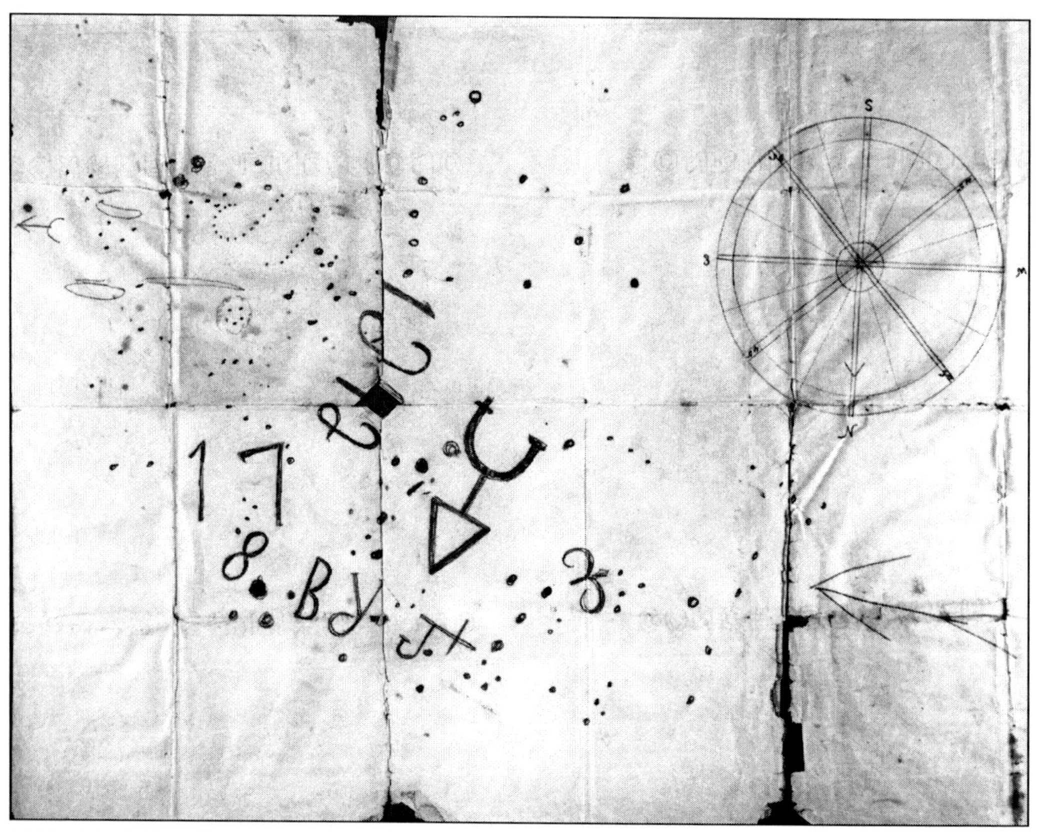

While living in Fort Worth, sometime prior to 1897, Dr. Terrell was given a map to lost Spanish treasure in gratitude for medical services. This may be a copy of that map, said to be dated December 12, 1783. (Courtesy Charles Terrell)

Once, a very ill Mexican came to him for medical attention. He was unable to pay for the services, but out of gratitude for the doctor's kindness, he handed him a map and a strange story of lost treasure. The doctor may not have thought much of the tale or map then, but in 1900, when his son Cabe was seventeen and recovering from scarlet fever, the doctor passed the map on to him.[4]

While the story the Mexican shared with Dr. Terrell has not been preserved, it is known that in the doctor's possession was a strange chart with cryptic letters and symbols. In one corner appeared a drawing, looking much like a mariner's compass, indicating directions by degrees. With the map was a letter written by Miguel Anhubta of Taos, New Mexico, to M. Dillon of Fort Worth on March 7, 1897. Anhubta explained how to interpret the map and arrive at the date December 12, 1783. He wrote:

"The arrow is pointing to the place where the money is buried. Number 17-8-3 means the year when the money was buried. Number 12-12 means the day and the month. B. Y. N. means the three corners of the survey and the J means the north corner. This] means a rock foundation in the same shape. The five dots mean five rocks put in the same shape around the foundation. Three dots means the ground. Put your needle where the arrow is and see how far it runs. Then measure from corner to corner of the survey. In the center is the place to look."[5]

Dr. Terrell was born in Paducah, Kentucky, in 1856, and grew up in Grayson County, Texas. By the age of twenty-three—in 1879—he operated his own drug store in Ranger in Eastland County. Three years later he married nineteen-year-old Frances Caroline Lutterloh, and their first-born the next year was Cabe. By 1888 the Terrells were living in Fort Worth.[6] On November 1, 1898, Dr. Terrell opened his drug store in Haskell. For years his advertisements graced the front page of the *Haskell Free Press*.[7]

Somehow Dave Arnold learned about Dr. Terrell's map. It may be coincidental that the topography now interesting Arnold lay a mere twenty miles to the west in the rugged cedar brakes near the boundary of Haskell and Stonewall counties. How much of a search Dr. Terrell had made prior to Arnold's arrival is not known. But that it began in earnest in 1902 was firmly imprinted in the mind of Charles E. Terrell, the doctor's second-oldest son, who was seven that year.

Two landmarks most interested Arnold: Kiowa Peak, a lone butte that could be seen for miles from every direction, and two rivers, one from the east and one from the west, that converged to form one running north. Those landforms, Arnold assured Dr. Terrell, would lead to a lost Spanish treasure beyond their wildest dreams. Arnold's own information may well have corroborated the Mexican's story and the chart given the doctor some years before in Fort Worth. It was only natural that they would join forces now.

The key to the mystery lay not in a document scrawled with ink, Arnold told Terrell, but in a curious stone etched with a map and the prescribed directions for anyone who could interpret it. That stone, that map, hidden for perhaps two centuries, was what Arnold now sought.

Arnold was careful not to reveal too much of his secret to any one person, never telling more than was absolutely necessary at that moment. The story of his search can be told today only by piecing together the many fragments of his quest, fragments left along a trail often ridden with seemingly insurmountable obstacles.

At first, and perhaps over many months, Arnold appears to have worked alone, traveling from ranch to ranch, landmark to landmark. He pursued many strange markings

Taos N. M.,
March 7th 1897

Mr. M. Dillon
Ft. Worth, Texas

My. Dear friend yours of the 28th of
Last Month is received I could not answer the Same
when received because I was sick in bed. I had been
sick in bed for the last twelve days. I am getting better
these is the first day I been out of the bed but I think
I will be out the house in a few days. I caught a-
bad cold. but I feel better every day: since last friday.
about the Man I could not see him he is out in the
Amizette mining Camp. but you can go. ahead
and work. on that place inclosed find a slip of-
paper with directions how to work. these Hidden Treasures, and you can write me the results of what you
done. I could not write you a long letter because I am
awfull. Weak but I hope you will be Satisfied with
what I write you this time I aint heard from Don Cesario
for a long time five feet snow between here and his place
I remain as ever your friend Miguel Anhubta

Above and next page: Miguel Anhubta of Taos, New Mexico, wrote this letter March 7, 1897, explaining how to interpret the cryptic symbols of the map he believed was dated on the twelfth day of the twelfth month of 1783. (Courtesy Charles Terrell)

carved on trees and stones, and some of the aura that surrounded him may have been due in part to others already on that trail. Just what Arnold sought was often confused and misleading, no doubt purposefully so, as evidenced by the stories told about him in later years and often even different versions by the participants. But many seemed sure of one thing: Arnold's sheepskin map called for chests of church plate, ingots, and candlesticks of gold, statuettes of silver, even pearl and diamond necklaces—all treasure of long-forgotten Spanish conquistadors.[8] Arnold is said to have referred to the sheepskin map as "the Circle of Fortune" and the chart carved into stone that he now sought as "the Wheel of Fortune."

Arnold was concerned with where and how the treasure was buried, more than with who buried it, or when or why. His own story about *who* is sketchy at best and leaves much

The arrow >→ is pointing to the place where
the Money is Burried.
No. 17-8-3. Means the year when the Money was
burried.
No 13 - 12 Means the day and the month
B.Y.N. Means the three Corners of the Survey and
there C Means the north Corner.
this] Means a rock. foundation in the Same shape
when you found there faundation you be sure to get
there Money.
there :·: five dots Means five rocks put on the
Same shape around the foundation this ·: three dots
Means the ground.
now put your needle where the arrow is and
see how far it runs then Measure from Corner
to Corner of the Survey and put a pin in the
Center of the four Corners of the Survey and
in the Center is the place to look. for this Money.
this Man say if he go there he can find it in
8 days. but I don't Know When I can see him
but I will do my best to see him soon.
Miguel Archuleta

to conjecture. This much, however, is known: Where the Double Mountain and Salt forks of the Brazos River meet—that natural landmark in an otherwise vast, uncharted wilderness of few landmarks and countless canyons—the Spaniards found deposits of much-needed copper and lead. Both minerals are as much in evidence today as they were in Spanish colonial times. Copper, and especially lead, meant life or death to the frontiersman, and to Spanish armies, it was essential. Copper was necessary for making vessels and for hammering into various ornaments. Lead was requisite for molding balls and shot for muskets and other weaponry.

Wherever there were mines and the crude smelters that were necessary to refine the ore into bullion, there were also stories of enough gold and silver, jewels and ornaments, to warrant leaving a trail of clues and coded marks that were often visible, but just as often had to be exhumed before a seeker was put back on that trail.

It soon became evident from Arnold's disclosure that had the Spanish conquistador Francisco Vásquez de Coronado found the fabled Seven Cities of Cibola and decided to hide the treasure until it could be safely transported home, he probably would have not gone to as much trouble to conceal it, then lay down a network of clues to relocate it, as did the Spaniards who left their mark where the Salt Fork and Double Mountain Fork merge to form Los Brazos de Dios—the Arms of God.

The fact that the Spaniards and even the French sought both gold and silver in this region in the seventeenth and eighteenth centuries is not disputed, and those who mined here scrawled their records not on parchment, but instead carved them into stone. The stone that Arnold now sought at the direction of his guarded sheepskin map was a curious, even mystical carving soon to become known as the Spider Rock. This was Arnold's Wheel of Fortune.

How long the Spaniards mined these copper canyons, where even today one can find fist-sized nuggets, or even complete logs metamorphosed into the bluish-green mineral, no one can say. But the evidence that they were here is yet plain to the careful eye, for the primitive smelter sites remain, and the ash, charcoal, and slag heavy in the mineral crudely smelted in those foundries can yet be found.

It is not so strange that the Spaniards sent out prospecting expeditions into this region at an early date, for legends of Spanish mines began circulating by the early 1800s. Those legends soon attracted parties of Spaniards, French, and finally, Anglo-American adventurers. The legends of Los Brazos de Dios tell not only of copper mines, but inexhaustible mines of gold and silver, a mountain of iron, and platinum. The Spanish *entradas* into the West Texas hinterlands were both early and late in Spain's New World glory.

Perhaps the first Spaniards in this region were Fray Juan de Salas and Fray Diego López. In the summer of 1629 they left Santa Fe to labor among the native Texas tribes. Many believe the priests' base of operations was the Middle Concho River near present San Angelo. It is known that Fray Salas returned to West Texas in 1632 with Fray Juan de Ortega to establish a mission among the Indians, the site of which is unknown today.[9]

In 1650 Captains don Diego del Castillo and Hernán Martín left Santa Fe to explore the land to the southeast for gold and silver. Their route is unknown, but in one of the streams, perhaps the Concho River, the Spaniards discovered freshwater pearls. After a six-month expedition, they returned to Santa Fe and presented the pearls to the Spanish governor. In 1654 still another expedition was launched by don Diego de Guadalajara. He collected more of the freshwater pearls and captured Indian prisoners along the way.[10]

Both Spanish and French records hint at the early mining activity. As early as 1725, the French were so intrigued by circulating stories of a Spanish silver mine in northern Texas that they mounted an expedition of five hundred men. From Natchitoches, Louisiana, they explored the North Texas region some ninety leagues beyond the Trinity River before turning back without finding the silver mine, reported to them by a Spanish deserter.[11]

While employed by the Spaniards, French explorer Athanase de Mézières visited the Wichita Indians on Red River in 1772. That site was a fortified village complete with moat when Colonel Diego Parrilla's Spanish army of five hundred men was defeated there in 1759.[12] Near present-day Spanish Fort, de Mézières reported the talk of the day when he noted that about forty leagues to the southwest (just over a hundred miles) were "red ochre beds, which persons versed in mining suppose to be deposits of greatest richness."[13]

Two years later, in February of 1774, a mysterious expedition left San Antonio for Red River in quest of "a rich mine" in that region. The sizable force consisted of thirty men, the report noted: twenty Spanish soldiers, seven civilians, and three Frenchmen. No record has yet been found describing the result of that search.[14]

The story of the "rich mine" continued to interest travelers to the Red River villages. While visiting the Wichita Indians in 1781, French trader Juan Baptista Bousquet was told about a silver deposit and managed to retrieve specimens that later assayed favorable. When Bousquet returned to the northern villages on a peace mission for the Spaniards in 1784, he let it be known he was interested in obtaining more of the silver ore. No one knows the outcome of that assay or its impact on other expeditions into the Texas interior.[15]

When Bousquet returned to San Antonio in February of 1785, two Frenchmen and a Spaniard who had been living at the Red River villages accompanied him back to the Spanish capital. The Frenchmen were Pedro Vial and Alfonso Rey, traders who had lived for some time among the Wichitas. The Spaniard was Antonio Mariano Valdés, who had lived with the Indians for eight years when he returned to his native San Antonio.[16]

Most important to the Spaniards was the intrepid Pedro Vial, a man of mystery who had lived among the Wichitas for six years. A skilled armorer, gunsmith, locksmith, silversmith, and blacksmith, his knowledge of Indians and the uncharted Texas interior made him valuable to the Spaniards for the next quarter-century. He was to blaze new trails between the Spanish capitals and keep journals of those explorations.[17]

From San Antonio northward to the Wichita villages on Red River, then westward to Santa Fe, Vial and a single companion blazed a trail in 1786–87 of eleven hundred miles. A year later, Vial and Francisco Xavier Fragoso explored another route eastward from Santa Fe, traveling down Red River to the Wichita villages, thence southeastward to Natchitoches, Louisiana. Vial covered nine hundred miles of uncharted wilderness between the distant provinces of New Mexico and Louisiana. In November 1788 the cavaliers returned to San Antonio, where they would rest before continuing on to Santa Fe.[18] During that interim, Vial became acquainted with another Frenchman, himself outfitting a prospecting expedition. Vial's services as guide and interpreter would be enlisted for that journey.

Hiring Vial was Alexander Dupont, adventurer, explorer, and mine hunter on the Texas and Louisiana frontier in the late eighteenth century. When he enlisted the aid of Vial, Dupont had lived in Texas for ten years. He managed to keep journals of some of his explorations into the interior. The journals were once discovered, then apparently lost or stolen from the archives in Mexico City.[19]

Dupont had combined prospecting and trading with the Indians and made himself knowledgeable about a great expanse of uncharted region. In what may have been the Ouachita Mountains west of the Little Missouri River near the present Oklahoma-Arkansas border, Dupont claimed to have discovered rich mineral veins. By the spring of 1788, he was seeking the silver mines worked intermittently by Spanish miners near the San Sabá presidio, a stone fortification abandoned by the Spaniards twenty years earlier near present-day Menard.[20]

When Dupont sought Vial's guidance into the *Comanchería* and Red River country, it can be assumed that Vial or other traders had told Dupont stories of the silver to be found in that region. The Frenchmen left San Antonio on February 5, 1789, accompanied by a dozen helpers and four Comanches. They reached the Wichita villages on Red River, or the Rio de Natchitoches, as they knew it, by April 20 and remained three days before heading southwestward. They later camped somewhere on Los Brazos de Dios.[21] If Dupont observed the deposits of copper and lead in this region, where already legends of rich mines hovered, there is no record of it.

It is known that Dupont returned to the abandoned Los Almagres mines near the confluence of Honey Creek and the Llano River, seventy-five miles east of the San Sabá presidio, and obtained ore samples for testing. In July, after more than a five-month prospecting excursion, Dupont and Vial returned to San Antonio with several pack mules bearing ore specimens. Less than a year later, Dupont sought permission to work the mines he had previously discovered in the Ouachita Mountains, but he was unsuccessful in that attempt, or so the records say. Interestingly, as late as February 1802, Dupont was seeking official approval to examine mines in the "Taovayas Mountains."[22] Might those discoveries have resulted from his and Vial's trip of thirteen years before, or subsequent investigation of the persistent stories of silver to be found?

The last Spanish *entrada* mounted through West Texas was a large expeditionary force led by sixty-nine-year-old Captain Francisco Amangual. Two hundred men with eight hundred horses and pack mules and cart train left San Antonio on March 30, 1808, to explore a route to Santa Fe while seeking water holes and spreading goodwill among the Indians along the way.[23]

Captain Amangual's sprawling force reached the stone ruins of the old Spanish fort of San Sabá by April 11. Once the largest garrisoned outpost in Texas, the presidio was abandoned by the Spaniards in 1768, or forty years before. It is difficult to follow Amangual's exact route, although he was heading north-northwest across West Texas. In May his force crossed both the Double Mountain and Salt forks of the Brazos in Stonewall or perhaps Kent County.

Several days' journey northward in rough country, perhaps between what is now Dickens and Quitaque, they traveled westward up a large canyon. Amangual wrote in his journal that the canyon was as wide "as an eighteen-pound shot range."[24] On a mesa to the west they found a spring of water and a cave large enough "that twelve men could stand in the entrance." It narrowed as it led inward, and on its walls were Indian pictographs.

Three Spanish explorers, Captain don José Agabo de Ayala, don Gregorio Amador, adjutant, and the chaplain, whose name was not given, carved their names on the cavern wall, then rejoined their squadron. If the Spaniards dated that carving, it would have been May 20, 1808. Amangual's army reached Santa Fe on June 19, after traveling 368 leagues, or about 957 miles.[25]

It is well known that copper deposits on the Brazos River became known to early Texas colonists. One such mine was located on the Stephen F. Austin map of 1836 at "the thirty-third parallel between the upper Cross Timbers and the ninety-ninth meridian."[26] The mine may have been in Young County, although the map showed it to be about forty miles south of Red River in Wilbarger County.

Early Texas surveyor Jacob Snively made one of the most interesting discoveries of a long-abandoned Spanish mine, smelter, and stone ruins. His discovery is more intriguing because of the man himself—and the fact that this site, too, is lost today. Snively's discovery also corroborates the early attempts by the Spaniards to mine precious metals on the upper Brazos and Leon rivers.

Jake Snively, also Colonel Snively, a rank duly won in the Army of the Texas Republic after a mere eighteen months, served as a staff officer for Presidents Houston and Lamar. Snively is perhaps best remembered in Texas history for having led a bold but unsuccessful raid on a rich Mexican packtrain crossing northern Texas from St. Louis to Santa Fe in 1843. After failing in that expedition in what is now Kansas (because of the intervention of U.S. Dragoons), Snively returned to his previous profession of surveyor.[27]

Surveyors were often explorers. Sometime in late 1843, Snively made an expedition up the Leon River, northwestward from the last Texas settlements in Milam County. Before his discovery was given widespread coverage in newspapers, Snively wrote his friend Dr. James H. Starr in Nacogdoches, revealing his excitement over that western journey. Writing from Milam County on February 19, 1844, Snively revealed that he and a mineralogist had found silver ore that appeared to be rich. In addition, he said, "We have found some of the old works where the Spaniards have been smelting."[28]

Clarksville's *Northern Standard* reprinted a story from the *Houston Telegraph and Texas Register,* reporting the discovery in its May 1, 1844, edition:

> Colonel Snively has lately returned to Milam County after a successful tour in search of a silver mine. He received information from one of the Mexicans captured by him near Santa Fe last summer, that a silver mine remarkable rich and productive was formerly worked by the Spaniards near the sources of the Leona, a tributary of Indian or Little River, which empties into the Brazos near Nashville. Immediately after his return from Santa Fe he went with a small party and after a very tedious and protracted search, found the mine in the bed of the stream. He found near it an old furnace, the remains of several crucibles and a number of crowbars, pick axes, etc., all nearly consumed with rust. The ore is of a dark grey color and resembles some varieties of iron ore. The vein is several feet in diameter and extends two or three rods along the bed of the stream. It is completely covered by the stream when it is swelled by the rains.
>
> The country around this mine is broken by remarkably high and steep hills, and the soil is very poor. The rocks most abundant are coarse grey lime stones and sand stones. The mine is situated about one hundred and fifty miles from Nashville and lies nearly west from that place. Colonel Snively we learn intends to engage a company of miners to reopen the mine in the course of a few months. If the description of the mine as furnished to us be correct, it must be exceedingly valuable and the ore, although yielding but a small proportion of silver, if found in such abundance, its products may rival those of several of the mines of Chihuahua.

The *Telegraph and Texas Register* of May 1 printed a follow-up to its story, placing the discovery on the Trinity. Snively's own letters, however, show that the Leon, as first reported, was the correct stream. The story also interjected more of the tradition concerning the copper mines on the upper Brazos:

> Colonel Snively has recently been on an excursion to the sources of the Trinity in search of a mine which was worked by the Spaniards many years since. It is said that he discovered the ruins of an old fort which had apparently been deserted for one or two centuries, and near the fort there were indications that a mine had formerly been worked. We doubt, however, whether any mine can be found in that section, unless it

be a lead mine. We have often wondered why the mine hunters of our frontier have never attempted to search for the copper mine on the Brazos above the Bosque.

That mine is laid down on all the old Spanish maps, and is described by old hunters who have visited it as exceedingly valuable. We believe it is more valuable than any other mine in Texas. It is situated on the East bank of the Brazos, about one hundred miles above the mouth of the Bosque River. An intelligent and respectable trader who visited it about twenty years ago, stated that there are thousands of tons of ore at this mine that can be removed with very little labor; and the ore is so rich that it will yield from seventy to eighty percent of pure copper.[29]

Snively became deputy surveyor in Milam County later in 1844. On May 20 he wrote his friend Dr. Starr: "Sometimes I work like thunder, and then again I examine the country for good land and minerals. I have two Caddo Indians with me who know the country well. They have given me information respecting the mines, formerly worked by the Mexicans. I can make surveying profitable, and if I can at the same time find the old mines, I can still make it more advantageous."[30]

Snively returned to the Leona, or present-day Leon River, prospecting for both silver and copper. It is difficult to determine just where he found the Spanish mine, smelter, and ruins of the stone houses, but the *Northern Standard* of Clarksville disclosed more of the tantalizing story on October 29, 1845:

Colonel Snively has discovered three large stone houses near the sources of the Leona in Milam County about sixty-five miles northwest of Bryant's Fort on Little River. They are situated in a beautiful and fertile valley which opens between the rugged and bleak hills that lie toward the mouth of the Leona. These houses are similar to those in Bexar and like them are built on the Moorish style of architecture with flat roofs. Their walls are still in a good state of preservation, although they appear to have stood for more than a century. They are placed in the form of a triangle. When discovered there were arrows or pointers on the roof of each house.

Colonel Snively noted the direction of these pointers and found traces of an old forge at the point where lines extending from the pointers would meet. We find no notice of these buildings on any of the old maps of Texas, but it is evident from their resemblance to the old Spanish buildings at Bexar and Goliad, that they were erected by Spaniards, and it is quite probable that they formed part of the chain of missions that extended from the Rio Grande to Nacogdoches.[31]

According to the newspaper, Snively's discovery was sixty-five miles northwest of Bryant's Fort, an early trading post established in 1840 on the north bank of Little River near the western boundary of Milam County. That distance northwest would have placed the ruins somewhere in present southeastern Hamilton County, through which the Leon River flows. It may be more than coincidental that Dave Arnold was living there in 1897.

Snively later wrote Dr. Starr that his discovery was near the headwaters of the Leon, which could place the mine even farther northwestward in present Comanche or Eastland County. Snively stated he had been elected county surveyor of Refugio County and would soon be leaving for that region. He revealed more of what he had found on the Leon in his letter of December 20, 1845:

> Now, my old friend I have a search to impart. When I was on the Leon the last time, I had an old friend with me who understands mineralogy well. He discovered considerable mineral nearly at the headwaters of the Leon, and after testing it he found it to be good copper, and very rich. We found four stone houses near the place, which had been made by the Mexicans many years since. I am satisfied there must be considerable silver in the vicinity.
>
> An Indian described the place to me precisely—and told me that he was there when the Mexicans were expelled. I am certain he was, because he gave a perfect description of the place. At the time I was there I had 14 men with me. These men suspected something of the kind. I had to deceive them and throw them off and to do so, the wild Indians assisted me. I intended to leave the same day in order to draw them from the place. The Indians appeared and gave them such a fright that no power on earth could have kept them there any longer.[32]

Although Snively apparently did not further develop his discovery, as late as December 15, 1846, he wrote Dr. Starr from Corpus Christi that the copper from their location on the Leon "will sooner or later make us a fortune."[33] Perhaps the discovery was not as rich as he thought, but if one could only find that site today! What secrets might the stone ruins have revealed of Spanish miners long forgotten? Surely, somewhere on the Leon today remains a legend of building stone that came from the ruins of ancient structures, near which was once found the residue of a smelter and tailings of a mine. Jake Snively himself went on to seek other bonanzas over much of the Southwest. He died by an Apache arrow east of Wickenburg, Arizona, in March of 1871.[34]

E. A. Reiman and his party of surveyors were working in the canyons near Medicine Mound north of the Pease River when they chanced upon an abandoned mine in 1882. Scrawled above the entrance was "Mercia Costello, San Antonio, A.D. 1847."[35] Many years after that discovery, Henry Ray of Vernon stumbled across a Spanish sword that had eroded on the bank of the Pease River. It was one of several such artifacts to come from the region.[36]

Any one of numerous Spanish expeditions may have been the miners on Los Brazos de Dios. Or, it may have been none of them. Complete journals of these expeditioners are lacking or no longer extant. There must have been many unofficial hunting parties who never recorded their stories on documents—at least not those made of parchment.

A record in stone would not disappear so easily. Such is the stone which Dave Arnold sought in early 1902. His story of the Spanish miners on the Brazos was sketchy. He did know that when the Spaniards abandoned their mines and attempted to erase the evidence of their crude furnaces—the telltale sign of mining—the master mapmakers buried key signs and coded rocks marking those sites. The largest, most beautiful, and intricate of those maps etched into stone was placed with many human bodies which would serve as permanent testimony to the vast treasure to be found nearby.

The chart made to guide the Spaniards back to the required geographic features was the sheepskin that Arnold now possessed. He said it had fallen to the custodianship of a faithful *mestizo* who had been a member of that Spanish party. The map had remained with him until he was near death, when he gave it to a member of his family "as a passport to immense wealth." The guarded sheepskin changed hands for two or three generations until Arnold fell into its possession in such a way as to arouse suspicion.[37]

Whatever means Arnold had employed, he was now the sole owner of a treasure chart that never left his sight. With the help of Dr. Terrell and the knowledge he had come into by chance, Arnold began to organize the most bizarre treasure hunt in Texas history. If he was not already aware of it, he soon discovered that his sheepskin map covered a large expanse, including both branches of the Brazos, Kiowa Peak to the northwest, and many minor topographic features. It also called for many marked rocks and trees, some of which he never could find.

There was often confusion in the search, for apparently no one other than Arnold and his closest companion, Dr. Terrell, knew just what appeared on the sheepskin, how one sign related to another, or their relationship to the forks of the river or Kiowa Peak. When signs were found, Arnold would study his map and the direction of the sign, then calculate numbers, distances, and degrees. After several months of searching, his calculations led him to the forks of the river.

Charles Terrell was a youngster of seven in 1902 when Arnold entered the lives of his family. At eighty-one, he recalled that the first time he became aware of the Spider Rock treasure was with Arnold's appearance. Charles remembers his many visits to the Terrell home and family drug store over a period of seven years. Arnold appeared to be in his fifties, rather swarthy, and had the habit of interspersing his conversation with the Spanish word *sí*.[38]

A man with a big paunch, he occasionally shared a meal at the Terrell home three blocks west of the courthouse. He never talked about himself, but always about the treasure. Many who knew him marveled at his ability at tracing the "marks" over the countryside, following the lines of signs and symbols for miles around. But his inability to completely unravel the mystery, to lift the final veil, became apparent early in his search. Hoping to solve the riddle, Arnold solicited the help of a Mexican from San Angelo named Saul Rodriguese.

Charles remembers Saul as a clean-cut fellow in his early thirties, who rode a beautiful copper-colored chestnut horse with a fine saddle. Saul remained in the search for about a year. Almost nothing is known about him, except that on October 19, 1902, Dr. Terrell wrote him this note: "Dear Sir: The Business out in the mountains, of which we talked about when you were here last, is now in good shape. When you return we will see what can be done. Hope you will be here soon."[39]

That letter was returned to its writer unclaimed. The business in the mountains must surely have referred to the quest for the now fabled Spider Rock. Although the mystery stone may have been discovered by that date, it is rather doubtful due to the strange turn of events that followed. There may have been others at that very time who were also seeking the Spider Rock, as Dr. Terrell himself may have, using the map given him in Fort Worth some years earlier.

Three letters that Dr. Terrell's son Cabe kept during his life are cryptic in content and written so that only the sender and receiver would understand the message. Appearing to relate to the treasure quest, one expresses the need of a certain individual to examine the site. All were written between November 10 and December 3, 1902, by R. H. McKee of Haskell to J. W. Matthews of Truby, Texas. The name D. M. Arnold appears on the envelope containing those letters. If either individual took more than a passing interest in the search, however, nothing further is known of it.[40]

No one today knows just when the stone around which the search was centered—the

Haskell Texas
Oct. 19-1902

Saul Rodriguese,
San Angelo, Texas.

Dear Sir:-

The Business out-
in the mountains, of which
we talked about, when You
were here last, is now
in good Shape.

When You return we
will see what can be
done.

Hope you will be
here soon.

Yours truly
C. L. Terrell
Druggist-

One of the first Mexicans to assist Dr. Terrell and Dave Arnold in their research was Saul Rodriguese of San Angelo, Texas. Dr. Terrell's letter to him of October 19, 1902, was returned unclaimed. (Courtesy Charles Terrell)

Spider Rock—was found, although it may have been early in the quest, sometime in late 1902 or early 1903. Charles recalls going with his father at that time to visit the diggings on the Salt Fork of the Brazos, a mile or so southwestward from the confluence of that stream with the Double Mountain Fork. On that early occasion, Charles and his father crossed the Salt Fork in a buckboard, and the doctor hurried the team of horses over the riverbed for fear of quicksand.

Charles remembers, too, a second Mexican who joined the search after Saul Rodriguese disappeared. No one recalls his name, but he was much older than Saul, had a peg leg, and caught rattlesnakes for their skins. Once, he made a hunting belt and bag from the skins for Cabe, Charles's older brother by twelve years, who often acted in his father's behalf. The Mexican remained three or four years before he was seen no more.

Slowly and cautiously, Arnold began forming a group of area ranchers and farmers to aid him in his quest for clues, landmarks, and strange markings carved on trees and stones, offering a percentage of the Spanish treasure when it was found. In addition to Dr. Terrell and Cabe, Arnold took into his confidence J. K. "Kelly" Johnson and his brother J. L. "John" Johnson, who owned farms just west of Munday, twenty miles or so downstream from the forks of the Brazos.[41] Then there were J. W. "Joe" Allen and his son Crawford, who at the time were among the few settlers living on the river west of Jud, just north of the forks.[42]

Also joining in was W. J. "Bud" Jones, whose family had settled on the north bank of the Salt Fork, just southwest of the confluence of the rivers, interestingly, on the opposite bank a mile or so from where most of the search would come to be concentrated. Jones's father-in-law, W. J. Carouth, would also participate, as would R. R. Davis and several others at one time or another.

Arnold often stayed with the Allens and Johnsons, using their homes as temporary field headquarters where he would remain overnight, or several nights, while seeking landmarks on some portion or tributary of the Brazos. Those relationships remained during most of his decade-long search in the West Texas brakes. Both families, along with the Terrells and others Arnold came to know, yet reminisce about the big man from Mexico who became legendary in their family history for revealing cryptic clues in a piecemeal fashion, then unearthing the evidence for all to see and ponder.

Kelly Johnson and his family purchased their West Texas farms from the railroad for $1.25 an acre in 1889. Kelly later donated land for the present Munday cemetery west of town. When Arnold appeared in 1902 seeking clues that led him to that part of Knox County twenty miles north of Haskell, Kelly was twenty-eight. His son Edwin was born a few years later. At sixty-eight, he recalled the stranger with his "plot rocks," as Arnold called them, and his many visits to the Johnson home three miles west of Munday. Many were the nights, Edwin remembers, that his father talked about "Uncle Dave," as the children knew him, and the almost fairy-tale-like search he led for lost Spanish treasure up and down the banks of the Brazos—and the tantalizing clues they found. Like so many others, Edwin laments that no one recorded those incredible events as they occurred over the years.

Joe Allen and his family settled 1,300 acres of land along the Brazos just north of the forks west of Jud. That was in 1899. Allen and his son Crawford took an interest in Arnold's search soon after his arrival, as did Allen's daughters Rhoda, Bertha, and Mattie, who all took turns cooking meals for Arnold whenever he arrived. The Allens would never forget the man from Mexico.

Above and below: The Salt Fork of the Brazos River, only a mile or so southwest of the confluence of the Double Mountain and Salt forks, where Dave Arnold, the Mexican sheepherder, and area farmers and ranchers sought the legendary Spider Rock. (Photos by the author)

Sometimes with the men he had chosen to share his secret—and sometimes alone—Arnold pursued the lost trail, following for miles at a time the strange rock piles found over the country, or the strange symbols blazed on gnarled trees or curiously cut on canyon walls. Up to this time Arnold may or may not have realized his activities had been quietly observed, especially his reconnaissance of the land where the Double Mountain and Salt forks merged.

It was here that the lone observer, a Mexican who, oddly, was herding sheep along the river, approached Arnold. It must have been as much of a surprise as it was a welcome when the Mexican offered his services. He may have fooled others in his sheepherder disguise, but it was obvious to Arnold that he knew too much about what was being sought, and too much about following the signs, to be merely a shepherd. His knowledge revealed him to be schooled in both the arts and sciences, and he possessed information that not even Arnold knew. Like Arnold, he divulged practically nothing of his past. He may or may not ever have given his name, but by some, he was remembered simply as Fernandez.[43] His association with Arnold would be a strained one.

The Mexican's knowledge proved uncanny to Arnold, who must have silently, if not openly, questioned how he came to know what he did. Fernandez revealed two points of interest that surprised Arnold. The Mexican government was aware of the treasure, for Fernandez had seen documents in the archives describing the rich mines in the West Texas hinterlands. And he knew, too, that priests in Mexico possessed the necessary information to find the treasure should others fail. How he had come by that knowledge, he did not reveal.

What they must find now, the Mexican said, drawing the letter H in such a fashion that it little resembled that letter of today, was the stone map bearing that symbol. Once that stone was located, he could lead them to the treasure, but the chart stone must first be found. With that revelation, Arnold knew he must include the Mexican in his search, for the stone he sought with the letter H in old Spanish chirography was the very stone that, up to now, Arnold had failed to find.[44]

The Mexican led Arnold to a wide-mouthed canyon running into the Salt Fork from the south. On either side of the canyon projected a small red promontory. Conspicuously, to the south and away from the canyon, as it narrowed heading southwestward, stood a lone small red hill, the natural point of an acute triangle formed by the three promontories. The two hills on the bank of the Salt Fork each overlooked a high cliff, providing superb vantage points for what appeared to be a natural river crossing into the canyon, itself sufficiently large to have once held a small settlement.

From that point the Salt Fork merges with the Double Mountain Fork perhaps two miles to the north-northeast. From atop the third hill to the south—the point of the triangle—Kiowa Peak could be viewed rising less than two hundred feet above the surrounding terrain, a few degrees west of north, about eight miles distant.

Arnold observed that the three red promontories were the highest on the riverbank, overlooking a broad, flat valley to the north and an equal distance up and down the Salt Fork. Only from atop the center hill was Kiowa Peak visible. There, the Mexican said, they would find the strange carving they now coveted, the same stone which Arnold's own sheepskin map called for.

2

The Spider Rock and Its Ingenious Clues

It has not been left to posterity just who was present that fateful day, but this much is known: toward the north end of the small hill lying between the two red promontories and some three hundred yards south of the Salt Fork, the Mexican sheepherder and those who accompanied Dave Arnold began to dig. Perhaps not more than two feet below the surface a stone was struck, and Arnold, as was his custom, knelt down to investigate. He removed the flat stone. It had been used only as a covering for what lay below.

Embedded in a layer of clay covering yet another stone were three flat objects of copper. Each had been placed in the clay with obvious precision. One copper piece was shaped like a dagger; another was a strange-looking key. The third, almost square object bore notches cut into its outer edge.[1]

Careful not to disturb the peculiar arrangement, Arnold lifted out the stone holding the clay veneer that imprisoned the three copper replicas. Those three artifacts may not have been removed with the precaution that was warranted that day, as later accounts seem to verify. Arnold or the Mexican sheepherder may have guessed at what lay below the clay holding the copper artifacts.

Delicately, Arnold peeled away the clay, revealing the surface of the underlying stone a piece at a time. Each of the workmen anxiously looked on as the weblike carving was exposed. Sixteen inches square and no more than two inches thick, the stone bore a diagram and symbols that were the meticulous work of a master mapmaker, who used sharp tools to skillfully cut a series of five concentric circles with lines radiating at varying degrees from the center.

Yes, Arnold said, this was the cryptic stone he had so long pursued, following an ancient trail all the way from Mexico. It was the Wheel of Fortune. Because of its weblike design, it would be called "the Spider Rock." Each man in the search party pondered its meaning. Its many strange symbols were unlike anything they had ever seen.

Arnold replaced the three metal pieces cut from the raw-beaten copper. Symbolic keys to following the directions of the Spider Rock, each bore an important message. Etched on the blade of the copper dagger were the numbers I8XII. The same figures were carved into the Spider Rock. The handle of the bottom side of the dagger bore a design that appeared to be a coffin.

The second copper ornament was a curiously shaped key with a backward F scratched into its surface. The third copper piece, called a leaf, proved to be the most complex. One side was rounded, while two sides were almost straight. Each of those sides had been cut with straight or rounded notches, as if some other object might fit into them in a symbolic

Sometime between 1902 and 1904 the beautifully carved Spider Rock was unearthed on the Salt Fork of the Brazos. About sixteen inches square and two inches thick, its mysterious symbols and concentric circles spawned a quest for Spanish treasure that has not ended to this day. This blueprint of the stone carving was later made. (Courtesy Dock Henderson)

puzzle. The surface of the plate bore a large square etched with single lines. Inside the square were more parallel lines separating the square into four sections, the center of which was marked with an X. The four sections were punched with a small instrument, eight times in each of three corners, nine in the fourth. Around the copper plate appeared thirteen more such punch marks.[2]

The positions of the copper replicas now imprinted in his own mind, Arnold once again removed them to study the legendary Spider Rock and its tantalizing web of con-

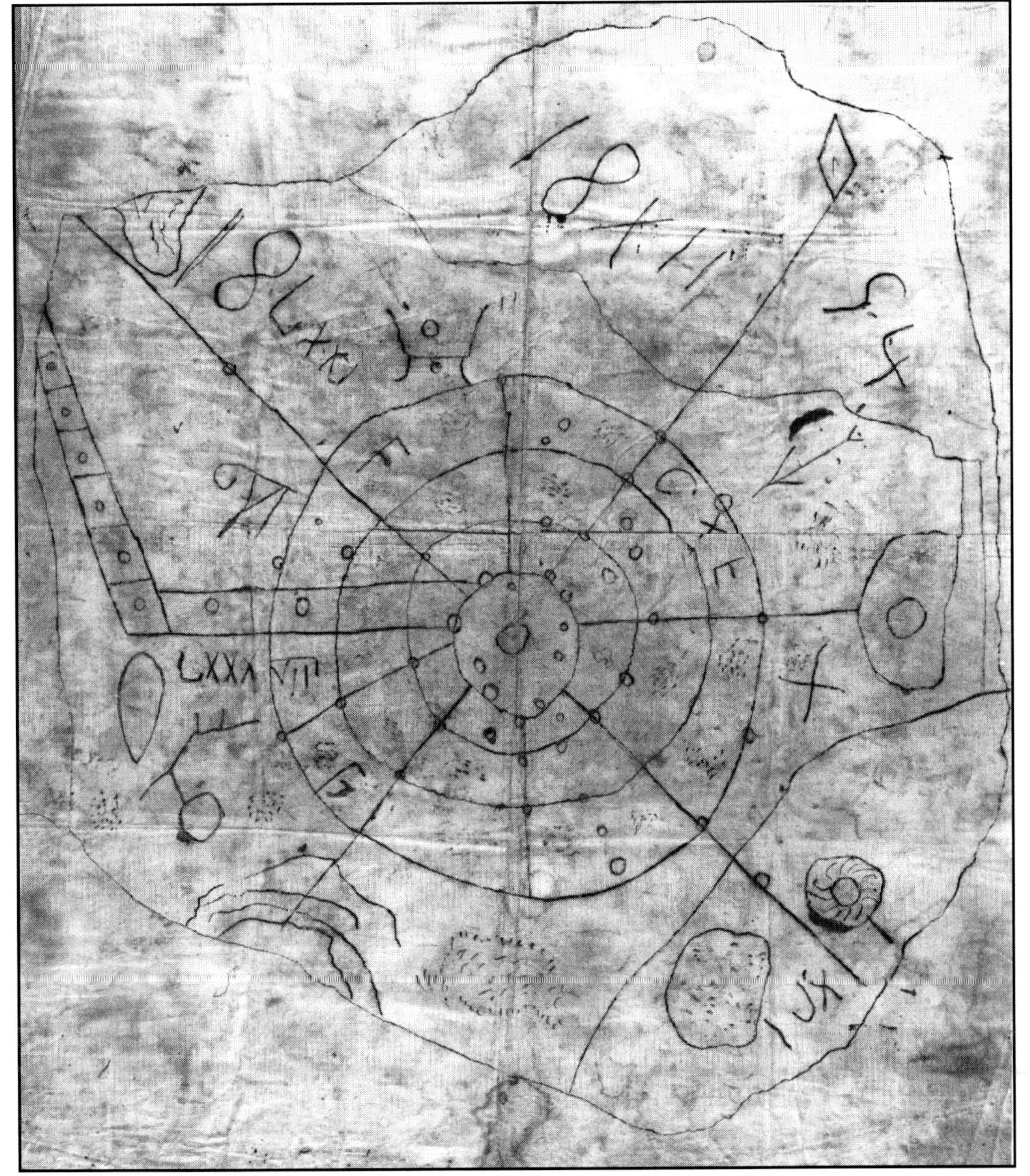

Cabe Terrell made this tracing of the Spider Rock soon after its discovery by Dave Arnold and the Mexican sheepherder. (Courtesy Charles Terrell)

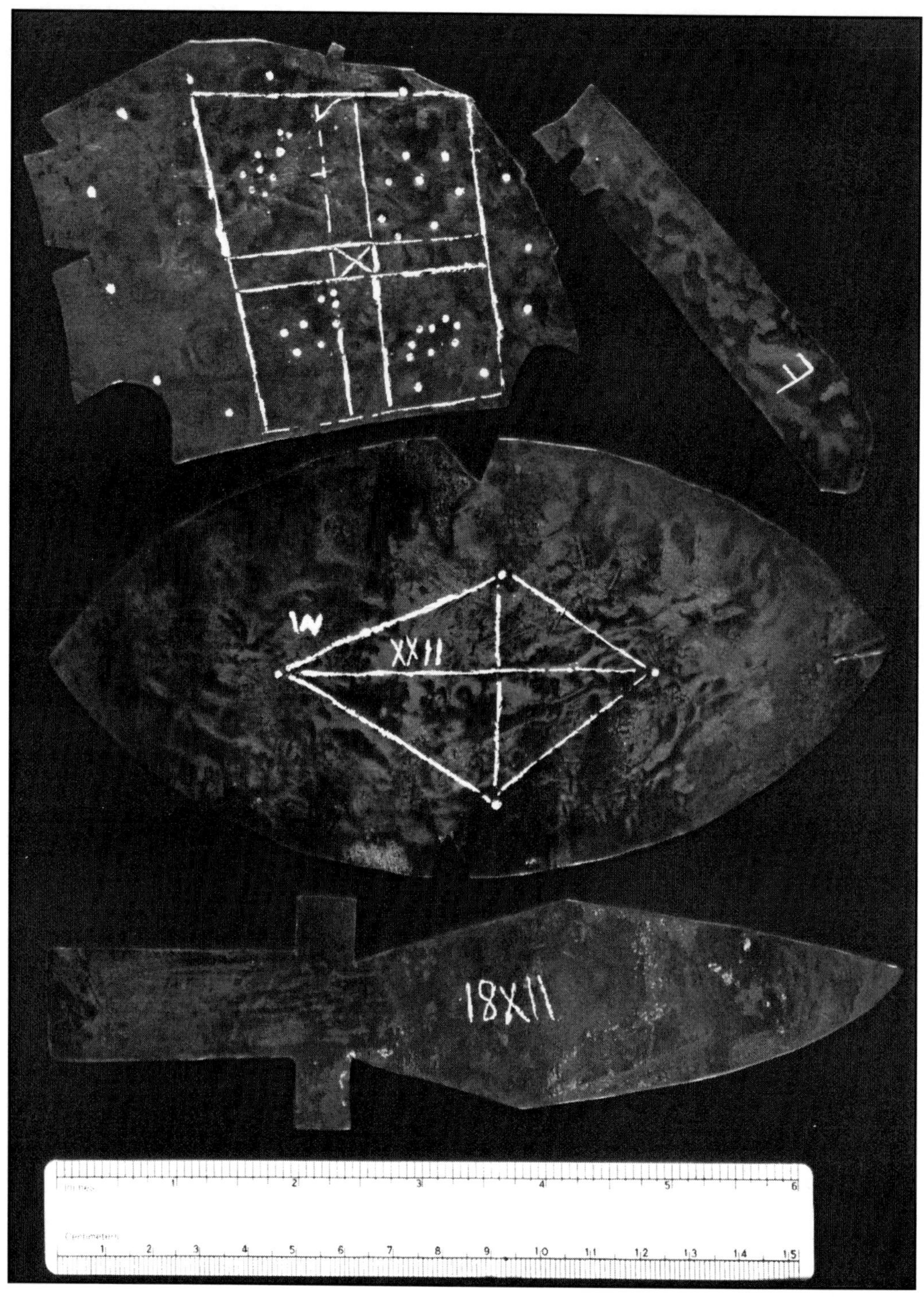

These symbolic objects of copper were embedded in clay atop the Spider Rock. The dagger and strange-looking key each bear incised symbols (outlined here in white). A third piece, with notches cut into its sides, bears punch marks and tracery. The oval-shaped copper plate, also bearing tracery, was uncovered a mile northeast. (Courtesy Charles Terrell)

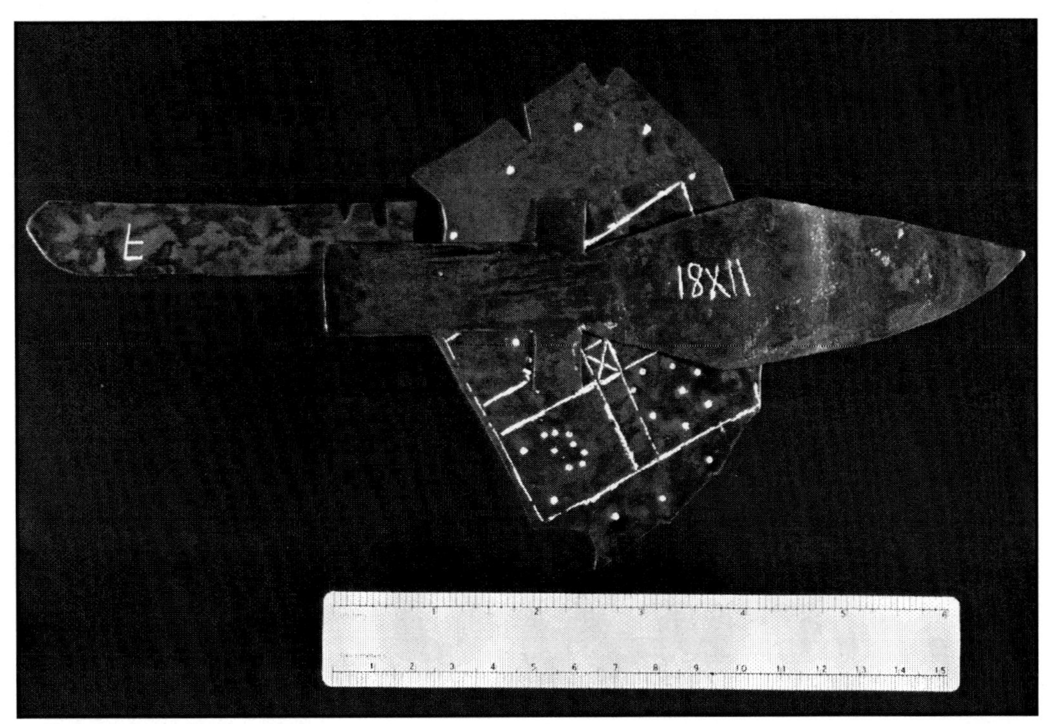

The position of the copper ornaments on the Spider Rock was believed important to following the stone's cryptic message. An old paper pattern kept by Cabe Terrell revealed this connection. (Courtesy Charles Terrell)

centric circles and array of numerals and symbols. Within the web of circles appeared many small circles. One row led down one side of the stone, then turned abruptly toward its center in an angular lane. Outside the circles appeared a mixture of Roman numerals, Arabic numbers, and curious Spanish symbols that may have been readily recognizable to the geographer, surveyor, mapmaker, or priest schooled in the sciences of the seventeenth or eighteenth centuries. And there was the letter H in old Spanish chirography, just as the Mexican sheepherder had said it would be.

None of those who witnessed the discovery of the hieroglyphic stone that day recalled either Arnold or the Mexican revealing its date of origin. Some believed the numerals I8XII indicated the year 1812, while others believed no date was given. If the date that Arnold would reveal later in his search was correct, they were the first to cast their eyes on the Spider Rock in more than 170 years—since 1731. Without realizing what may have been the archaeological discovery of the century, and fearful that his discovery might now become known, Arnold sat cross-legged on the red clay hill with the Spider Rock in his lap, studying its cryptic symbols, numbers, and directional lines. It was the most majestic, ingeniously coded document chiseled into stone that he had ever cast his eyes upon. How well he could interpret it now was as much a mystery.

To Arnold, finding the Spider Rock must have been akin to Napoleon's armies finding the ancient Rosetta Stone, the key that unlocked Egyptian mysteries. To the one who could read the Spider Rock, Arnold was just as sure would go the secrets of a forgotten time, a gilded age. A colossal Spanish trove now seemed to be within his grasp after years of following its trail. Unfortunately, archaeological discoveries were of no interest to

Arnold, and despite the fact that each of his followers witnessed that historic find, it was treasure—not ancient stone maps or symbolic copper plates—that interested them now.

Some of the intricate carving on the Spider Rock exhibited the singular craftsmanship of its Spanish engraver and mystery creator. At one side of the stone map, near an incised arrow, a hole had been gouged and plugged with a stopper rock. In the top of the stopper rock was still another depression, about the size of a cherry. The diamond-shaped figure in one corner that connected to the concentric circles by a long single groove was in fact a thin copper plate cut and fitted into the stone.[3]

Arnold or the Mexican may have offered answers for the Spanish riddle. However, if either of them knew, it is safe to assume those answers were given piecemeal at various stages, as shown in later years by varying accounts of the participants. Perhaps most puzzling of the ciphers, and the group to spawn the most speculation, was the angular lane of small circles that led down the left side of the stone about midway, then abruptly turned inward to the side of an inner circle. Each of the circles within the angular lane were depressions, or drilled holes, and each was filled with a different colored substance. One hole was filled with charcoal, one with red clay, another with yellow shale, and so on, all taken together to indicate that a tunnel must be followed through those various layers of substance.

The Mexican sheepherder had shown Arnold and his followers a tantalizing road map that was the ingenious creation of someone schooled in the ancient arts, combining cartography, mathematics, perhaps even astronomy, all symbols of his trade. Angles by degrees, distances by coded computation, landmarks by symbolic representation. All were part of that secret combination, one that Arnold was sure he possessed sufficient knowledge to break.

Not all members of the party Arnold selected were always present during the search, but during the early stages, each man spent as much time at the diggings as he could spare from his farm. It was perhaps easiest for Bud Jones to participate almost daily. He lived but a mile from the diggings, on the opposite side of the river. Joe and Crawford Allen lived a couple of miles more downstream, north of the forks. Dr. Terrell occasionally rode out to consult with Arnold, or Jones, or the Allens. Cabe Terrell assisted as he could. Brothers Kelly and John Johnson actively participated.

After the discovery of the long-sought Spider Rock, Arnold learned that the land, located about twelve miles northwest of the settlement of Rule, still remained state land upon which no one had obtained a patent, but Hoy Smith, a landowner nearby, now leased it. Arnold drew up a contract between Smith and the participants in the secretive search, and although that document does not survive, it may be assumed that each man was to share equally in the treasure they were convinced would soon be found.

As was Arnold's custom, he chose a special name for the Spider Rock diggings. It would be known as Mount Lama Vista. That name is an intriguing choice, for *lama* can mean the dust of ores in mines, or gold or silver cloth. Letters written from the diggings would bear that place-name. To conduct that search in a businesslike fashion and draw no more attention to himself than was necessary, Arnold incorporated his company of treasure seekers, calling it the Arnold Mining and Milling Company.

The sheepherder appeared less troubled at interpreting the Spider Rock than did Arnold, for he now directed that they dig still deeper on the small hill that yielded the stone. Here they should find an underlying stone the Mexican called "the base rock." Beneath the base rock would be found "a great many bodies," Indian slaves, he said, whose spirits had guarded the treasure since its interment. In excavating, he explained, they should find "a kind of wall," such as a trench filled with a hard substance. Then nineteen steps westward, the large bone of a prehistoric animal should be found.

Almost frantically, Arnold's followers dug for the base rock, soon finding the wall-like wedge of hard substance—wide at the top and narrow at the base. Then, at a depth of between fifteen and nineteen feet, their spades unleashed a stench that made it almost impossible to proceed. It was a smell unlike any ever encountered by the men. There lay the many human skeletons the Mexican sheepherder said would be found, and among the remains were many personal articles of various kinds.[4] How many skeletons were found that day, no one seemed to know, or perhaps care. It was not an archaeological excavation, and bones and simple artifacts had little significance when those things seemed to be commonplace just after the turn of the century. Such is the tragedy of haste.

Moving nineteen steps westward from the human graves as the Mexican directed, Arnold's men again resumed their digging and soon unearthed the large bone of a prehistoric animal, about the thickness of a man's body and extremely porous. To the casual observer, such a bone might appear suspect, but to Arnold's followers, who knew the West Texas canyon country, and to the inhabitants of this rugged region today, such bones are not uncommon. The bone Arnold's men found was probably the leg bone of a mammoth, or prehistoric elephant, perhaps eight or ten thousand years old. Other similar bones would later be found near the diggings.[5] That the Spaniards found them is not so strange.

At this juncture, the Mexican directed Arnold to a small bluff at the head of the canyon at the foot of the Spider Rock hill on its western side. The canyon was shallow and narrow at that point, but as it led northward toward the river, it deepened and broadened until it served as a natural crossing on the Salt Fork, overlooked on either side by the two red promontories that had first attracted the Mexican sheepherder to the site. On the east side of the canyon, just below a small pour-off, several daggers and arrows were carved into the stone ledge. On the opposite side of the pour-off, the sheepherder said, they should find another great bone like the first, and other ornaments the Spaniards had buried.

On the west side of the bluff, well hidden beneath a stone ledge, the second huge bone was found. With the prehistoric bone were the tarnished but well-preserved relics of a distant past. The first was a Spanish sword with a wide, long, curved blade and handguard or hilt that must have been a cavalryman's saber. With it were two ornate silver epaulets, each still bearing its gold tassel. Seemingly they were the distinctive ornaments of a Spanish cavalry officer's uniform. Also retrieved from the stone ledge cavity were several unidentified silver ornaments, perhaps more personal decoration, a large number of glass beads used to trade with the Indians, and finally, forty-two gold buttons strung out in a long row.[6]

What any of these things meant to Arnold or the Mexican sheepherder, no one knew, or they soon forgot in the excitement. Perhaps they meant only that the Spider Rock had been interpreted accurately, that its directions were followed correctly. If the seemingly personal effects of a Spanish officer were symbolic in nature, as were the three copper replicas found atop the Spider Rock, the sheepherder did not offer an explanation. He now directed the search party to move immediately across the canyon onto the small hill that gradually sloped to the canyon's edge.

The symbolic copper dagger, key, and plate found lying atop the Spider Rock seemed to be the guiding influence. How they were positioned on the stone determined how they were to proceed. The Mexican sheepherder interpreted them to mean that they should follow a tunnel into the hill, where the treasure chamber would be found.

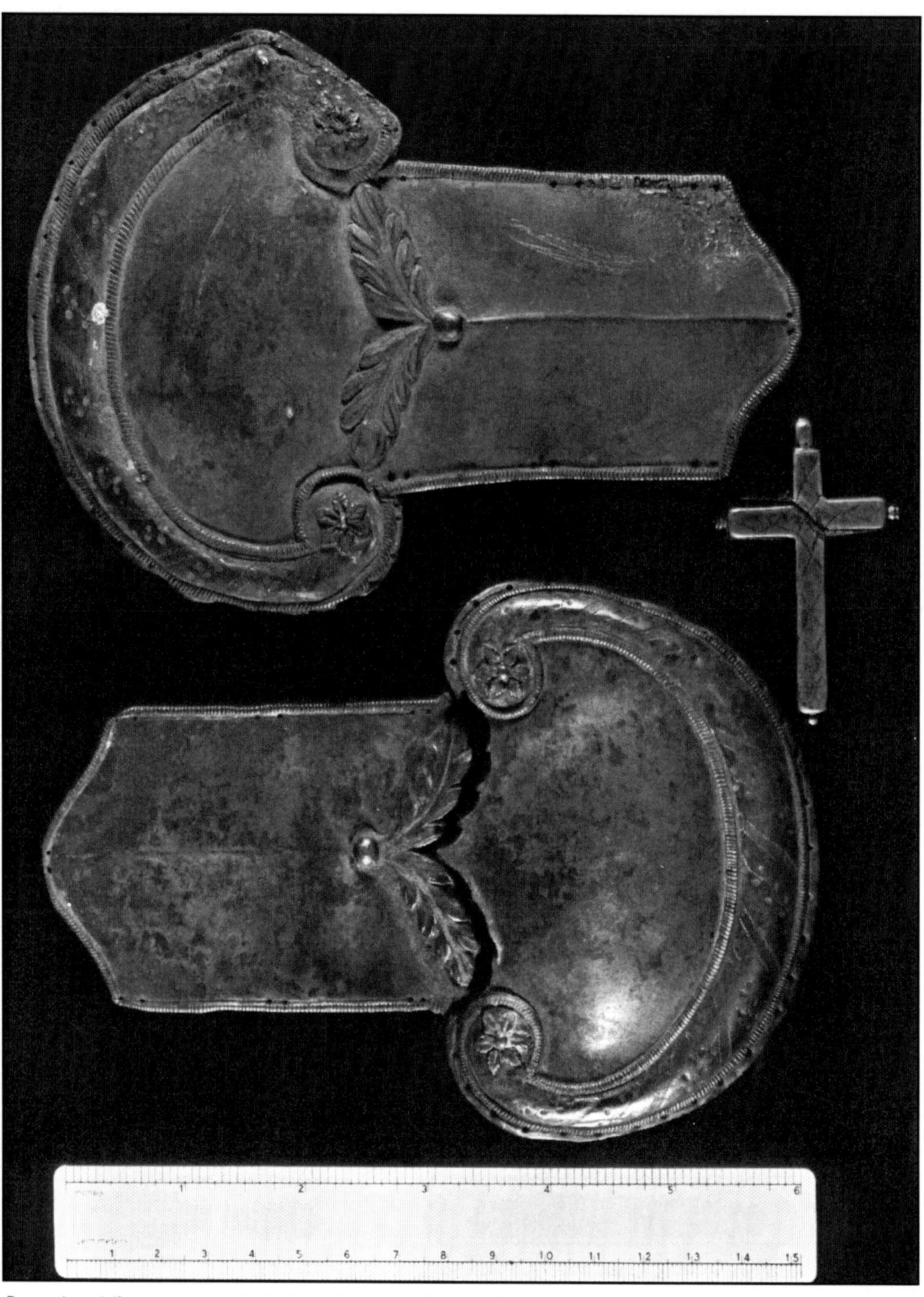

Dave Arnold's party unearthed these silver epaulets, at the time still bearing their gold tassel. A Spanish sword, gold buttons, and other articles were also found. The silver crucifix was found at a separate site. (Courtesy Charles Terrell)

Bud Jones, who lived across the Salt Fork from the diggings, was not present the day the Spider Rock was freed from its long entombment, but he saw the stone and its copper artifacts shortly afterward. Jones himself may have been enlisted early in the quest because of the discovery of a clue on his river farm that undoubtedly was part of the Spider Rock mystery.

That clue was another copper plate with cryptic tracery, oval-shaped, and about seven inches long by three and a half inches wide. Whether it was found before or after the Spider Rock and its copper ornaments, the plate from Jones's farm was from the same hand-hammered copper and bore notches on either side with a small notch at one end. On one side were four punch marks, two opposite each other near either side, and two more opposite each other near either end. Lines were etched from one punch mark to the others, forming four equal sections. In one section appeared the numerals XXII, and to the outside, the letter W.

The copper plate was uncovered between two rocks on the side of a bluff, only about a mile northeast of the Spider Rock and about three hundred feet from Jones's house.[7] It is assumed that Arnold or the Mexican recovered the copper plate, but what part it played in the cryptic puzzle, apparently, not even Jones knew. Nor could he remember in later years, when he tried so hard to recall the details of that intricate search, exactly how the other three copper ornaments fit together atop the Spider Rock.

Jones always believed that the half-round, half-square copper plate, called "the leaf," had lain halfway on the concentric circles and halfway on the angular lane leading into them. The copper dagger fit into one notch of the leaf inside the angular lane, while the copper key fit another notch of the leaf within the circles of the Spider Rock. The arrangement of those three copper pieces would be argued by the participants in later years, evidence of their lack of concern at the moment of their discovery.

Cabe Terrell, who assisted Arnold intermittently from 1902 to 1909, kept among his personal possessions the paper patterns of the three copper ornaments, each pinned together in what may have been their arrangement at the time of discovery. The pattern shows the copper leaf with its etched side up as the bottom figure. Placed diagonally across it was the copper dagger with its blade pointing outward. Opposite the dagger's handle was the copper key, the teeth of the key just beneath the dagger. Each member of that search party seemed sure of one thing: how the copper pieces were arranged was crucial to the direction they followed.

That direction led them to the head of the canyon west of the red clay knoll and the discovery of the Spanish sword and epaulets beneath the stone ledge. The bedrock outcropping on the west side of the canyon ran underneath the hill, a hill that had to be manmade and that seemingly concealed the secret treasure chamber. The pieces of the ancient puzzle seemed to be fitting together when the Mexican sheepherder led Arnold to the peculiarly unnatural hill.

Following the direction of the already recovered saber, and digging just above the bedrock, the Mexican began unearthing small, round clay balls, and he followed them northward along the canyon rim some forty feet before they turned abruptly westward into the hillside. It was now obvious to Arnold that the angular lane of circles, represented by the clay balls, was the same lane as depicted on the Spider Rock. Surely the center of the circle beneath that hill provided the key, perhaps the entrance to the treasure chamber itself.

To clear that hill to the bedrock would necessitate moving from a few inches to as much as fifteen feet of earth that a century or more before had been placed there to conceal the same pattern of symbols carved into the Spider Rock, found atop the hill to the east. To level the manmade hill would require teams of draft animals and scrapers, and each of the participants furnished their share.

Edwin Johnson recalls his father's story of that massive excavation. Kelly and his brother John furnished several of the eight or ten teams and fresnos they used to remove the overburden from the bedrock.[8] The excavation covered perhaps a square acre. The soil and all it contained were dumped over the bluff twenty feet or so into the canyon below. The farther they went into the hillside, because it led upward from the canyon rim, the deeper the excavation became, until at its western side, fifteen feet of earth was removed.

During the excavation, portions of the exact replica of the Spider Rock were uncovered lying atop the bedrock, matching the weblike circles and symbolic figures of that stone, but re-created from clay, stone, and metal, or occasionally carved into the bedrock itself. The workmen initially began following the angular lane of clay balls that led into the center of the circle. One of the first symbols they found, where the angular lane turned inward, was an oval-shaped stone eighteen inches or so high—representing the same curious symbol that appeared on the Spider Rock.

The symbols found in the excavation matched that placement on the Spider Rock and how it was oriented when discovered. The concentric circles were formed from red, black, and blue clay balls about five or six inches in diameter. The outside circle was about twenty-one feet across. The center was reached about forty feet from the edge of the canyon. The strange-looking symbol just outside the south side of the outer circle, similar to the zodiac sign of Pisces, was found carved into the surface of the bedrock.

However, many of the symbols were not found, and, in Arnold's haste, were probably graded up and pushed over the bluff into the canyon. The letter H, which the Mexican sheepherder first revealed would lead him to the treasure once the Spider Rock was found, was not located in the new diggings. Nor were many of the numerals, nor the arrow, nor the stone with the stopper rock on the west side of the weblike pattern. Arnold perhaps did not think those symbols were important to finding the underground chamber.

The clues found thus far did not seem to be taken as seriously by Arnold as by the Mexican sheepherder who had led him to this juncture. The sheepherder was careful to interpret each discovery, often referring back to the Spider Rock or the copper ornaments found atop it for their symbolic message. Although Arnold possessed the sheepskin map that led him here, it became more apparent that he knew far less about its interpretation than did the Mexican sheepherder, who was much more careful in fitting together every piece of the Spanish puzzle.

Anxious to dig beneath the bedrock thus far exposed in the hasty excavation, Arnold conceded when the Mexican directed that they dig still farther westward for other clues. By then some twelve to fifteen feet of overburden had been removed, and instead of leveling the rest of the hillside to that depth, two shafts were dug a few feet just outside the excavation near the northwest corner. One shaft yielded nothing. But at twelve feet in the other, two human skulls were unearthed, resting upright and back to back on a stone base. One skull looked back toward the excavation, while the other faced northwest. The Mexican did not offer an explanation for the skulls, or if so, it was soon forgotten.

Arnold seemed more positive than ever that the angular lane appearing on the Spider Rock, and again found made of clay balls atop the bedrock, indicated the presence of a tun-

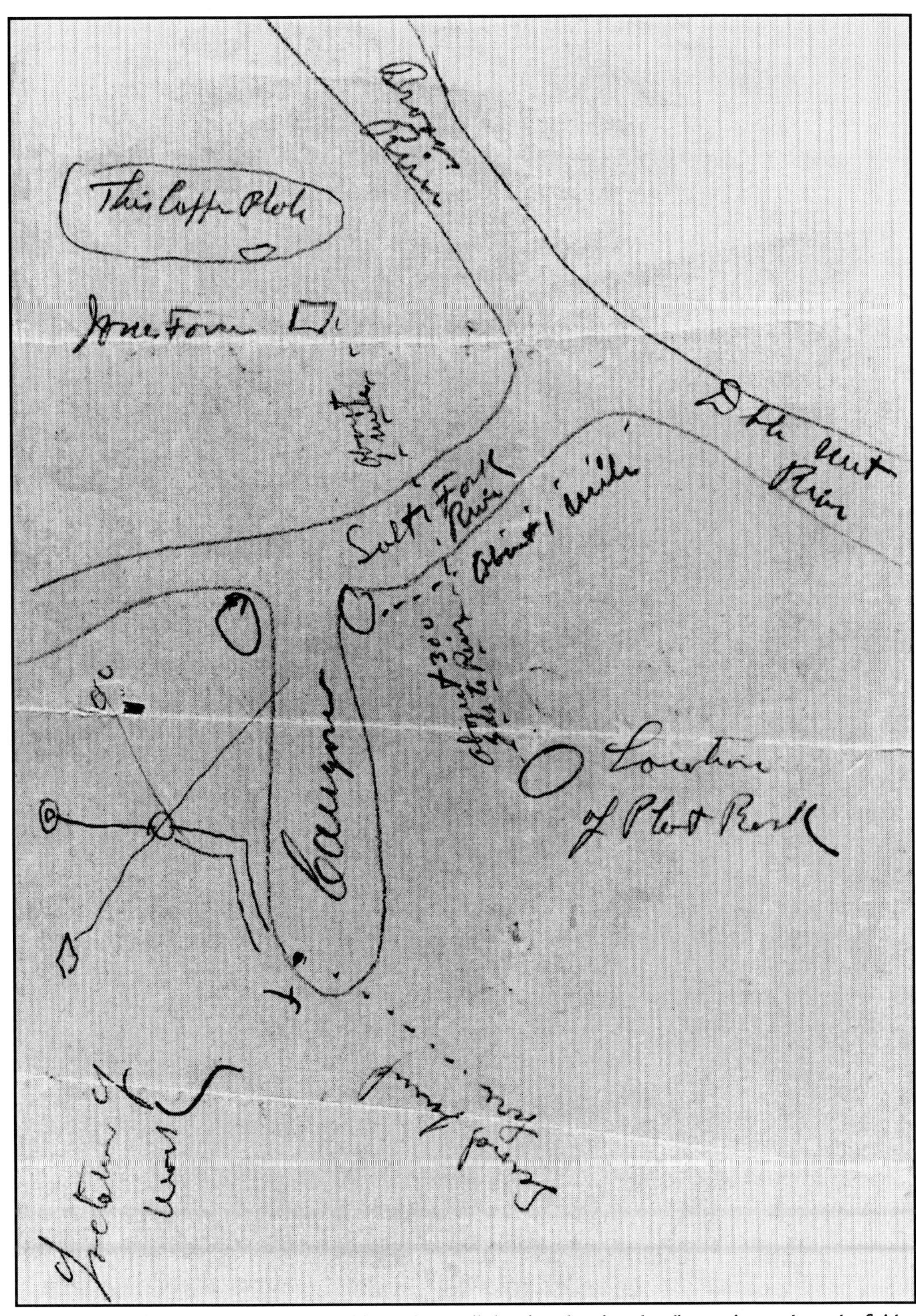

Among Cabe Terrell's possessions was this crude pencil drawing showing the discoveries made at the Spider diggings. The Spider Rock was found about 300 yards south of the river, the oval-shaped copper plate a mile away across the river, the Spanish sword and epaulets at the head of the canyon. The large excavation was made just west of the canyon. (Courtesy Charles Terrell)

The Spider Rock hill, the south promontory that yielded the mysterious stone map which Dave Arnold believed would lead to the Spanish treasure. (Photo by the author)

nel that would lead them to the treasure chamber. He directed that they sink a shaft through the bedrock in the center of the concentric circles, where he believed the underground vault would surely be found. The men sank a shaft through the bedrock and several feet beyond, but nothing unusual was found. Arnold and each man in his party believed beyond any doubt that the treasure must be close, within a few feet of their grasp. They believed that too much had been found for it to be otherwise. A closer search of the canyon would be made.

Just how closely Arnold followed the directions of the Mexican sheepherder is open to conjecture. It is not believed he always followed him, or it may have been that the Mexican, whoever he was, did not intend to fully share the knowledge he had brought from Mexico, seemingly following in the footsteps of Arnold himself. The digging was not always organized or in sequence after the Spider Rock was unearthed. While random digging went on, Arnold, often alone, would ride over the countryside seeking yet another clue. No one ever doubted his ability to follow the surface signs. His rides almost always took him north or west.

During much of his search at the Spider diggings, Arnold lived with Joe Allen and his family, whose 1,300-acre F-2 Ranch lay four miles northeast of the diggings, downstream from the forks on the east side of the Brazos. It was a convenient place to stay, since both Joe and his son were participants in the search. The Allens came to know the aging Arnold well over the months and years. They never doubted that he possessed an incredibly accurate Spanish document in the sheepskin map he harbored, or an uncanny ability and mania to follow it.

Allen's three teen-age daughters viewed their guest from south of the border much differently from their father or brother. Rhoda, Bertha, and Mattie each shared in preparing meals for Arnold at almost any hour of the day. Rhoda was eighteen when she first met Arnold. In recalling those events more than sixty years later, two of the Allen girls, Mrs. Rhoda Epply and Mrs. Bertha Worley of Haskell, shared their impressions of Arnold, his ability at unraveling part of the mystery, and his inability to solve it.

"He could trail those markers, following one to the other without any apparent difficulty," Bertha said. "He often talked about tracing those lines from here to yonder." The lines consisted of marked stones, trees, landmarks, and cairns that led Arnold over a complex network that only he fully understood. But that he did not fully understand the complexity he sought to unravel was evident time after time. When the Spider Rock was found, Bertha recalled, Arnold "couldn't read a foreign thing on it."[9]

The Allen daughters remember Arnold as a gentleman and always honest, "but as fat as the town dog," Bertha quipped. "I'd have to go in at three o'clock to cook his dinner," Rhoda chimed in. "I was so mad at him all the time I could have killed him." Arnold's habit was to ride into the ranch at midafternoon, and even at near sixty, he had a tremendous appetite. "Whenever I saw him coming, I'd go cook him a meal," Rhoda said.[10]

The Allen sisters remember that their father or brother and Arnold would often talk long into the night, planning their next day's work. Often Dr. Terrell and Cabe would come and stay all night. Their talk always concerned the Spanish treasure, or an interpretation of "the plot rock," as the Spider Rock was often called. The Allen girls saw it often in their home. It was truly a work of art, and it enraptured everyone who came into contact with it.

Arnold might stay at the ranch for two, three, or four days at a time, then disappear for as many days and be back again. Neither of the Allen girls ever glimpsed the sheepskin map he guarded so well, although it came up in his conversation with their father or brother. However, Rhoda remembers one grisly relic Arnold always kept in his room, and her disgust with it. That was a human skull he had brought in from the diggings on the Salt Fork. Once, while Arnold and the search party were excavating, he rode in excited one afternoon and told Rhoda he was borrowing her team and wagon to haul in the gold, believing it would be only a matter of hours. She had just bought that wagon and it was brand new, Rhoda recounted, but the hours dragged on—into days, weeks, and months.

There were many times over the following weeks that Arnold and his co-workers believed they were on the verge of finding the treasure. Edwin Johnson recalls his father's anticipation when they were excavating the hillside with the teams they helped furnish. On one occasion they uncovered a small clay statue of a human figure.[11] Arnold interpreted the figurine as meaning that it guarded the entrance to the tunnel leading to the treasure. Each man believed likewise.

So sure was Arnold of finding the treasure, that he and most of the participants strapped on six-shooters and kept rifles within quick reach. A strange aura of uneasiness penetrated the diggings about Mount Lama Vista. Bertha Worley recalled when "they carried those big guns because they were afraid they'd be robbed when they found the treasure." Those same weapons made a similar impression on Dr. Terrell's son Charles.

At what time during the search the Mexican sheepherder began to distrust members of Arnold's party, no one now knows. But no one seemed to trust the Mexican, least of all Arnold, and although the Mexican continued to direct the search, he remained distant and aloof, almost as if he would furnish the necessary knowledge only at the last moment.

Looking east down the Salt Fork from the red promontory at the mouth of the canyon near the Spider Rock diggings. (Photo by the author)

Seemingly, the more clues Arnold and his men uncovered, the more intricate the search became. More and more, the sheepherder was suspected of knowingly guiding them away from the treasure, and his movements were closely watched.

The Mexican lived a few miles downriver below the forks with a family named Stuart. No one knew much about the Stuarts. But even though they were not members of Arnold's party, they obviously knew about his search and the Mexican's guidance in it. It was not until many years later that anyone learned how much the Mexican had shared with the Stuarts. The atmosphere about the diggings was one of suspicion. Bud Jones suspected treachery and believed, as many may have, that the Mexican sheepherder was misleading them.[12] That distrust was reinforced when Jones spied two Mexicans running down a canyon not far from the diggings, carrying something between them. Their presence worsened an already perilous turn of events.

Just how much Arnold or any of his men may have voiced their suspicions to the Mexican sheepherder, no one can say. But that the Mexican feared grave consequences in the offing was revealed years later. It was at this time that the sheepherder directed the workmen to dig right up to the side of the excavation made by the teams and slips, and stop until the following day. That seemed peculiar at the time, but everyone went along with it. The next morning, the Mexican did not appear. It was discovered that where they had stopped digging the afternoon before, someone had slipped in during the night and dug a hole just beyond the excavation. It was impossible to tell if anything had been removed from the hole, but every man in the party had his reason for believing that something had.

That suspicion seemed to be verified when not long after the Mexican vanished, a human skeleton was found several miles away on the east side of the Double Mountain Fork. There seemed to be little doubt that the remains were those of the Mexican sheepherder. Nearby "were two small, heavy copper pots, one shaped oblong somewhat in the form of a canoe, the other round, and of the capacity of a gallon and a half, built much stronger than any vessel now made for commerce and capable of holding itself full of the heaviest metal."[13] Each copper vessel was empty. Faint buggy tracks of the possible murderer led into and out of that river pasture, but no clue was found to the driver's identity.[14]

Kiowa Peak, a prominent landmark, lies eight miles distant a few degrees west of north from the hill that yielded the Spider Rock. (Photo by the author)

With teams of draft horses and scrapers, Dave Arnold and his followers leveled this hillside to the bedrock where they found symbols made from clay, stone, and metal, or carved into its surface. They matched the same symbols on the Spider Rock. (Photo by the author)

No one recalls just who found the skeleton, but Crawford Allen later took possession of the antiquated copper vessels and for years exhibited them outside his home, until finally they, too, disappeared.[15] Many pondered the probable contents of the two copper pots. Whatever they may have contained, Arnold was sure the real treasure had not been found. Neither Arnold nor any of his followers would ever know of the mysterious letter the Mexican sheepherder scrawled late one night in the Stuart family dugout before his disappearance. The Stuarts would keep that message secret for many years to come.

Without the Mexican sheepherder and the knowledge he provided, Arnold appeared to be at a loss in a quest that was far more encompassing and complex than anyone had fully realized. Arnold later brought a clairvoyant to Mount Lama Vista. No one now alive can tell what transpired that day. Arnold may have carried the Spider Rock with him, as well as the symbolic copper dagger, leaf, and key, or the plate found a mile to the north. He may have shown the clairvoyant the Spanish sword and silver epaulets with their tarnished gold tassel.

It cannot be said with certainty, but part of what occurred that day at the Spider diggings may have been chronicled on the back of a yellowed envelope Cabe Terrell kept among his personal papers. One side of the envelope shows a diagram depicting the three hills at Mount Lama Vista—the hill that yielded the Spider Rock and the two promontories on either side of the canyon on the Salt Fork. It shows, too, a drawing of the Spanish saber and its discovery site at the head of the canyon. The major work, or excavation of the hillside, was indicated on the west side of the canyon.[16]

On the back of the envelope appear these questions and answers: "Ask about sword—just what she thought. Ask about deep well—put monument in center so can locate exactly. Ask about plot rock—wait later. Ask about red peak—wait later." In one handwriting appears the statement, "A polished rock will be found 10 feet left of point of sword. About 9 feet underground between track and sword it is placed in hard dirt—point towards money and a few feet from the track."

In yet another handwriting is the message, "I will go on the ground ... [writing here is too faint to read] men and locate the exact place. I will be a little confused as to the exact location but then I will be exactly right. I will have some trouble with one of the men as to the location, or he will try to bear me off a little bit to where he thinks it ought to be, but do not let that bother me in the least. Some man enveys [*sic*] me but tries to act as one of my best friends (watch him very close). I will be one of the ... appointed, this man will get out of heart a great deal, either 51 or 52 or 58 will ..."[17]

Although that message reveals little about what transpired, perhaps it shows better than anything how much Arnold was groping for any possibility he may have missed. Two shafts were dug under the supervision of the clairvoyant. Each was sunk to a depth of a hundred feet and dug principally by Crawford Allen. The first shaft was dug atop the Spider Rock hill, at the very place where the chart stone was found and the human skeletons beneath it. The clairvoyant believed the treasure chamber Arnold was seeking would be found there. When that excavation failed to yield anything, the red hill or promontory overlooking the Salt Fork on the west side of the canyon was chosen. At its base, another shaft was sunk to the hundred-foot level, but the results were the same as before.

Although Arnold's search at Mount Lama Vista had temporarily halted, he would return to those diggings periodically over the next five years, as existing letters and documents describe. Meanwhile, he had more of the ancient trail to follow, more of the Spanish mystery to unravel. The trail led him twenty miles downstream, northward from the forks. Sometime earlier, Arnold had found the next site he now wanted to dig. Over the months he had come to know Kelly Johnson and his brothers, John, Moss, and A. J. V., and their families.

While Arnold ran the trail on the upper Brazos, he would stay with one of the Johnson families three miles west of Munday. Kelly's son, Edwin, was born in 1908. Today he lives at his father's homestead where Arnold often made his headquarters while prowling the breaks. When the work lagged at the Salt Fork diggings, Arnold resumed his search on Wild Horse Creek, where he sought the grave of a Spanish priest that he said was indicated on his sheepskin map.

When he found that site on the east side of the confluence of Wild Horse Creek and the Brazos River about six miles northeast of Knox City, Kelly and John Johnson were among those who participated in the excavation. No one remembers just how Arnold came to locate the gravesite, but the human skeleton was buried sitting up facing east. The body had been interred with a burro, as those animal bones were also present, as were the artifacts that had been worn or carried.

No inventory has survived of those artifacts of a former age, but in later years Kelly remembered the decayed parts of a packsaddle, bridle bits, buckles, a pipe, a small engraved ebony and silver crucifix, a walking cane, a small clay lamb, a pearl necklace, a diamond necklace, and buckles, rings, and earrings all made of gold. Edwin, who remembers Arnold being at his father's home toward the end of his search, recalls that he placed a value of $13,000 on the discovery.[18]

Many of those artifacts, in addition to the copper ornaments, sword, silver epaulets, and the Spider Rock itself, were entrusted to Dr. Terrell. Although much secrecy always surrounded the search, occasionally Dr. Terrell would show a wide-eyed youngster or trusted friend some of that discovery. Marvin H. Post of Denver City remembered such a treat.[19] He lived just across the street from the Terrells. Another Haskell resident recalled seeing early in 1906 a copper plate with tracery, the hilt of a sword, some gold fringe, and the small ebony and silver crucifix, which he believed bore the date of 1767 or 1778.[20]

During the months Arnold lived with the Johnsons, and over the years he periodically visited them, Kelly and his brothers came to know the aging man from Mexico perhaps better than anyone else. Kelly learned that the upper Brazos was not the only region that Arnold was guided to by the sheepskin map. He confided to the Johnsons that he had also pursued the same trail in Comanche County near the headwaters of the Leon River. Might he have been seeking the same site that Colonel Snively discovered in 1844?

If so, Arnold might well have found it, for he unearthed more than $12,000 in Spanish gold, he told the Johnsons. It may be more than mere coincidence that the *Taylor County News* of June 29, 1888, picked up such a story. It stated: "The *Comanche Chief* related that last week nearly $20,000 in gold and silver coins were found near that town."[21] If the subject of *that* search was in fact Arnold, the date may indicate the length of time he had pursued that trail to the Spider Rock and the mysterious grave on the bank of the Brazos. Interesting, too, that where Arnold lived in 1897 near Evant was not that far from Comanche.

Arnold and the Mexican sheepherder may both have possessed knowledge that neither was willing to share with the other. But for the moment, Arnold was puzzled, or appeared to be so. He may not have been as lost for an explanation as his followers believed. In the winter of 1904–05, Bud Jones, W. J. Carouth, Joe and Crawford Allen, and Kelly and John Johnson had their own farm chores to tend to. Dr. Terrell's son Cabe had left sometime before to work for his uncle Horace Terrell at his drug store in Baird, thirty miles east of Abilene in Callahan County.

That may have been only coincidental, but if so, it was to Arnold's advantage, for both Dr. Terrell and his son would play a major role in Arnold's next search on that bizarre trail. If he did not know the location of that site by the late winter months of early 1905, he spent those months pursuing the trail to a farm perhaps no more than five miles from Baird—or roughly sixty miles southeast from where the Spider Rock was found.

It may be assumed that Dr. Terrell and Cabe were aware that Arnold now sought a second stone map—another piece of the Spanish puzzle that somehow dovetailed with Arnold's own sheepskin map. Neither the doctor nor his son could have foreseen the ominous turn of events that was to occur there.

3

Cryptic Symbols to a Lost City

John and Lucretia Sembritzki and their eight children moved from Indian Territory in 1899 to a farm they purchased in northwestern Callahan County, three miles northeast of the hamlet of Clyde. The Sembritzkis had no way of knowing that their north central Texas farm was any different from those around it, sandy, with gently rolling hills of mesquite and post oak.[1] They could not have known that one day a stranger would appear, and that the bizarre story he would tell would change the lives of everyone drawn into his fold. That story today, just as it did almost a century ago, haunts men's minds in quest of answers to an age-old riddle.

The south eighty acres of the Sembritzki farm were considered by John to be the most unusable portion of his land. It would require complete clearing before it could be worked. The soil was deep, loose white sand veneered with an almost impenetrable growth of underbrush spotted with huge oak trees. That portion of the family farm, recalled Sembritzki's daughter Verne at eighty-one years old, "was such wild country, it seemed that we were the first inhabitants on earth ever to explore it."[2]

Lucretia Sembritzki had a special curiosity for that portion of their farm, and one day while John did not require her assistance, she spent her leisure moments walking over that wilderness. When Lucretia returned home that day, she took a story of a strange discovery.

While the family of ten ate their evening meal around the long wooden kitchen table, Lucretia explained that while she had passed through the dense brush and huge oak trees a quarter-mile southeast of the house, she found a peculiar pile of stones. A large, single stone stood upright like the headstone of a grave. That would not have appeared so unusual, except there were no other similar stones on their farm. Near the stones grew three trees that appeared to have been braided together when small, and had grown entwined into large trees.

Little more attention was given to Lucretia's discovery and the incident was all but forgotten, but about two years later, in the late winter of 1905, two strangers drove up to the Sembritzki house about dusk and asked if they could have shelter for the night. John and

John and Lucretia Sembritzki and their eight children about the time Dave Arnold entered their lives in his quest for the second of the stone maps. Their daughter Verne stands next to her father, and Ann, behind on left. (Courtesy Verne Sems)

Lucretia never turned away a traveler, and, considering the cold weather, invited the strangers in. The younger of the two men, who drove the buggy, introduced himself as Sam Hart. His family worked a farm a few miles away. The older man, a big, paunchy fellow clad in overalls, was Dave Arnold.

Around the dinner table the two men made small talk as the eight Sembritzki children sat wide-eyed in wonderment, occasionally giggling at the fat man's apparent penchant for home-cooked food. After dinner, the older girls cleared the table while the Sembritzkis and their guests sat around the iron stove and talked. Arnold's casual talk soon took the form of questions concerning peculiar markings on trees and unusual rock formations. He asked if the Sembritzkis might have found some trees that had grown braided together near a large pile of rocks. Lucretia, still remembering her discovery, replied that she had found such a place about two years before and felt confident she could direct him to it again.

Arnold's eyes beamed. The place Lucretia had found appeared to be what he now needed to complete a trail that he said he had followed all the way from Mexico. He had lived in Mexico for some years, he explained, and while there learned to read Spanish signs and symbols carved on rock and trees. He had followed such a trail of markers to their farm, where he was sure would be found a treasure beyond their wildest dreams. He would know for sure once he had seen Lucretia's discovery.

In his excitement, Arnold asked Lucretia to describe again everything she had found, querying her about certain markings blazed on the trees. It was all Arnold could do to con-

The Sembritzki home three miles northeast of Clyde, Texas, where Arnold headquartered early in 1905 while seeking the buried stone map and other clues. (Courtesy Verne Sems)

trol his enthusiasm. The fact that Lucretia's discovery was in a thick undergrowth of brush was all that prevented him from leaving the house at once with a lantern. When the Sembritzki family and their two guests retired to bed that night, the big man slept restlessly. Arnold was first to rise the next morning, only to encounter his first disappointment. That night a heavy snow had fallen, making it impossible to do anything for almost a week while it thawed. All Arnold could do was pace the floor with impatience. Sam Hart, who had brought Arnold to the Sembritzki farm, returned to his own.

In the anxious days that followed, in what must have been late February or perhaps early March of 1905, Arnold revealed still more of his story. He gave no hint as to how long he had been in Texas but said his wife and daughter were living in San Angelo, 120 miles or so southwest. He mentioned nothing of his more than two-year quest on the Salt Fork or of the Spider Rock he had found there. The Sembritzki family was enraptured with Arnold's story. He especially made an impression on two of the Sembritzki girls, nineteen-year-old Annie and ten-year-old Verne. Both of them in later years would recall Arnold's visits and the bizarre events that resulted from them. Without their memories, little of Arnold's next search would be known today.[3]

Arnold said he was seventy-two, but his ruddy complexion and sandy blond hair, and his lack of dentures or glasses, gave him the appearance of a much younger man. He was probably not yet sixty. His dark blue eyes were as penetrating as his story was convincing. He divulged almost nothing of his past. The overalls he always wore showed him to be a man used to outside work, yet his obesity and manner revealed he was not as used to manual labor as his clothes might indicate. To a God-fearing, hard-working German family like the Sembritzkis, whose only luxury was an organ and whose only reading materials were the family Bible, school books, and a semiweekly paper, Arnold was especially interesting and entertaining.

"Clean-shaven, and clean personally, he did not drink or smoke," remembers Verne. "His conversation was clean at all times, and it showed him to be a man of some education. In short, he was a gentleman at all times." Arnold did reveal one characteristic that none of the Sembritzki children ever forgot. He was a talented ventriloquist and amused and intrigued the family for what seemed like hours at a time. He gave no hint about his skill's former use.[4]

In his usual soft-spoken manner, Arnold revealed that while living in Mexico, he had come to know a very old Mexican who had a wooden leg. The Mexican had taught him all he knew about reading the marks on trees and the meanings of rock piles that he had followed to the Sembritzki farm. He had fallen heir, he said, to a sheepskin map that led him to the hidden treasure he was convinced would be found on their farm.

Arnold's sheepskin chart would always be the subject of much mystery. Few people ever glimpsed that map. The Sembritzki family members were among those few. He sifted through his luggage and pulled out the folded sheepskin. When he spread it out over the tabletop, it appeared to be at least three feet square. In recalling that map, Ann Sembritzki Fuqua, at ninety years of age, remembered the sheepskin was laden with a strange network of diagrams and symbols on one side, and circles and peculiar signs on the other. "It was as foreign to them as anything could be," she said. It was so old and faint that Arnold later had one of the older Sembritzki girls "go over the entire thing with an indelible pencil," remembers Ann's younger sister, Verne.

Almost a week passed, and the snow had nearly melted when Lucretia and John guided their guest to the entwined trees Arnold so anxiously awaited. Lucretia had no difficulty refinding them or the nearby stone marker. Arnold became excited upon seeing them. "Yes," he muttered to himself, "yes, this is it. This is exactly what I'm looking for."

At the cairn, Arnold eased down on his hands and knees and gently brushed away a thick layer of sand covering the stones, finally blowing the sand away to make a clean surface, painstaking in his efforts not to disturb a single stone. He found the sign he wanted and then sighted from it. Without revealing the meaning of the symbol he found, Arnold would say only that it meant so many *varas* east or north, south or west. Always his measurements were in *varas*.

Arnold continued to look for markers, putting together in his mind an ancient puzzle that told him a story only he seemed to understand. He left no stone unturned, no tree of size unexamined, always sighting, always pacing in great strides. Many of the symbols blazed into the trunks of huge, regal oaks were unlike anything John or Lucretia had ever seen. There were circles, half-circles, long straight lines, crescent moons, triangles, even spiral marks that began high up the trunk and wound around it to the base, terminating in a head. Arnold called them "snakes" and noted the direction they pointed. Upon seeing what Arnold was now showing them, John and Lucretia became as excited as he. The story he imparted was from another time. That he had found something that somehow had remained hidden to modern man, they were sure, and time after time he would show that what he said was true.

Arnold explained that the Spaniards had buried a vast trove in gold ingots near where they had walked that day. He did not attempt to hide the figure he believed would be found. On many occasions, Verne, even though only ten, recalled Arnold saying they would find gold valued at $60 million. But first, he said, he must find "the plat rock," a map carved into stone that would guide them to the treasure.

Arnold was too old and too heavy to do much manual labor, and John Sembritzki agreed to help him as long as he could. For a week or more, he dug holes where Arnold directed, chopping out brush, clearing a path at one place, then another. Nothing was found but deep white sand that showed no indication of ever having been disturbed. Still Arnold would check and recheck the symbols blazed into the huge oak trees that appeared to have withstood the sifting sand for perhaps centuries. The days continued to pass, and still nothing more was found. John felt he had given Arnold all the time he could spare. His chores were piling up, and spring planting would soon be upon him.

In the days ahead, Arnold worked alone, digging shallow holes. His pace was slow and arduous. Finally, one day about dusk, the Sembritzkis saw him scuttling down the road to the house as fast as his legs would carry his heavy body. Breathlessly he gasped, "John, I've found it! John, I've found it!" and sat down to catch his breath. John dropped what he was doing and ran to him. Attempting to calm him, John helped him to his feet and returned with him to see what he had found.[5]

At the base of a large oak, Arnold had dug a hole three feet deep, where he discovered the stone map, imprisoned in the roots that had grown over it. To free it would require several hours' work, and it was now almost dark. Arnold wanted to remain there that night and free his prize, but John persuaded him to wait until morning, when, he said, he would help him. One night more would not matter. Even so, Arnold slept restlessly.

At daybreak they were back at the huge oak. On his knees, John carefully chopped the roots that had grown around the stone, buried in a mass of oiled, pulverized charcoal. It was animal fat, Arnold said, that the Spaniards had mixed with ground charcoal to keep the stone just like it was the day it was buried. It required almost the full morning to free the stone. Arnold carefully noted its position before allowing John to remove it from its long entombment. At any time it might easily have been broken, for the white sandstone slab was a mere fifteen inches long by perhaps twelve inches wide, and little more than an inch thick, with irregular edges.

Arnold brushed off the charcoal that clung to the stone. It was perfectly flat and smooth, and carved on both sides with skillful craftsmanship. Holding it possessively in his lap as he sat at the edge of the hole from which it came, Arnold carefully examined it as John looked on in awe, convinced now that Arnold actually did know what he was talking about. The stone was carved with three concentric circles, the outer circle being eight and a half inches in diameter. The circles were divided into eight equal portions by four radial lines. A small gouge or hole appeared in the center where all lines converged, as well as where the lines intersected each other circle. In all, there were twenty-five such gouges, the largest being in the center.

That design, Arnold told Sembritzki, represented the surface groundwork—the symbols carved on trees and rock piles that led to the treasure, all converging over it from miles in every direction. The underside of the stone showed the most intricate carvings. Arnold said it represented the map to the underground workings, which he would describe once the stone was cleaned. Arnold and Sembritzki went home that day with their long-buried prize, a bizarre Spanish document carved into stone that had remained hidden for almost two centuries. Sembritzki, as much as Arnold that day, believed his days of grubbing brush and farming deep blow sand would soon be no more. At last he had seen with his own eyes what Arnold promised they would find.

That evening Arnold took great care to clean the stone until every delicate etching came into plain view. The care he took was no less than if the map had been on ancient parchment. Then he placed the white stone on the kitchen table as the Sembritzki family gathered around him to hear its enigmatic story. Verne, recalling that memorable event, remembers, "It was the most beautiful and most delicate carving in stone that I have ever seen. Everything down to the smallest detail was perfect. It was truly a magnificent work of art."[6]

As Arnold explained the mysterious stone with its cryptic ciphers, he unraveled a Spanish cryptopuzzle no one had read about in the history books. With the intricate design face up, he revealed in an almost solemn tone, as if reading the last will and testament of a lost people, a story that someone had wanted preserved for centuries. The stone, he said, was a map to an underground village, a fortification once inhabited by a colony of Spaniards. Each of the sections marked off in squares represented rooms. The large room with the cross was the chapel. The dots in all the rooms represented the quantity of gold bullion, and each room appeared to be almost filled. The Spaniards had mined the gold elsewhere and brought the treasure to this hidden city.

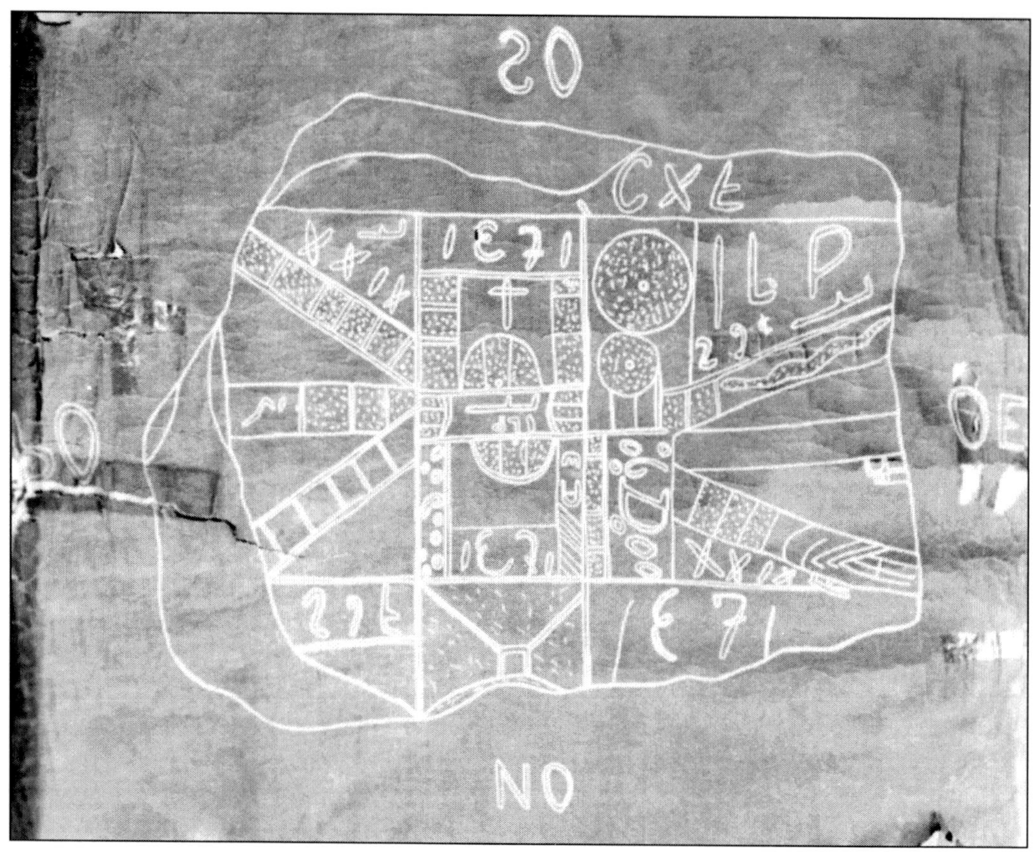

Dave Arnold hacked the second of the stone maps from the roots of a huge oak tree. About fifteen inches long by twelve inches wide, the white stone was perfectly smooth and carved on both sides. Reading from right to left, Arnold interpreted its date as being 1731. Others would read it as 1671. This blueprint was later made of the stone carving. (Courtesy Dock Henderson)

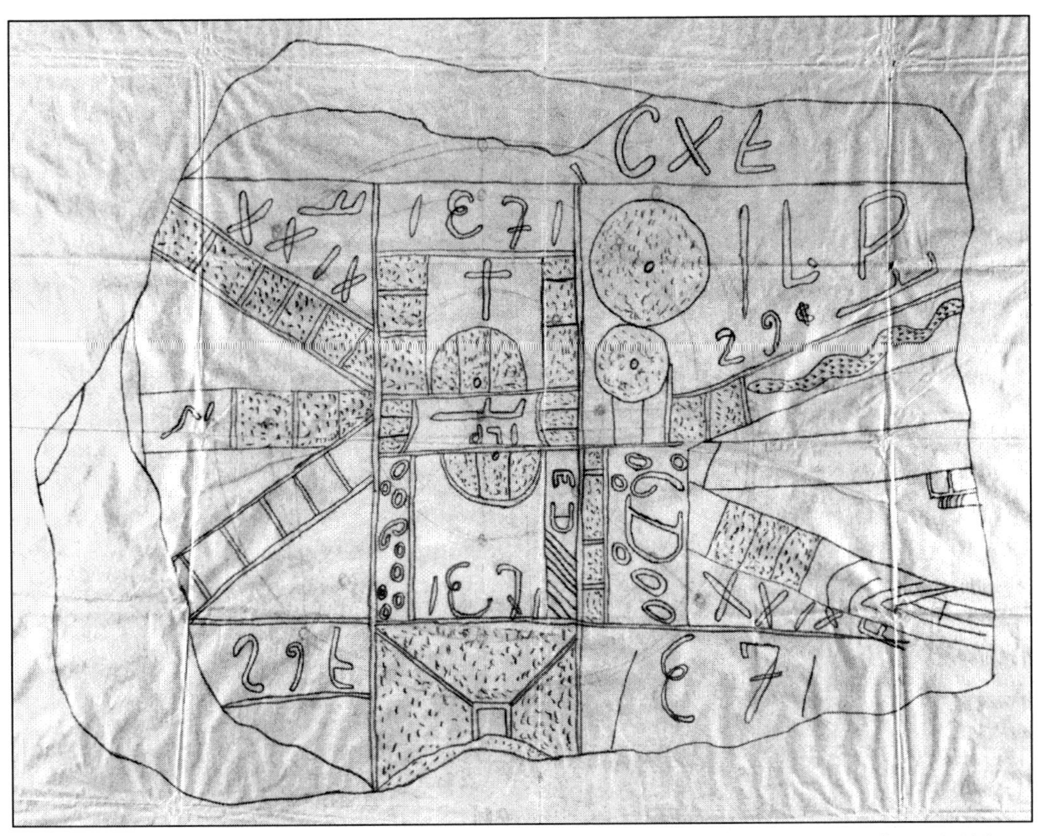

In Cabe Terrell's possessions were tracings of each side of the stone map unearthed on the Sembritzki farm. It appears that the later blueprint was made from this tracing. Some of its symbols also appeared on the Spider Rock, found sixty miles away. (Courtesy Charles Terrell)

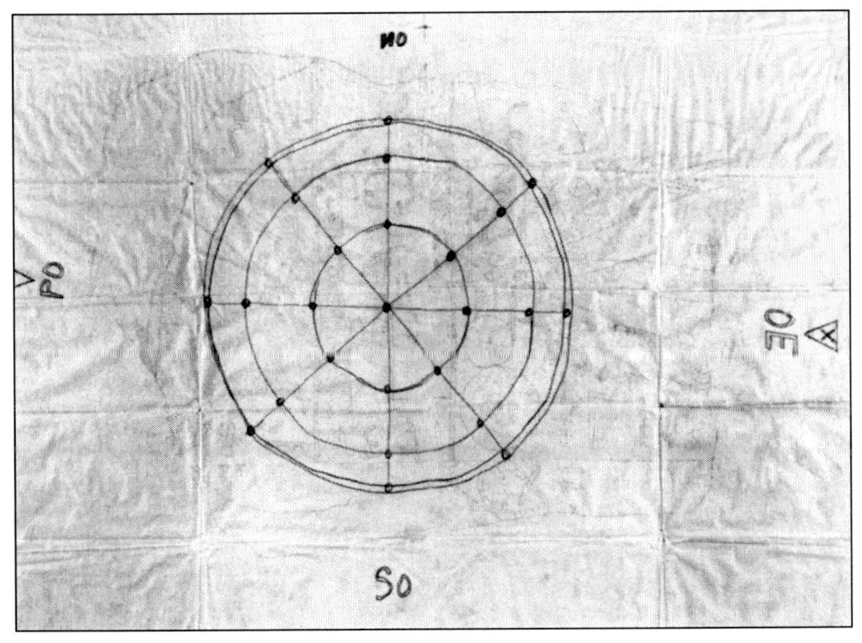

On the opposite, or bottom, side of the stone appeared only the concentric circles and directions. (Courtesy Charles Terrell)

Because the Spaniards suffered violent and regular attacks by Indians, they were forced to abandon their underground stronghold. With their treasure trove placed in each of the rooms, they directed an underground water source into the city so that no one could reach the gold or avoid the water, except by finding the secret passage or tunnel leading to the treasure chambers. There were two air vents, Arnold said, but one chimney is broken. The year of this event is found near each of those vents. Arnold arrived at the date by reading right to left, for 1731, or exactly 174 years before.

The upper left and right corners of the stone, he said, indicated that water would be encountered at twenty-nine feet, shown on the stone twice in both Roman numerals and Arabic figures. The secret tunnel into the underground network could be reached at one point only. That was shown on the stone at the far right center. The long, empty, narrow space was actually a small, hollowed-out groove indicating the secret tunnel and was the only entrance by which the hidden rooms could be safely reached, Arnold cautioned.

That was the story of the stone map as Arnold revealed it. Unfortunately, all the details as he made them were not recorded until more than sixty years later, and many of his revelations were forgotten. Arnold did not know or did not disclose the meaning of many of the cryptographic symbols. For example, the ILP found twice on the stone, the CX and inverted F, what appears to be the number 6 and letter D surrounded by six circles, and to the right of one of the three dates, the letters ED and seemingly eight bars or slashes were among the unexplained ciphers. And then there were the two half-circles in the center, each with three compartments. What might they have represented?

And what about the two large circles near the top center? What kind of underground compartments were those? It is interesting that the ancient alchemical symbol for gold is a circle with a dot in the center. And what about the six lone F's? What did they signify? And the snakelike figure in the upper right corner? Sembritzki may not have cared what all the symbols meant. Arnold seemed to have the knowledge to follow the directions to something so wondrous that no one would have gone to such meticulous pains to conceal it unless it was indeed incredibly valuable—a prize truly beyond their wildest dreams.

No doubt Arnold revealed more about the stone than has been remembered, but there are many things, too, that he did not tell. He told the Sembritzki family nothing about the Spider Rock unearthed sixty miles to the northwest, or the eight concentric circles that formed its spider web design. Considering his precision, he must have recognized immediately that only one-half the circles formed that same pattern on the stone he had just found. He must have recognized, too, the CX and inverted F that appeared on both stones, and the many F's and use of both Roman numerals and Arabic numbers. The top of each stone—unlike a modern map—seemed to indicate south, and the right side, west.

On the face of the stone bearing the four concentric circles and apparent directions, the letters NO, apparently for *norte,* appeared at the top, and at the far right, the letters OE. Arnold may or may not have explained those directions. Did the OE stand for *oeste,* Spanish for west? If so, then what about the letters PO at the left side? Another Spanish word for west is *poniente*. Cabe Terrell later made tracings of the stone, and only the side with the concentric circles bore directions. However, the blueprint of the opposite side also includes those directions, with NO at the bottom. Of course, when the stone is turned over, SO—seemingly for south—is then at the top.

It was always Arnold's custom to reveal only bits and pieces of the story that only he may have fully understood. The Sembritzki family would never know of his quest for the

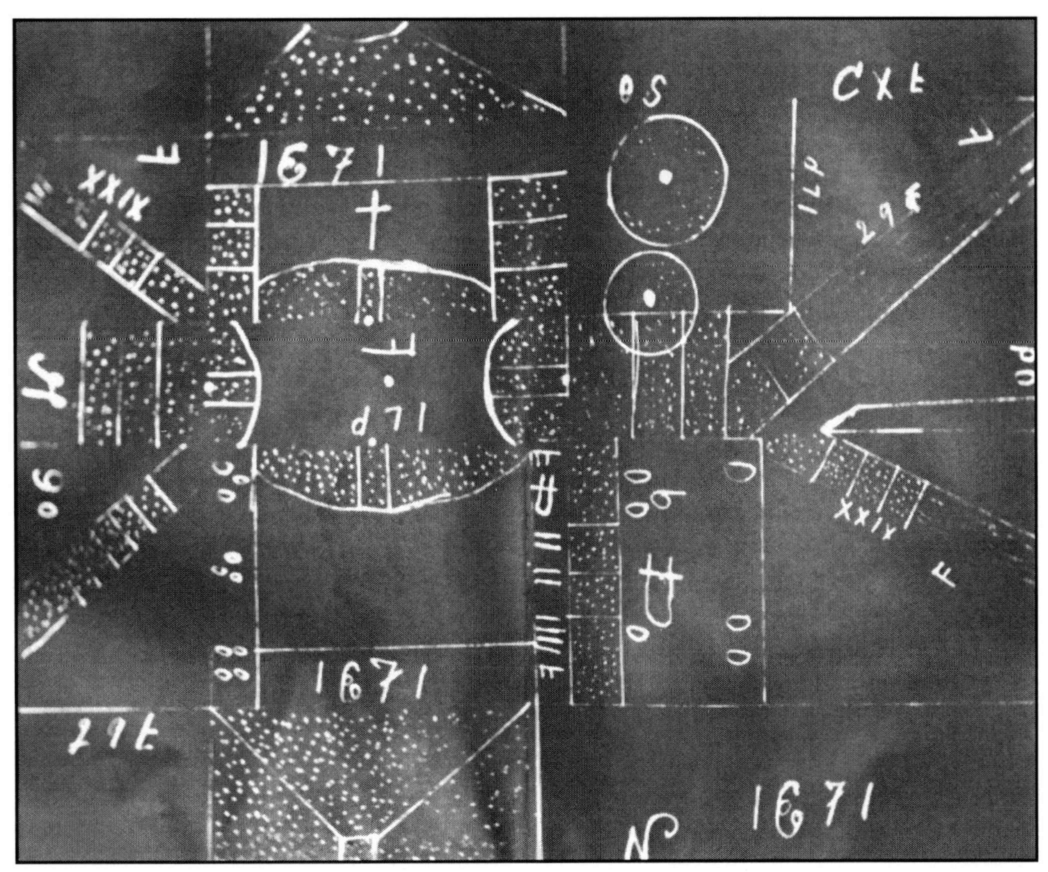

A similar blueprint emerged in later years, showing some subtle differences in the stone carving. The date looks more like 1671. The Sembritzkis made their own tracing of the stone, and this blueprint may have been made from their copy. (Courtesy Joe Woods)

Spider Rock, or the relationship of one stone map to the other. It may be assumed that only Dr. Terrell and Cabe knew that relationship, as it must be assumed that Arnold soon made Cabe aware of his latest discovery, for Cabe now clerked in his uncle's drug store in nearby Baird.

Arnold found the stone map perhaps a quarter of a mile from the three trees that had grown together as if they had been braided when young. Many of the older oak trees on that portion of the Sembritzki farm bore the strange symbols that guided Arnold from one place to another. Always his manner was to sight from them, and simply say that so many *varas* east, west, north, or south, they would find the next clue. Almost always he identified that object before it was found.

Arnold stepped off that Spanish measurement "in ground-devouring strides," remembers Verne, would stop at still another sign or rock pile, and instruct her father to dig to find a certain stone pointing down or pointing south, never failing to be correct. "It was uncanny and almost unbelievable the way he could stand near a rock pile and tell you what you would find there," Verne recalled, "and he could do it quickly. He read signs at a glance. My parents remarked later that he was like a hound dog on a scent when he found a mark on a tree or a sign in a rock pile. His vast knowledge of Spanish marks was encyclopedic."[7]

Most of the digging was now confined to an area seventy-five to a hundred feet square. The stone map unearthed at the oak tree served as the northwest corner of that square. Near the northeast corner, at the base of another large oak, Arnold directed John to dig until he found the object he sought. John soon struck something hard with his shovel, and, careful not to disturb it as Arnold requested, he cleaned the dirt away from it. He had found an almost perfect stone replica of a duck, placed as if resting on its nest. It was perhaps ten inches long and five inches across at its breast. On hands and knees with his face almost to the ground, Arnold sighted from it. Then he lifted the stone duck and found beneath it three small, round stones that he called "her eggs," without offering further explanation.

The days dragged on for Sembritzki, who could not understand the unusual and strange formality in arriving at the secret underground passageway. Arnold's method was almost that of a careful archaeologist, always considering every object, always careful not to disturb it before he had its pattern and its message firmly imprinted in his mind.

Still working within that hundred-foot square of dense brush and oak, Arnold stepped off a predetermined number of *varas* due south of the oak tree where they had first chopped out the stone map. Stretching his legs as far as he could in stepping off that measurement, he stopped at a distance of about a hundred feet. With pick and shovel, John Sembritzki sank yet another hole. Both were soon confident that the distance had been correctly measured, for the same oiled, pulverized charcoal was encountered. It seemed to fill a wedgelike hole, wide at the top and tapering downward.

At a depth of two or three feet, John struck a stone. Carefully he cleaned away the charcoal and found, lying atop the stone, a small half-disc cut from a thin sheet of copper. It was straight on one side, and deep notches were cut around the curvature, forming sharp points. The jagged piece of copper, little more than three inches long by two inches wide, represented "the setting sun," Arnold said.

John completed cleaning off the stone before removing it. Arnold always stressed the importance of each object to the other and directed that nothing be disturbed until he had observed it. The stone proved to be about eighteen inches long by ten inches wide and little more than an inch thick. It was white sandstone, smooth and flat, like the stone map found earlier. Carved upon its face was the single word *OESTE*—another Spanish word for "west."

Arnold then moved an equal distance to the east, forming a fourth corner of the imaginary square. Clearing a path through the brush along the way, John again dug into a wedgelike hole filled with oiled, pulverized charcoal, wide at the top and narrow at the base. At the same depth as before, he found another small half-disc of copper with irregular, pointed edges. It represented "the rising sun," Arnold explained. Again they found another stone like the last. Upon its face was carved the single inscription *PUENTE*—Spanish for "bridge."[8]

Arnold did not explain the significance of the stones with their messages, or the copper half-discs symbolic of the rising and setting sun, perhaps used as boundary markers. Or, if he did, the details did not seem important. All that mattered now was finding the secret passageway that led to the underground rooms filled with gold—a vast treasure hidden by the conquistadors.

Calculating measurements and directions by a method that only Arnold understood, he stepped off an equal distance between the two stones and their half-disc sun symbols.

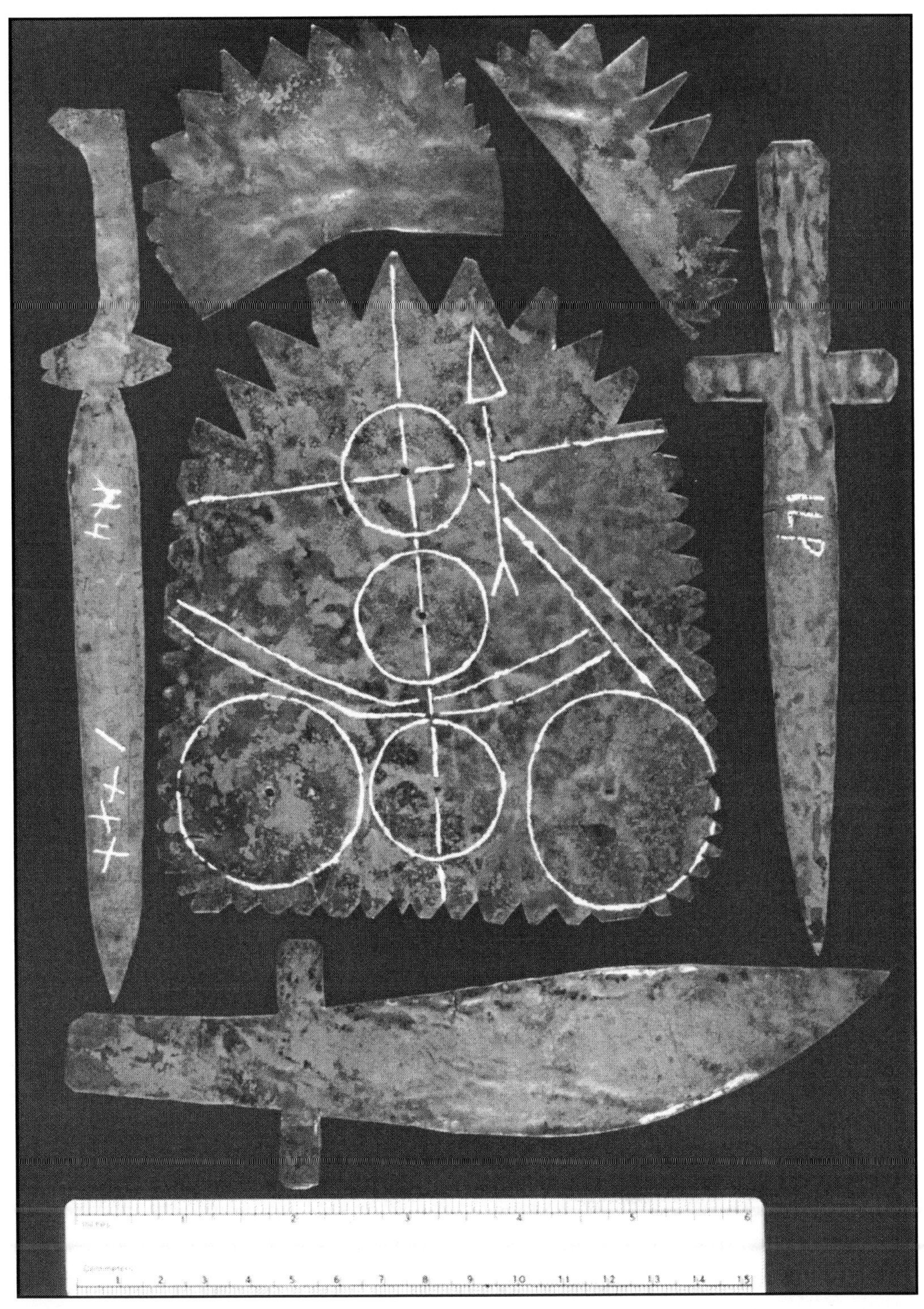

Working within a hundred-foot-square of dense brush and deep sand, Arnold unearthed these symbolic clues cut from sheets of copper, all buried several feet deep in oiled, pulverized charcoal. The half-discs represented the rising and setting sun. The center plate with tracery (outlined in white) was called "the crown." The three daggers were found in separate locations. (Photo by the author)

Once again, John hit the mass of oiled, pulverized charcoal that tapered downward. Soon he exposed something metallic, and on his hands and knees, he cleaned away the charcoal that would have preserved the object for centuries. Arnold watched carefully as the replica of a beautiful dagger was exposed, its blade pointing downward.

Arnold lifted the dagger from the charcoal. Cut from the same raw-beaten copper from which the sun bursts were made, the dagger was a mere seven inches long, with a blade not quite three-quarters of an inch wide. On its blade appeared the letters *ILP*, formed by minute dots pricked with a sharp instrument. "Each prick looked like a fleck of gold," remembers Sembritzki's daughter Verne, who took a fancy to the copper dagger soon after its discovery.[9]

Arnold interpreted the knife to mean to dig still deeper, which they did. At four or five feet deep, they encountered a yellow clay, different from any soil they had yet found, and strangely, almost as smooth as glass. Upon that discovery, Arnold asked John to let him take over. Carefully he peeled off the darker soil a little at a time, until finally he had exposed a perfectly arched doorway of yellow clay, about two feet wide and five feet high. The smooth, glassy appearance of the archway had been the result of piecing it together with the ochre-colored clay when still wet. It was the craftsmanship of a skilled artisan, who also filled the arched doorway with pure white sand. They were destroyed as Arnold directed the digging to continue in that direction.

Arnold seemed sure he had now found the secret passageway to the underground rooms, but further digging yielded nothing. Even so, he remained undaunted, saying only they would have to dig elsewhere for other signs that would guide them back to the underground chamber. Many days had now gone by, and Sembritzki believed he had neglected his farm for much too long. Spring had come, and the harvesting of his crops would soon be upon him. Arnold would leave temporarily to enlist a select crew of men to pursue the labor that he knew would lie ahead.

Over the weeks that Arnold lived with the Sembritzki family, they learned little of his well-guarded past, but on one occasion, perhaps regretfully for Arnold later, Verne recalled, "he either indicated to us, or told us outright, that he had killed the Mexican with the wooden leg in order to get the sheepskin map. I was only a small child when Mr. Arnold was working on this hidden treasure on our place, and I loved him because he was so kind to me. I used to sit in his lap, what little he had, because he had a big paunch like a blown-up balloon. He wasn't very tall, but he was awfully fat. He said he was in his seventies at that time, but in spite of all this, he was very active and mentally keen."[10]

Because of Arnold's paunch and apparent difficulty in bending over to tie his shoes, the younger Sembritzki girls often delighted in taking turns to do that for him. Once Arnold gave one of them a small gold ring for that gesture.

The Sembritzki family observed Arnold's patience firsthand. "He was slow to anger and very secretive," reflects Verne. "He did not divulge any more information about anything than he wanted to."[11]

Arnold often spoke of living in Mexico, where he had cultivated the friendship of the Mexican from whom he had received the sheepskin map. Various versions have been told about how he obtained that map, all of which may have been told by Arnold himself. Sembritzki's daughter Ann Fuqua recounts a different story, which she heard from Arnold when she was about nineteen.

Ann is perhaps the only person who can say she once glimpsed Arnold's sheepskin map when he spread it out on the bed to study. Everything about it was mysterious, with its many diagrams and symbols and circles. Arnold revealed that an elderly Mexican who lived with his sister possessed the sheepskin. Everything Arnold knew, he had learned from him. When their house burned, Arnold saved the sheepskin from the fire, but its owners did not know that. Later versions were watered down from the story Verne had overheard from Arnold's conversations with her father and mother, a story that strongly hinted at foul play.

The Sembritzkis did not pry for details about the map, but each member of that family knew Arnold guarded it with his life. Sometime before, he had moved to a tent that he set up in the backyard of the Sembritzki home. There they knew that Arnold slept with two heavy revolvers by his pillow. "And when he was away," Verne recalls, "we had specific instructions not to go inside his tent." No one ever questioned that order.

4

A Company to Dig $60 Million in Gold

When Arnold saw that extensive excavation would be necessary to find all the clues that led to the secret passageway, and it in turn to the treasure chamber that he believed guarded $60 million in gold, he gathered around him a select group. Among those who had worked with him at the Spider Rock diggings, only Dr. Terrell and his son Cabe would become members of the search that now continued at the Sembritzki farm.

It is known that Dr. Terrell financed much of Arnold's pursuit, but to what extent is not known. Into his fold Arnold now brought Jo A. Hodges, an area farmer, and John F. Hart, a longtime Callahan County rancher, the father of Sam Hart, who had first brought Arnold to the Sembritzki farm.[1] Dr. W. M. Crume of Munday also became a member. Dr. Terrell served as secretary-treasurer and saw to it that all transactions were handled in a businesslike fashion.

The first item of business came on May 20, 1905, when the executive committee of the Sembritzki Mineral Company held its first meeting. On the motion of John Hart, John Sembritzki was elected chairman. Again on the motion of Hart, Dr. Terrell was elected secretary-treasurer. The committee appointed Hart general manager. The minutes of that meeting reveal just how well organized the West Texas treasure quest was to be. No record exists showing who contributed the money or how much, but there were a total of ten shares of stock, and it was decreed that one share of the company would be used to pay Sembritzki, Hart, Hodges, Dr. Crume, Arnold, Dr. Terrell, and others "for the purpose of discharging all claims held by said parties or others against the company for any and all labor, money, or materials furnished by them in all the work or money furnished by them for company prior to the organization of this company on May 20, 1905."[2]

The committee decided that "D. M. Arnold [would] be relieved from paying any part of the expenses, or performing any of the manual labor from this date, his duties being defined as follows: He shall assist in an advisory manner to the best of his ability in any and all ways in the promotion of the work; to look after the locations, signs, and marks pertaining to the secret work."

Expense accounts and time sheets were to be kept by each participant, with each man paid from the company treasury. It was decreed that "the value of a day's work performed shall be 45 cents per day at 10 hours; value for a day's work for a man and one horse shall be $1.50; and a man and two horses shall be $2 per day." Finally, it was agreed that "John Hart, as general manager, shall have credit on the books of $1.50 per day for the days he works as manager, this concession is made in order to pay for the extra time and work devolving upon him."

That same day, John and Lucretia Sembritzki signed the lease papers with Arnold, Terrell, Hart, Hodges, and Crume. The lease included "twenty acres in a square body situated in the SW corner of Sec. 73 and SE corner of Sec. 82, the premises to be held and possessed by lessees for the purposes of prospecting, exploring, investigating and mining, for all minerals, metals, ores, valuables and things to be found in and upon said premises, with full power and authority to take, possess, and carry away and dispose of all, or any part, of said valuables subject to: that said lessees shall commence the work within 30 days from the date hereof; if there shall be anything of value found the lessees shall pay over and deliver to owners five per cent of any and all things of value so found on said premises; all of the maps, plats, marks or surveys of the works found by parties hereof on said premises, shall be and remain the property of said lessees."[3]

Subject to those conditions, the lease was to be in force for one year, "beginning the 20th day of May, A.D. 1905." It is strange that indenture was not witnessed until October 27, not filed for record until November 15, or duly recorded until December 2 at the Callahan County Courthouse in Baird.[4]

Work began immediately on the hundred-foot-square piece of deep blow sand a quarter of a mile south of the Sembritzki homestead. Five days before signing the contract, Arnold purchased a shovel, a barrel, three pick handles, a box of pepper sauce, black pepper, and peas at a cost of $3.25, and Jo Hodges a bucket, potatoes, a lantern globe, oil, sugar, lard, syrup, salt, and coffee for $2.65. Four days into the project, expenses showed powder, coffee, bacon, flour, dynamite, a coffee mill, and a rope at $12.[5] Arnold moved his tent to the diggings when the excavation began in earnest, guiding and directing the covert treasure quest every inch of the way, with all the care and excitement of digging in an Egyptian pyramid.

Again Arnold studied the curious stone map he and Sembritzki had dug from the roots of the regal oak tree. Again he remeasured the varas between the copper replicas of the rising and setting sun, and the beautiful yellow clay arch they had uncovered five feet below the surface. Over the days and weeks that followed, Arnold's efforts were rewarded with the discovery of at least three other objects cut from the same thin copper used to make the half-discs and dagger. Two of those metallic pieces were additional copper daggers, each of a different pattern and unlike the first he had found. Although each dagger was about the same length as the first (seven to eight inches), the blades and handles all differed.

Incised into the blade of one dagger were the Roman numerals XXXI and what appeared to be II4, or perhaps W4. This blade was less than three-quarters of an inch wide, while the blade of the third dagger, bearing no inscription, was fully one and a half inches wide. What these artifacts symbolized, Arnold did not say, or did not know.

Perhaps the most peculiar of the discoveries was a small copper plate almost six inches long by five inches wide. Its top was rounded and trimmed into sharp points, while the remainder was almost square and trimmed with short, narrow points. Made from the same raw-beaten copper as the other objects, the cryptic tracery it bore proved to be a mystery

The State of Texas }
County of Callahan } This Indenture Witnesseth
that we, the undersigned parties hereto, have
this day, jointly and severally made and entered
into the following agreement and compact, to Wit:-
We do hereby agree to make, form and enter
into a firm Company or Partnership to be
Known as The Sembritzki Mineral Company
with General Office and Headquarters at
Haskell Texas, with such branch offices
at other place or places as may be necessary.
The purpose and object of said Company
is the prospecting for, mining, recovering and
disposal of all ores, minerals, metals, valuables
and things and to explore, investigate, and to
search for, secure, possess and dispose of and
distribute any and all such ores minerals, metals
valuables and things, resulting from such labors
and found within the scope and extent of the
operations of said Company.
It is hereby agreed that the control and
management of all the business and affairs
of said Company shall be and is hereby
delegated to and vested in an Executive Committee
of Three members, who shall have full
legal powers and authority to direct, manage and
control all the business, affairs and proceedings
of said Company, and it is hereby mutually agreed

Above and next page: On May 20, 1905, Dave Arnold, Dr. W. M. Crume, John F. Hart, Jo A. Hodges, and Dr. C. L. Terrell drew up this contract with John and Lucretia Sembritzki in their quest for lost Spanish gold. (Courtesy Charles Terrell)

This Indenture Witnesseth:

County of Callahan

That I. Sembritzki I. Jno Sembritzki Joined by my wife Lucrecia Sembritzki party of the First Part of the county and state aforesaid, Lessor_, for and in consideration of the sum of One Dollar, Cash to me in hand paid by Wm. Arnold W. M. Cumnes, John F. Hart, Jos. A. Hodges And C. L. Terrell Party of the Second Part,

Lessees, the receipt whereof is hereby acknowledged and confessed, and the further consideration of the undertakings and agreements hereinafter stated, to be kept and performed by said lessees, their successors and assigns, as well as for the labor and expenses heretofore performed and incurred, and hereafter to be performed and incurred, do by these presents, demise and lease unto the said party of the second part, Lessees all of the following described real estate and premises, situated in Callahan County Texas, , and more particularly described as follows: Twenty acres in a square body situated in S.W. cor. of Sec 73. and S.E. cor. Sec 82. of The B.B.B.&C. R.R. Co. Surv. and being an equal amount out of each survey, and is the land now owned and controlled by party of first part here to

the said premises to be entered into, held and possessed by said lessees, their successors and assigns, for the purposes of prospecting, exploring, investigating and mining, for all minerals, metals, ores, valuables and things to be found in and upon said premises, with full power and authority to take, possess and carry away and dispose of all, or any part,, of said minerals, metals, ores, valuables and things found in on or upon said premises, subject to the conditions hereinafter stated, to wit:

The said Lessees, their successors and assigns, shall commence the work of prospecting, exploring, investigating and mining for minerals, metals, ores, valuables and things in and on said premises, in good faith, within Thirty days From the date hereof, and shall continue to prosecute said work until they shall be satisfied that there is or is not minerals, metals, ores, valuables and things in and on said premises in sufficient quantities and value to justify the labor and expense required to prosecute said work, and if there shall be any thing of value found in or on said premises, then and in that event, the said parties of the second part, Lessees, their successors and assigns shall pay over and deliver, or cause to be paid over and delivered unto ~~the said party of the First Part, Lessor his heirs or assigns~~ Five per cent of any and all things of value so found on said premises, all of the maps, plats, marks or surveys of the works found by parties hereto on said premises, shall be and remain the property of said lessees.

The said Lessees shall have the right to erect all ~~necessary~~ buildings and machinery and requisites on said premises for the purpose of properly prosecuting and carrying on the work, and shall also have free access to over and through adjacent premises belonging to said lessor to the nearest public road.

If party of the second part shall fail to comply with the terms and conditions of this lease, then and in that event said lease shall end and determine, and said party of the first part may declare an ouster, and re-enter upon and hold said demised premises.

Subject to the conditions herein mentioned, this lease shall be and remain in full force and effect for the term of One Year, and thereafter, as long as necessary from date hereof.

to all who viewed it. Three circles, lined up one below the other, were etched down the center of the plate. A single line ran from the top of the plate down through the center of each circle. Another line intersected the center of the top circle. To its right appeared a large arrow and a kind of lane leading off to the right. It intersected still another lane that ran across the plate between the two bottom circles. On either side of the bottom circle appeared still larger circles. In the center of each of the five circles was a hole or puncture through the copper plate.

What did the curious tracery mean? Five hills? There are no hills within sight of the Sembritzki farm. In fact, there are no landmarks of any kind. Only the marks, the signs, could have led Arnold to that plot of deep blow sand in a wilderness of mesquite and scrub oak. If he knew the meaning of the strangely shaped copper plate, he did not share that information, or no one alive today remembers an interpretation of it.

A later search would refer to the copper plate as "the crown" and state that it was unearthed near the beautiful clay arch. Of all the tantalizing objects found on her father's farm, Verne, as a young girl, did not view this piece. It may be that once it was uncovered, Arnold concealed it, sharing it only with Dr. Terrell and Cabe, who by this time were visiting the diggings.

It was obvious to Arnold that the half-discs, copper daggers, and plate were all made from the same thin copper as the oval-shaped plate, dagger, key, and leaf found atop the Spider Rock sixty miles northwest. The three daggers, each cut from a different pattern, were all from an ancient design, as was the dagger originally found with the Spider Rock. It was probable, too, that both stone maps, with many of the same symbols, were carved into carefully chosen thin stone slabs. All these things Arnold must have noted and discussed with the Terrells.

Also found among the recent diggings were the copper trimmings left by the coppersmith who cut the symbolic objects from the thin sheets. In practically all the excavations were countless small blue glass beads that Arnold called "prayer beads." Verne remembers, "We picked them up by the handfuls, played with them for a day, then discarded them. None of us ever had any idea of their historic value."[6]

As Arnold continued to direct the digging, the excavations mounted, and the area took on the appearance of a diamond field dug helter-skelter in an attempt to find its gems. Several shafts were sunk in an effort to find the underground rooms, but at twenty-nine feet, as Arnold predicted, they always struck an abundant underground water source and were forced to abandon the shaft.

Arnold never fully explained the hidden city or underground fortification he sought that contained the rooms of gold in such quantity to cause him to arrive at a figure of $60 million. Of course, no one seemed to know exactly what Arnold was thinking much of the time. The size of that subterranean sanctuary could only be conjectured, but Sembritzki believed that such an underground lair was possible on his farm.

He had attempted to find water prior to Arnold's appearance, and each time failed. Whatever Arnold knew about reading Spanish marks and interpreting the stone map, he had been correct about recognizing the depth to water. To reach that twenty-nine-foot level, one had to dig beneath a deep layer of sand, and a still deeper layer of yellow clay, before finding a stratum of blue shale, and finally one of solid blue rock. If an underground chamber had been dug there, or a natural one found, discovering it would be like seeking a needle in a haystack, unless one were able to follow a trail of markers to its entrance.

As the time sheets kept on each man's work reflect, work was erratic the summer and fall of 1905. Each man could not spend all his time at the treasure site, and Arnold himself would disappear for days at a time, evidently seeking the clues he needed to accurately guide his course. Between May 22 and July 19, Sembritzki devoted ten days' labor to the diggings, and between May 20 and August 12, ten and a half days under Hart's supervision and eight more under Arnold's guidance. For those dates, Hart turned in thirty-three and a half days, and Hodges, between May 22 and July 19, twenty-two days. Dr. Terrell's account book of July showed expenses of $125.45, those shared on the basis of one-fifth for each man.[7]

Perhaps only Dr. Terrell and Cabe knew where Arnold disappeared to when he left the Sembritzki farm. Or perhaps only Arnold knew what story he was piecing together in his own mind in July and August of 1905, and whether any part of the discovery at the Spider Rock would help him at the Sembritzki farm. Or did the stone map and copper symbols found there in some way dictate his actions back at the Spider diggings?

Whatever the significance of one site to the other, Arnold traveled back and forth between them in the summer of 1905. In mid-July he left the Sembritzki farm to redirect the search at Mount Lama Vista. All the original members were back at the Spider diggings by the second week of July, as the account books and time sheets kept by Dr. Terrell reveal. The work performed there was business of the Arnold Mining and Milling Company, and among the supplies were twenty-eight sticks of dynamite, fuses, and caps purchased by Joe Allen and his son Crawford in Haskell.[8]

By August 14, a newcomer named Lester Smith had accumulated thirty-five days' work at Lama Vista. John Johnson had invested twenty-seven and a half days, and his brother Kelly, twenty-one. Bud Jones tallied thirty-six days with assistance from his father-in-law, W. J. Carouth. R. R. Davis spent twenty-four and a half days in the renewed quest that Arnold thought important enough to again enlist each of the original party.[9]

Work at the Spider diggings continued through part of August and at least into September, when the dissatisfaction of another newcomer, named Alberta Epllis, prompted him to write Dr. Terrell this note from Mount Lama Vista on September 6: "Kind Sir, I hope you will not think that I am meddling with your affairs, but Mr. Smith wants to lease his land to some one and I think that the Company can get it by trying and having you see him. And if they don't get it now we won't be able to dig much. I hope that I will see you out here before long. That is all."[10]

When the lease with Hoy Smith expired is not known, nor is anything else of that intensive search back on the Salt Fork. What is known is that Arnold promptly returned to the diggings on the Sembritzki farm, no later than August 17, where his full efforts, and those of the members of his party there, were concentrated as never before. Between August 17 and September 21, Hodges logged twenty-seven and a half days' labor. He was followed by Dr. Terrell for twenty-seven days; Dr. Crume, twenty-four and three-fourths days; Hart, twenty-three and a half days; and Sembritzki, fourteen and three-fourths days.[11]

Lucretia Sembritzki and her children visited the diggings more often during that summer. A well-worn wagon trail led past their house for a quarter of a mile or so south to the diggings, where mounds of white sand and deep holes replaced what was once a wilderness of impenetrable brush. To anyone who did not know what had been found in that geometric pattern of shallow and deep holes, some still black with the charcoal dug from them, the mounds of sand, cleared brush and trees, and workmen's tents nearby would have made absolutely no sense in a region devoid of landmarks and stone outcroppings of any kind. By now even the huge oak, whose roots had so long guarded the cryptic stone map, had been felled and dug out to clear it from the site. The Sembritzki children continued to fill their pockets with the many small blue glass beads dug from the shafts that littered the white mounds.

Perhaps because the expense of the diggings continued to mount and the work seemingly would not soon end, the executive committee of the Sembritzki Mineral Company—Sembritzki, Hart, and Dr. Terrell—met at Baird on August 10 and resolved to transfer two and a half shares of the company stock to Dr. John Collier of that city. In return for that stock, equal to twenty-five percent of the stock, Dr. Collier agreed "to supply and furnish all money, means, provisions, supplies, tools, machinery, appliances and all other requisites necessary for the execution, promotion, and completion of all of the work to be undertaken and performed by said company." In addition, Collier was also "to furnish 25 percent of all the work and labor."[12]

It is probable that Dr. John Collier was invited into the search because Hart or other locals hoped he could translate the mystery stone map. Collier had come to Baird in 1898 and founded Baird College. He retired in 1904 when the school was destroyed by fire.[13] Collier obviously took an interest in the search, but he would soon learn that Arnold would not share anything with him.

As the weeks dragged into months, it became more apparent that Arnold was having difficulty unraveling the Spanish puzzle. His interpretation of the cryptic drawings and each of the stone and copper replicas never changed—yet somehow he lacked the final key that would lead him underground, and the holes dug to find that secret corridor were many.

When one clue seemed to be the last, Arnold sought still another, with little explanation as to his method or reasoning. It was his way. It seemed to be understood that the big man from Mexico was purposely not revealing everything he knew. "I think we all sensed that, and took for granted that was the way he handled his affairs," recounts Verne. "Arnold was not a talkative person, especially regarding his personal life and affairs. He confided in no one."[14]

Perhaps that covert custom, coupled with other problems Arnold encountered at the Sembritzki farm, only magnified tensions among the members. John Sembritzki's jealousy of Arnold certainly must have become a major factor in the turn of events in the fall of 1905. Sembritzki was German-born and originally settled near Fredericksburg. Although he spoke English, it was always with a heavy German accent, and few people could understand him. That, coupled with the fact he was almost deaf, made it almost impossible to carry on a conversation with him.

For those reasons, Arnold did most of his talking with Sembritzki's wife, Lucretia. That led to jealousy and grew into a seemingly violent hatred of Arnold's presence. Those tensions must in part explain the chain of events that resulted in a series of letters to members of the search party on October 16. Both Dr. Terrell and Dr. Crume received the following letter, signed by Sembritzki and Hart:

> Dear Sir: We the undersigned members of committee of Camp Sembritzki, hereby notify you that in compliance with an agreement heretofore entered into between ourselves, J. A. Hodges, C. L. Terrell, and W. M. Crume, with reference to the works and excavations being made on the land of John Sembritzki about six miles north of Baird,

Baird Texas
Aug. 10th 1905
The Executive Committee
of the Sembritzki Mineral
Company. Met in Executive
Session at Baird Texas
and passed following
resolution to wit:
Resolved That we the
Committee hereby agree
to transfer sell and
deliver to Dr. John Collier
of Baird Texas Two and
one half Shares of the
Stock set apart of Co
for Expense and incidental
accounts as expressed in
our articles of agreement
of May 28th 5 — He to
furnish all supplies
needed, from and after
this date for the successful
operations of the works
pertaining to the business
of the Co and to be fully
defined in agreement
of assignment of the
said Shares of Stock

On August 10, 1905, the executive committee of the Sembritzki Mineral Company met in Baird and agreed to sell Dr. John Collier two and a half shares, hoping that he could help translate the cryptic stone map. (Courtesy Charles Terrell)

> Texas, we do this day declare said works stopped and abandoned by you on your failure to come up with your portion of the expense necessary to operate said works and excavations, and that hereafter you fail to have any interest therein on account of said failure to furnish funds, and are hereby notified that we propose to continue said works, and that should anything of value be discovered, that you can only come in for a part to the extent of $24.75, the amount of funds you have furnished in operating said works and excavations.[15]

Dr. Terrell's amount of funds furnished was placed at $35.20. It may be that Hodges also received such a letter, and perhaps Arnold a similar one. Three days later, on October 19, Dr. Crume wrote Dr. Terrell this message:

> Dear Doctor: Received your letter yesterday evening. Will say that it will be impossible for me to go to Baird now. I think Cabe could do more than I could since he is there and onto how everything has been working and better acquainted with those fellows. Smith [no doubt Lester Smith] told me to tell you that he thought the best thing to be done would be to send some one to take charge of the work and go ahead with it. If Collier fails to do what he agreed to do, it seems that that would be the best way out of the trouble.[16]

The original contract of May 20, allowing the search to proceed on Sembritzki's land, was finally witnessed on October 27. The following day, Cabe wrote his father that he was sending the lease and contract. They were filed for record on November 15 and recorded December 2.

Cabe had become disgusted with his position in Baird, clerking in his uncle's drugstore. Apparently his uncle did not think much about his preoccupation with Spanish maps and clues, as Cabe revealed to his father on October 28: "I have a great deal of trouble getting things fixed up here. It seems as my *Boss* is all ways taking so much stock in our business, and says no body but a D. fool would monkey with such things. I am full up with his foolishness myself, and am going to quit the D. Store."[17]

On November 20 another contract was made, giving Lester Smith two shares of the company stock, in exchange for twenty percent of all "money, labor, and expense necessary" to carry on the work and operations during existence of contract, effective until July 1, 1906.[18] Perhaps it was the financial boost Arnold needed to carry on. He had engaged Smith the previous July when the search was renewed at the Spider diggings. Perhaps brought in to serve as an impartial mediator amid mounting tensions, Smith would keep the account books and turn in the time sheets to Dr. Terrell.

Although differences appear to have been overcome, Arnold must still have had cause for concern. That his thoughts also turned to the work developing back at the Spider diggings is reflected in a letter he penned to Dr. Terrell from Baird on November 23, 1905. It was written without punctuation, which has been added here for clarity. The spelling is his own.

> Dear Sir and friend: I will answer your leter. Would of did so sooner but have bin so buzey that I could not. Will say in regard to the work, we just got the contract all rite and will send you the contract and the Collier contract. Dr. Collier turned it over to

W. M. CRUME, M. D.

MUNDAY, TEXAS, 10/19 1905

Haskell Texas.

Dr. C. L. Terrell.

Dear Doctor Received your letter
yesterday evening. Will say that
it will be impossable for me to go
to Baird now. Think Cabe could
do more than I could he is there
and onto how every thing has been
working and better acquainted with
those fellows. Smith told me
to tell you ~~that~~ he thought the best
thing to be done would be to send
some one to take charge of the work
and go ahead with it if Collier
fails to do what he agreed to do
it seems ~~that that~~ would be the
best way out of the trouble.

Yours Truly. W M Crume.

October 19, 1905, Dr. W. M. Crume of Munday writes Dr. C. L. Terrell of Haskell his concerns regarding the progress at the Sembritzki farm. (Courtesy Charles Terrell) me and Smith, and sayed he was out, and that he, Collier, had never signed it. As you will see, he, Collier, did not sighn it. So we have the contract.

Will say Lester started to Dallas on the 12 o'clock train and will stop at Cisco and see the little girel and have hur to look up the Haskell and Salt fork work and rite to you at once.

Now in regard to the cliping you sent me, I am shur Dr. Collier is the man that roate it. He, Dr. Collier, wanted me to give him some dater. I just told him I would when you and I conculted to gether. I am pumping him. I am geting all the dater and giving out nothing. You can bet you botom dollar that.

Well, Dr., we have it all our way. Me and Smith has our tent on the ground and a chimney to warm by. So you see we are in possession, whitch is 9 points in law. Hart readley sighn the contract and sayed if Symbriskey diden, he would, and we would go ahead with out John S. But John S. come over; all sighned it.

I will rite Bud in regard to the old Salt fork and the Peak. Now I think the work will go on all rigte. Mr. John Willson told Hart he was going to stop us if we dident give him one-half sheare. I told Hart I dident have nothing to do with he, Wilson, and for him to just go ahead if he had any standing in the company. So he stopt his racket. I dont know any one but what is in this company. Rite me at Clyde.[19]

The John Willson mentioned by Arnold remains otherwise unidentified. "Bud in regard to the old Salt fork," referred to Bud Jones at the Spider diggings. The little girl whom Lester Smith planned on seeing in Cisco is a mystery, unless she was the clairvoyant he had enlisted at the Spider Rock site, or even at Sembritzki's. Obviously Arnold did not like or get along with the learned Dr. Collier, and because of it, Collier decided not to become involved with him.

In late 1905 and early 1906, Arnold's troubles continued to mount. To have come so far and found so much, it seemed as if every avenue of approach was leading nowhere. Seemingly what had previously occurred at the Spider diggings was now happening at the Sembritzki farm. It was as if his sheepskin map, the stone charts, and the many copper clues all led him to the brink of discovery, only to withhold it from him. Arnold must have realized his own shortcomings, his own lack of knowledge, when at last he brought a strange Mexican to the Sembritzki diggings, showing him the stone map and all they had found in the past months.

The Mexican interpreted many of the signs as Arnold had but told him nothing that he wished to hear. "The treasure is cursed," the Mexican lamented, "guarded by evil spirits." Arnold summoned other Mexicans to the diggings, and at long intervals between, they came, examined the stone map, and always announced the same belief: Arnold would never find the Spanish treasure, because it was cursed—and all who tried, each Mexican warned, would surely meet with disaster. In every instance they left, wishing not to be involved any further.

Arnold knew he had found too much to have misinterpreted the stone drawing. His own sheepskin map had never been wrong. Yet, somehow, after all he had seen and discovered, again he was failing. Perhaps because of that failure, because of Arnold's seemingly devious method of arriving at where to dig, his co-workers more and more doubted he was leading them to the treasure at all, and they began digging on their own.

Tensions at the Sembritzki farm rose so high that one morning Hart, a crusty fellow

1)

Baird Texas
November 23rd 195
Dr C L Terrell Dear Sir and
friend i Will answer
your leter Would of Did So
Sooner But have Bin So
Buzey that i Could Not Will
Say in Regard to the Work Wee
Just got the Contract all
Rite and Will Send you the
Contract and the Collier
Contract Dr Collier Turned
it over to me and Smith and
Sayed he was out and that
he Collier had Never Signed it
as you Will See he Colier Did
Not Sighn it So Wee have
the Contract

2)

Will Say Lester Started to Dallas
on the 12 ocolck train and Will
Stop at Cisco and See the litte
girl and have her to look
up the haskell and
Salt fork Work and Rite to
you at once Now in Regard to
the Cliping you Sent me
i am Shur Dr Collier is the
man that Roate it he Dr
Doctor Collier Wanted me to
give him Some Dater i
Just told him i Would When you
and i Conculted to gether i
am Pumping him i am
geting all the Dater and
giving out Nothing you Can
Bet your botom Doller on that

3)

Well Dr Wee have it all our
Way me and Smith has our
tent on the ground and a
Chimley to Warm By So you
See Wee are in Posesion Whitch is
9 Points in law hart Readly
Sighn the Contract and Sayed
if Symbriskey Diden he
Would and Wee Would go a head
With out John S But John S
Connover all Sighned it i Will
Rite Bud in Regard to the Bald
Salt fork and the Peak i
think the Work Will go one all
Rite Mr John Willson toald
hart he Was going to Stop us
if Wee Dident give him one half
Sheare i told hart i Dident

4)

have Nothing to Dow with
he Willson and for him to
Just go a head if he had any
Standing in the Company
So he Stopt his racket
i Dont know any one But What
is in this Company Rite here
at Clyde

Yours Truley

D M Arnold

Dave Arnold wrote this rare letter to Dr. Terrell on November 23, 1905, telling of the work on the Sembritzki farm. It is the only known letter in his own handwriting, and reveals his dislike of, and refusal to work with, Dr. John Collier. (Courtesy Charles Terrell) who seemed to resent taking orders from Arnold, appeared wearing two six-shooters. Arnold said nothing that day, but the next morning he wore his own heavy revolvers. Sembritzki had already made his sentiments known, due to his jealousy of Arnold. But when it fast became evident that Arnold would not back down, Sembritzki intervened, demanding that Arnold and Hart leave their guns at the side of the hole being dug that day. The two consented but continued to bring their weapons each day.

Work continued through December and January. Lester Smith sent December time sheets to Dr. Terrell showing that Dr. Crume had amassed sixteen and three-quarter days' work; Hart, sixteen and one-quarter days; Sembritzki, twelve and three-quarter days; Dr. Terrell, twelve days; and May (not otherwise identified), five and three-quarter days. On New Year's Day of 1906, Smith wrote Dr. Terrell from Clyde: "We are getting on very well I guess, considering bad weather. We are down some thirty-seven feet. Will let you know if anything develops."[20]

In January, work continued at about the same rate. Dr. Crume logged sixteen and three-quarter days; May, thirteen and a half days; Hart, thirteen days; and Sembritzki, six and a half days. Smith tallied $13.65 for his labor. Total expenses for labor amounted to $164.35. January of 1906 or perhaps a short time thereafter appears to mark the end of Arnold's quest at the Sembritzki farm. That was the last month time sheets were sent to Dr. Terrell, and a February 1 letter from Smith to the doctor stated that Sembritzki no longer wished to be a part of the search that had now stretched out for most of a year.

"We are getting on very slow with the work," Smith wrote, "as we have had and still get some very hard rocks to contend with. Mr. Sembritzki isn't helping us anymore. We have offered I think everything fair and reasonable to him. We offered, if he would help us finish this hole, we would let him go to work on his crop and not lose anymore time, and he would not accept that proposition, and therefore we have had to work as you see the statements show."[21]

It may have been Sembritzki's way of telling Arnold he no longer wished his presence, an attitude that may have been egged on by some members of the party. Tensions being what they were, and Arnold, perhaps confident that nothing would be found without his guidance, temporarily disappeared from the Sembritzki farm. Although he would return, perhaps out of spite, he would never knowingly step foot back at the diggings he had directed for almost a year. A check stub shows that Dr. Terrell last paid Lester Smith $15 on February 12, 1906, for "Sembritzki Company work."[22]

"I remember Dave Arnold as a kindly, soft-spoken man who was very kind to me as a small child, and I loved him," recalls Verne. "On the other hand, he carried two big six-shooters with him constantly, and I don't believe he would have hesitated a moment to use them if he thought it was necessary. There has never been any doubt in my mind but that Dave Arnold knew exactly what he was doing, and he knew the location of the secret passage to reach the underground village. Otherwise, how on earth could he have located all of these things in a wilderness of thick brush and deep sand where there were no traces of human habitation since the world began. The reason he abandoned the project is that he received no cooperation from my father or any of the workmen. There was tremendous friction among them, almost to the point of hate and murder. He simply quit and left."[23]

Arnold returned to Stonewall County, and in the months ahead, Hart and Hodges continued their random digging, sinking shafts in an area that already gave the appearance of being dug with no plan or purpose. Arnold returned briefly to the Sembritzki farm from time to time, but he was obviously upset and disturbed, remembers Verne. It was almost as if he had lost all interest in the search, although he seemed to enjoy the fact that no one else had found anything since his departure.

About this time it was learned that Arnold and his wife had divorced and he had remarried. That was *his* story, but for some unexplained reason, Arnold lied. His wife, Martha, whom he had married forty years before, died on March 9, 1906, at age fifty-six. Her brief obituary reveals almost nothing, simply stating: "Mrs. M. A. Arnold died at Water Valley at 4 o'clock Friday afternoon. Burial will be there on Saturday. The deceased was well known in San Angelo."[24] Why Arnold would tell anything other than the truth is as much a mystery as the man himself. The Sembritzki family would have no reason to doubt his story, nor would they ever meet his new wife.

It was obvious Arnold knew more than he was ever willing to share. An example of that knowledge was later shown during one brief visit when he took young Verne with him to examine an oak tree a hundred yards north of the digging site.

"When we arrived at the oak tree," Verne recalls, "Mr. Arnold stopped, looked, and sighted, then walked briskly to another. He pointed to a mark of this tree and remarked to me, 'See this mark? This means to go east ten *varas*.' He stepped off these *varas*, which led to another old oak, the mark on which meant so many *varas* south. When he stepped this distance off, we came to still a fourth such tree. I presume the mark on the last tree meant the termination point, because he said this was the place.

"Originally, two oak trees had grown from one trunk, but years before, one had been cut down. Between that stump and the trunk of the tree was a cradlelike indentation. Mr. Arnold took the ax which he had, chopped into the indentation, and opened a hollow space. He reached inside and pulled out a handful of copper trimmings, which he gave to me."[25]

The small copper strips were like many others they had found at the diggings. That Arnold knew where they would be found showed his uncanny ability at interpreting the strange symbols etched into the tree trunks so prominent around the diggings. Later, Verne's mother asked her to take her to the tree. Lucretia dug around the base and found still more copper strips like those Arnold had found, but nothing more.

Arnold returned once more to the Sembritzki farm. The Sembritzkis thought it strange that he had come then, but they were glad to see him, especially the children, whom he always treated with kindness and generosity. Up to then, the Sembritzkis had kept all the artifacts found on their farm, including the beautifully carved stone map Arnold had so patiently sought. He asked if he could examine the stone once more, and the Sembritzkis naturally agreed. But after he had gone, they discovered that he had taken all that had been found on their farm: the stone map, the two large stones with their single-word inscriptions, the copper daggers—everything considered important. Arnold had missed nothing, except a tracing of the stone map one of Sembritzki's daughters had made.

So far as the Sembritzki family knew, Arnold disappeared from the country. None of them would ever see or hear from him again. What John and Lucretia would never know was that he had not disappeared at all. It was more than sixty years later before any of the Sembritzki children knew his search had not ended at their farm.

With Arnold apparently gone forever, Jo Hodges and John Hart continued working for a time on their own. They persuaded a clairvoyant, a Mrs. Matlock of Abilene, to visit the diggings. She performed her trance at the site and directed more digging, none of which yielded anything. The final blow to the partnership came when Hart and his wife divorced.

Someone who knew about some of the discoveries at the Sembritzki farm told a reporter in the fall of 1907, who dispatched it to the *Fort Worth Telegram*. Although not completely accurate, the story reveals Arnold's name for the first and perhaps only time during his entire search, and it offers yet another version of how he acquired his map:

> *Special to The Telegram.*
>
> ABILENE, Texas, Oct. 26.—Out one hour's ride east of Abilene a most wonderful find, that of an old mine, has been made. Three years ago a Mr. Arnold located this place by the aid of a chart furnished him by an old Mexican he had befriended, and who, when it dawned upon him that his hours were numbered, feeling appreciation of the kindness shown by Mr. Arnold, called him to his bedside and placing the chart in his hand, told just enough to give some faint idea of where this mine was located, and expired.
>
> It appears from characters and figures found on copper plates already excavated that this mine was in operation in 1731, tho if such was the case, the chart given Mr. Arnold by the old Mexican had been handed down from generation to generation. Be this as it may, every article called for by this chart has been found at the exact point mentioned.
>
> Among the articles so far excavated are the following: An adobe door twelve feet from surface of the ground; four copper daggers, each at supposed corners and of equal distance from the door; a copper key; a copper plate about three inches by five inches, arched at top and so indented as to represent the rising sun; a similar plate was also found indented to represent the setting sun; on the underside of one of the plates was the word "Ariente," on reverse side of the other plate "Poiente."
>
> A visit to the place will fill one with wonder as the mind runs back to the ancient times these relics represent.
>
> That this is either an old "Aztec" house of worship or a long lost mine, no one can doubt.
>
> That it contains an enormous deposit of silver seems to be beyond any doubt whatever, as specimens already tested show rich in silver oxides.
>
> It is stated that the old archives of Bexar county contain many hints of old Spanish mines, hidden treasure, etc. The facts stated in this article are backed by absolute proof.[26]

Little more than a year after Arnold left, Gurney E. Ward, a photographer and mining promoter in Abilene, became interested. In the summer of 1907 he began his own search, which in some ways was as secretive as Arnold's. Whether Ward ever knew Arnold cannot be determined, but it is doubtful the two ever met. Yet Ward had more than a passing interest in Arnold's actions, in fact, in his every step, a fact that came to light over the next two or three years.

Ward and J. B. Ely signed a lease with Sembritzki on May 27, 1907, "for the purpose of seeking and procuring supposed hidden treasures or mines," claiming two-thirds of "any hidden treasures such as valuable metals, minerals, precious stones, valuable relics, or records or coins or any other valuable treasures." The lease further stated, "if any valuable mines shall be found, John Sembritzki, J. B. Ely and G. E. Ward shall own and operate such mines, each owning one-third interest. . . . "[27]

"Gurney Ward planned everything on a large scale," remembers Verne. To finance his search, he drew up contracts and sold shares in what he claimed was six thousand pounds in gold ingots. Ward no doubt steeped himself in his subject, questioned Sembritzki about everything Arnold had told him about the stone map he had unearthed, and every meaning of its host of artifacts.[28]

No one remembers just how Ward became involved. Perhaps he had read a story on it or somehow heard about it. He is remembered as a handsome fellow with a promising photography business in Abilene. A good promoter, he was persuasive in manner, and the stock he sold in the enterprise contributed heavily toward his quest over the next two years. Even so, neither Sembritzki nor his wife fully trusted Ward.

Ward moved in his own crew of pick-and-shovel men, set up a tent camp nearby, and hired a male cook to keep the workmen fed. Over the months that followed, the Sembritzki children often played with Ward's three: Gurney Jr., Otis, and Jewel.

Ward may not have seen the stone map that Arnold and Sembritzki hacked from the roots of the huge oak. The odds are good that he never saw any of the other copper and stone replicas from the diggings. All those articles were locked away for safekeeping in a masonry vault in Dr. Terrell's drug store in Haskell, where Arnold had placed them, along with the Spider Rock, its copper artifacts, the Spanish sword, the silver epaulets and crucifix, and jewels. Ward probably had only tracings or sketches drawn from memory of the articles found on the Sembritzki farm. However, in all his promotion, Ward would tell his story as if he himself had discovered those clues, saying nothing of Arnold's earlier quest.

Ward sought articles that Arnold may or may not have hunted. Among those things were the body of a high priest buried in a silver casket and the log book listing the mines under his jurisdiction. Ward wrote a newspaper article early in 1908 that shed more light on some of the clues Arnold had found only a year or so before. Titled "The Old Spanish I.L.P. Mine," the story appeared in Abilene's *Taylor County News* on January 13, 1908. Unfortunately, this edition is no longer extant, but a clipping of the story was preserved by Sembritzki's daughter, Ann. Ward described the search:

> The chart stone was found on the northwest line at the base of a large oak tree. It was lined with small rocks, buried about five feet deep, and surrounded with charcoal. It was found because of two rocks which were leaning against a third located at the base of the tree. On the northeast line at the foot of another large oak tree, was the sandstone duck sitting on three eggs. It was buried two feet deep.
>
> On this same line was a copper dagger with "I.L.P." stamped on the blade in gold dots. Its blade was up and pointed five degrees off of center. In the direction it pointed, a few feet away, was the adobe arched door. It was 12 feet under the ground, and was five feet high and two and one-half feet wide. The adobe was two inches thick. Behind the door was a copper key. It was four feet from the door and angling toward it. It was made from a flat piece of copper. It was three inches long and one inch wide. A little to the west of the key was a copper crown with marks on it. It was five inches by five inches.
>
> The center of the plot was marked by a pile of rocks on the surface. Fifteen feet deep, under the pile of rocks, a hollow drill hole was found. A rock covered its top and it was 18 inches deep. To the southwest and pointing toward the center was a charcoal cross. It was five feet under the ground. Beside the cross was a stone turtle.

> Also on the southwest line and pointing toward the center was another copper dagger. A stairway was found near the southwest line. It was five feet below the ground and the three steps angling toward the adobe door. A third dagger was found on the southeast line also pointing toward the center. It had the date "1731" stamped on it. The daggers were all buried about 18 inches deep. They were about eight inches long and made from thin copper.
>
> To the west a copper disc was found which was slightly tilted by a stone. It had the word "porient" written on it. Another disc was found to the east. It was a sheet of copper two and one-half feet wide, and was tilted about 20 degrees by a flat rock. It had the word "orient" cut on its bottom side, and was 14 and one-half varas from the center.[29]

Although Ward appears to have been accurate in some of his description, he far overestimated the size of the flat half-discs made from copper, which Arnold interpreted as representing the rising and setting sun. Each of those was only about four inches long. Also, his inscriptions on the two stones found with the copper pieces were wrong.[30]

There were other details that Ward confused, although without an accurate accounting of the items discovered at the time, it is impossible to say precisely what all was found. Verne remembers no stone turtle but recalls distinctly the sculptured stone duck resting atop a nest of stone eggs. The copper dagger bearing the inscription *ILP* was in fact found in the center of the diggings, between the rising and setting sun symbols, with its blade pointing *down*. Arnold always "referred to it as the center," recounts Verne.

The clay arched doorway lay directly below the copper dagger, and it was filled with pure white sand. Again, Verne remembers no copper key, but neither did she ever see the copper plate with jagged edges cut around it and bearing five etched circles, which Ward apparently referred to as the copper "crown." The charcoal cross and stone stairway are other items of which Verne has no recollection. Ward was correct that three copper daggers were found, but none bore the date 1731, as did the stone map when Arnold read the numbers right to left.

It was Ward's belief that the numerical system on the stone map had been doubled from its correct meaning, that twenty-nine actually indicated fourteen and a half *varas* (or about forty feet). In his newspaper account, he said he had gone east of the old diggings one-half mile, found "slabs of burnt concrete," and there "sunk a shaft eight feet and found a mesquite limb sticking straight up with its bottom sunk in a drill hole some eight inches." He did not interpret the meaning of that discovery. He stated further that at 3,000 *varas*, or about one and a half miles to the northeast, he found evidence of "field packed clay," and at fifteen feet down he found running water. Again the significance went unexplained.

Ward concluded his account by saying that the stone chart "called for over 6,000 pounds of bullion together with the bones of the high-priest buried in a silver casket along with a log book which showed all the mines under his jurisdiction. This log book was encased in layers and layers of hides."

Ward was aware of the abundant underground water source at the twenty-nine-foot level, and in an effort to bypass it, he moved about three hundred feet to the east of the earlier diggings. There he sunk shafts nearly to the water level, then began tunneling westward, hoping to break into the treasure-filled rooms. Other newspaper accounts publicized his efforts, and it can be assumed, too, that Arnold, at that very time continuing his own quest elsewhere, kept himself informed of Ward's progress.

After almost two years at the diggings, Ward received a brief flurry of publicity on his pursuit, perhaps generated in part to raise additional working capital. He took complete credit for translating the stone map originally unearthed by Arnold. The *Abilene Daily Reporter* chronicled his latest efforts on May 13, 1909, in its page-one story, "Death to Those Who Enter without Right—Was Evidently the Theory on Which the Ancient Spaniards Planned the Works Found by Ward." The story filled much of the right-hand column of this edition, and unfortunately the only copy existing today has that portion of the page torn away. The part remaining, however, captures some of the drama of the moment:

> A trip to the scene of the buried Spanish treasures in Callahan County, near Clyde, is amazing to the most skeptical and rivals in interest the tales of the "Arabian Nights." While the latter is fiction, the former is fact. Then one stands astounded as he hears of the months and months of study it took to locate, by the use of an old plot, the hidden "chart stone," and then to translate it after it was found—how many failed and how the task was for years abandoned, and how it finally fell to G. E. Ward of Abilene to successfully solve the puzzle, after nine months of incessant efforts.
>
> Then, after Mr. Ward had translated the "chart stone" and thus located the spot where he was to dig for the hidden treasures, for fourteen months he toiled, endured the trials and encountered the dangers in order to bring the wealth to light. . . .

On page seven of that edition appeared a photograph of the treasure diggings on the Sembritzki farm under the headline, "The Old Spanish I.L.P. Mine Abandoned in 1731." The picture showed Sembritzki standing in the northwest corner of the diggings where he and Arnold had first chopped out the stone map four years earlier, and identified the holes in the hundred-foot-square of wilderness that yielded the various clues.

If Ward had not in fact seen the stone map and copper artifacts from that site, he would never see them now, for six days earlier the Terrell Drug Store in Haskell had burned to the ground. On the morning of the next day, May 8, 1909, Dr. Terrell died after a lengthy illness. The Sembritzki family later heard that everything found at their farm—the stone map, the copper artifacts, all the clues that Arnold had taken—was destroyed in the fire. Only tracings and memories of those discoveries remained.

On several occasions, Ward's workmen barely escaped cave-ins in the tunnels he dug three hundred feet east of the original diggings. At least once, Ward himself was overcome by gas that he said came from the Spanish tunnel. The *Abilene Daily Reporter* covered the story on June 12, 1909. "Overcome by Gas in the Old Spanish Mine. G. E. Ward Carried out Unconscious but Recovers. Expects to Uncover $100,000 in Short Time," headlined the page-one story:

> Overcome by gas and knocked out for half an hour was the experience of G. E. Ward, according to a report that comes from the old Spanish mine he is working near Clyde.
>
> Mr. Ward was engaged in digging in the mine trying to find the old tunnel, and the presence of the gas is taken by him to mean that he is nearing it, as he believes he will find it full of gas when he strikes it. Other workmen in the mine carried Mr. Ward out and resuscitated him, after which he returned to his digging.
>
> Strong indications of an early find of stored wealth have been struck in the old

This photograph by Gurney Ward shows Dave Arnold's diggings on the Sembritzki farm. The photo and Ward's story appeared in the Abilene Daily Reporter *on May 13, 1909. John Sembritzki stands at the site where he and Arnold unearthed the stone map four years before.* (Author's collection)

mine. Mr. Ward has found two or three more sets of stones, one being found in one locality and the other in another, but when they are put together they fit like a hand in a glove. The chart in the possession of Mr. Ward indicates that soon after the finding of the last set he found this week, he is to find the first money which will be about $100,000 in Spanish coin.

Mr. Ward installed this week a five-horse power engine, with which to run his mill and pump, and he expects to be ready by next Wednesday to begin working on the large body of packed sand containing a lake of water.

Quite a number of persons interested in the work of the old mine have visited it this week and are elated over the prospects of an early find of a big sum of money. They think the $100,000 will be uncovered in three weeks if not sooner.

Ward continued to encounter the water at the twenty-nine-foot level, but the pumps and windmill he erected to remedy that problem did little good. No one knows how much money Ward sunk into his treasure hole, but Verne remembers that "at the site where he began his work was absolutely nothing on earth to give the slightest indication of a hidden treasure. But for that matter, the same conditions existed where Arnold decided to explore, too. But Arnold knew what he was after, Ward did not. He was working blindly."[31]

By now Ward had received considerable publicity across the country. A newspaper reporter discovered one visitor in Abilene in November 1909 who had traveled from out of state, and he was so impressed that he chronicled the event in the local newspaper:

> William E. Larnes of Philadelphia, Pennsylvania, arrived in Abilene yesterday afternoon with a view of inspecting the gold mine he had heard of being situated near this place. When informed that the mine was near Clyde in place of Abilene, he decided to remain overnight in Abilene and then go to the site of the diggings. "I have heard a great deal about the old Spanish diggings through my home papers and they gave the location as Abilene," said Mr. Larnes, "and in fact they talked so much about it that I decided to come here and look the place over."
>
> Mr. Larnes has with him several charts which he will tell about but not show and states that he obtained them in much the same way as Mr. Ward got hold of his charts. Mr. Larnes believes that he could help Ward in locating the treasure and after looking over the site near Clyde, will probably see what can be done in that line. "I am a little disappointed in the country," added Mr. Larnes, "as from the newspaper stories I had heard great things of Abilene and the gold mine both. I expected to find a large city here and the treasure already found. I may return to Philadelphia tonight because I don't believe anything would induce me to live out here." And with the assurance that he meant no slam on the citizens, but merely the country, Larnes boarded the eastbound Texas and Pacific for Clyde this morning.[32]

Apparently nothing more became of Larnes' interest, as there appears to be no further association. Like a true promoter, Ward continued to tout the fortune he knew he was about to discover. In September 1910 the local press reported his latest belief, more sanguine than ever:

> "Victory is in sight" was the message brought to Abilene Thursday afternoon by Gurney Ward who came in from his Spanish mine claim near Clyde and spent the night in the city. Mr. Ward wore a smile as large as that which adorns a school boy's mug on a holiday. He says that his mining force broke into the entrance of the passageway which will lead into the long lost and hidden mine Wednesday afternoon, and he is prepared to believe that within three weeks and maybe less time, the way into the treasure storehouse will be effected. For nearly three years Mr. Ward has given his time almost exclusively to unraveling the mysterious route on the charts which he has in his possession, and directing the men who have been carrying out his instructions with picks and shovels, and he is more jubilant and confident today than he has been since he entered upon the work.[33]

Ward and Dave Arnold's paths must have crossed often in 1910, for that year Ward was virtually retracing Arnold's footsteps. Ward appeared at the John Metcalf farm on the Salt Fork northeast of Aspermont not long after Arnold had left it after several months. Arnold had dug several holes east of the Metcalf home, and strangely, Ward dug holes of his own nearby. Ward made a couple of trips from Abilene, and Metcalf let him copy the Spider Rock map, which Arnold had made on oilcloth, and left with Metcalf, along with replicas of the copper artifacts found atop it.[34]

Apparently Ward was also visiting the old diggings downstream on the south bank of the Salt Fork and claimed to have leased the land. It is known that Ward followed Arnold to other sites in the cedar brakes. There is no record of the two ever meeting in person. What is known is that Ward was becoming more desperate to find something. He wrote the Abilene newspaper in April 1911, offering shares in his company and proof that he was on the verge of finding the treasure. He claimed to have unearthed another "chart stone" near Kiowa Peak. Ward explained:

> Now it's The Old Spanish Works Developing Company, Incorporated for $16,000.00, with headquarters in Abilene, Tex. The purpose is to finish the work at Clyde, Tex., and then on the other end of the W. W. line in Stonewall Co., Tex., where we have under lease the ground where was found the chart stone, from which from this, it was traced some 12 miles from there; another large chart stone which was buried at 40 feet depth, a few miles south of Kiowa Peak. My trip in that country was very successful in all runs and I have resigned a good position with a large oil company as their expert in charge, in order that I may keep my promise with my faithful shareholders who have for nearly 3 years stayed with me until now.
>
> We find it expedient to capitalize to complete this wonderful work and to do so I have as their president and manager agreed to prove to the people the true and wonderful proposition this is. Therefore I have now displayed next door to F. & M. Bank many wonders found, also a true log of past work done, showing and proving it is great; and on Monday and Tuesday, April 17 and 18, at hours 8:30 a.m. and 3:30 p.m., will give to all a full history of all. Explain how I found, where I found each sign and will prove I have not only translated this chart, but have successfully worked sign and sign for over 2 1/2 years steady, and not once have I made a miscalculation and if this is true and this same chart tells us of the vast riches there, then have we not the right to expect it. Further I will say in selling the limited amount of shares—800—these shares are at par $10.00 and include the Cylde property, also the Stonewall and anything appertaining on this line which we develop, etc.
>
> I beg all to but come and see, listen to the wonderful story and after I am through I will be pleased to explain everything in reason, and I ask the wisest person to try to tear down my chain of proven evidence and if you fail, why then I must be right. If so is this not then a good business proposition and a scientific course as well. I offer you the most liberal advantage to fully investigate everything. As a chance like this may never again occur, besides now since we have proven beyond doubt this is a true and original work. We prove to you it is in many particulars the lost Tamped in old rich mine called Los Almegras, which we will prove is on record in Santa Fe, N.M. Come, everyone is welcome. You will surely learn much any way and if you are interested I will be pleased to talk to you personally at anytime.[35]

If Ward had leased the Spider diggings on the Salt Fork, he did not remain there long. If in fact he found another stone map near Kiowa Peak, witnesses, copies, or photographs do not remain to document it. A more plausible possibility is that Ward knew that Dave Arnold was seeking another such stone, and Ward used the newspaper to publicize that he had found it. If Arnold read the story, he must have been amused by it.

Ward found nothing in the shafts and tunnels he continued to dig near Arnold's older diggings, except water. For that, the Sembritzkis were grateful, as they had been hauling their drinking water in large barrels from a mile away. Ward's windmill now allowed them to retrieve it there. Family troubles now plagued Ward, and as had happened before, he and his wife soon divorced. His funds gone, Ward abandoned his quest, removing everything but the windmill. He soon moved to Lampasas 150 miles southeast and opened his photography studio there.[36]

Ward did not end his search for Spanish treasure at the Sembritzki diggings. Scattered stories placed him in the Sacramento Mountains of New Mexico. One might wonder if Ward followed Dave Arnold into those mountains, because he is known to have opened his photography studio in Alamagordo, New Mexico, about 1914, close to the same time Arnold disappeared from West Texas. Certainly Ward had a penchant for following in Arnold's tracks, but no evidence has yet turned up showing that Arnold went into the Sacramentos.

Historian Eve Ball of Ruidoso, New Mexico, was told one such story by Archie Frame, who as a boy lived on a ranch near Clyde, Texas. Frame's tale garbles the facts and is long on imagination, but on the other hand, it may well be the very story Ward told him.[37] It must have been about 1911 that young Archie Frame ran into Gurney Ward on the streets of Abilene, where he had set up a sidewalk stand and was selling stock. "I joined a Saturday crowd listening to Mr. Ward's story, and I begged my father to put fifty dollars into the project, but he laughed at me. I borrowed it at the bank, and gave my horse and saddle as security, and did some visiting with Mr. Ward."

Ward told Frame that he and his wife had lived in Clyde, where they ran a boarding house.[38] One night a "Spaniard from Mexico" boarded with them, carrying a small leather-covered chest. He bought a mule and digging tools and occasionally stayed away overnight. He would leave each morning and spend his time at a grove of unusually large oak trees several miles away. After searching for three months, unable to find what he had come for, he asked Ward for money enough to return to Mexico, where his wife waited for him.

The Spaniard offered his burro and unlocked his small chest, removing "a flat stone upon which were cut signs that looked like those in the almanac. Picture writing, he said. Yes, he could read them."[39] The Spaniard left the stone with Ward and shared the key to reading it. He showed Ward the grove of trees he had frequented, and a stone with three small holes drilled into it. He told Ward he had found two other such markers: one on the Pecos River, and another in the Sacramentos, where the mines and smelter were located.

Ward told Frame that the Spaniard's stone chart "indicated the number of varas from one corner to another of the equilateral triangle which he sought. The points would be indicated by trees, each containing a bar of silver the thickness of his wrist and as long as his forearm." The tale that Ward weaved became more complex and showed almost no similarity to the actual events that occurred at the Sembritzki farm prior to his own arrival on the scene.

Ward continued that he had found one huge oak that he believed to be one of the three oaks of the triangle, and the huge stumps of two others. He said he knew that the chart stone would be found "in the center of the equilateral triangle" of the huge trees. He attempted to locate the felled trees and eventually found one at the local cotton gin which burned wood for fuel. Ward said he received permission to drag it from the the rest and have it split. In it he found one of the three silver bars. It was then, Ward explained, that "he bisected the sides of the triangle and drew intersecting lines to establish the center."

He dug down a yard through red clay, hit white sand, and found the chart stone. With the stone was "a ruby the size of a quarter."[40]

Ward told Frame that the chart stone indicated forty muleloads of gold, silver, and other treasure buried within that triangle. The stack of gold bars would measure ten feet by twelve feet by fifteen feet. Ward went to the local bank to borrow money. The banker had no confidence in his chart stone with the mysterious signs and symbols, but he had the large ruby tested, and it was genuine. Ward got his loan and continued his work for two years. That was when Archie Frame heard Ward speak about his chart stone, and Frame joined in the quest—a quest that he did not realize then would consume much of the rest of his life. Frame apparently never knew anything about Dave Arnold or the search that he led, and of course he had no idea that Ward had not found the stone at all.

Frame knew that Ward and his workmen had dug a shaft to bedrock. When they broke through, one worker barely escaped ahead of the water that flooded it. Ward returned to the banker, who this time saw no future in Ward's money pit. Archie Frame said Gurney Ward went back on the street, sold more stock, "and hit for the Sacramentos." In fact, it may have taken longer for Ward to migrate westward to New Mexico. In 1911 Ward was living in Lampasas, so further work at Clyde would have been more difficult. The actual whereabouts of Ward for the next few years are difficult to trace. But it would be several years before he was known to be in Alamogordo and blasting away in the nearby Sacramentos.

There were those who remembered the predictions of the Mexicans Arnold had solicited to read the stone: the treasure was cursed and would bring only ill fortune to those who pursued it. They remembered, too, when Ward abandoned the diggings, leaving only his windmill. An abnormally strong whirlwind struck the windmill, ripping off the wheel and driving it into the sand with such force that it was half-buried. A short time later, a bolt of lighting struck the tower and split it to the ground.

Well over a decade passed without anyone searching further at the Sembritzki farm. The next person was not a treasure hunter, but a wildcatter in the oil business. He knew about the Sembritzki farm, knew about Dave Arnold and Dr. Terrell's quest, and perhaps believed that if anything were to be found, he could do so with his drilling rig. Charles Terrell was thrity-two when he signed an oil and gas lease with John Sembritzki in August 1927. Terrell never shared his father or brother's interest in the Spider Rock treasure, but he probably knew more about the search at the Sembritzki farm than the one on the Salt Fork, simply by virtue of being older when his father and brother worked with Arnold at Sembritzki's.

Charles Terrell's August 24 mining lease agreement was a catch-all, "for the purpose of mining, digging, drilling, prospecting and investigation for copper, silver, lead, zinc, coal, gold, whether in a natural or unnatural state, relics, and antiques and every other kind of mineral or ore."[41] His lease included all 320 acres of Sembritzki's land for four years, and Terrell would pay one-quarter of all found. It can be only assumed that Terrell brought in his rig, drilled, found nothing, and left, for no one ever recalled the incident.

In the mid-1930s, James and Laura Miller of Abilene began the search anew. Laura was a clairvoyant who believed her supernatural powers would lead her to the hidden treasure chambers. The Millers' permit allowed them "to search and dig for hidden treasure," covered 160 acres, and would give John Sembritzki "one-half of anything found." Signed on July 30, 1934, the contract ran to April 2 the following year. That was later ex-

In the 1930s, still other seekers dug deep canyons in the 1905 diggings first done by Dave Arnold. (Photos by the author)

Huge mounds of earth on the horizon show where later hunters attempted to uncover the treasure Dave Arnold was sure he would find. (Photo by the author)

tended to October 2, 1935.[42] The Millers directed a crew of men intermittently for over a year without finding anything. Finally, the search ended with Miller and his wife divorced.

By the 1930s, heavy equipment and tractors were available, and one of the first to dig with them was a stranger named Kessler, who used bulldozers to make a trench through the original diggings thirty feet deep by a hundred feet wide. He installed large pumps to draw out the water, and some say that at twenty-nine feet he uncovered waterways arched at the top and filled with sand. In his massive excavation, he reportedly found three stone steps similar to those Gurney Ward said he had discovered.

At about that time, Kessler, who always drove a Stutz Bearcat, ordered two armored cars parked at the massive trench, ready to load with the gold he believed they would soon uncover. But when nothing more was found, Kessler left for Florida. It may be that Kessler proceeded on the story of Laura Miller, who ended her search in the fall of 1935.[43]

Dave Arnold would not have approved of Kessler's large earth-moving equipment at the site he had painstakingly dug with the perseverance of a detective. For much like an archaeologist, Arnold "was very, very, careful that nothing be disturbed when found, because he wanted to read the signs," remembers Verne. Arnold realized the significance of the signs, the replicas, the artifacts—each told a story to the one with the knowledge to read them. What else that plot of earth on the Sembritzki farm may have told antiquarians may never be known, for with Kessler and those who followed him, interest was not in history or archaeology, but in finding the gold.

Joe Woods and Joe Cauble followed the rainbow most of their lives. Much of the time, they followed the trail Dave Arnold had left. In June 1936 they arrived at the Sembritzki farm. Their equipment included a large earth-moving crane, and the hole they left among older diggings was forty-five feet deep. Cauble maintains that they uncovered a spider web of tunnels filled with sand, but copper shavings and a Spanish sword were their only reward.

As late as November 1942, Joe Cauble was still involved at the site. At that time Cauble, then living in Clyde, and Melville E. Peters of Wichita Falls signed an agreement with William Ramos to allow him six months to search. Ramos agreed "to do such work in the presence of J. M. Cauble who has charge of the lease." Ramos would not "do any excavating within a radius of 300 feet of the center of the excavation now being made by J. M. Cauble." The agreement also stated that "upon discovery of such treasure, the same will not be removed except upon the consent of Cauble, and then only with the consent of the United States Government." Twenty-five percent would be delivered to the Sembritzki heirs as a royalty, Ramos would receive forty percent, and Cauble and his associates sixty percent. Ramos was to furnish a man to work on the excavation, and Cauble would work

During the last attempts to find the Spanish treasure on the Sembritzki farm, seekers dug this huge excavation a quarter-mile northwest of the original diggings. (Photo by the author)

concurrently.[44] Joe Cauble invested over six years in the quest, but the results were no different from previous efforts.

Little more was done at the Sembritzki farm. Gradually the wilderness of deep sand and brush reclaimed the diggings of almost three-quarters of a century. Then, after more than thirty years, Joe Woods returned for another, more extensive attempt to uncover the treasure. With backing from others in Abilene, Woods moved in a drag-line, a bulldozer, a backhoe, and a pump in late 1970 and early 1971. A quarter of a mile northwest of his earlier diggings, and just southwest of the Sembritzki farmhouse, he carved out a hole thirty feet deep or more, creating a huge mound of earth and stone reaching above the treetops on the neighboring farm of W. H. Walker. No one knows just what prompted Woods to dig on this occasion, but he was known to carry out such excavations on a whim. Just as three decades before, his efforts were unsuccessful.

No one can say with what hesitancy Arnold abandoned his pursuit, nor can they say with what accuracy he had interpreted the stone map and its host of symbolic clues. Arnold had yet other trails to pursue, other stone maps to find, beckoning him at a time when he seemed lost for answers. Always guiding him in that continuing pursuit was the one item he never allowed out of his sight—the sheepskin map that had brought him from Mexico.

The tragedy of Arnold's triumphs and failure at the Sembritzki farm is that so little of it was recorded when it was fresh in the memories of all who saw him uncover those antiquities. Where were those who might have preserved that tantalizing chapter of perhaps the most bizarre quest for lost Spanish gold in the American Southwest?[45]

Recalling those memories so firmly imprinted in her mind as a child, Verne Sems offers one other tantalizing clue to the mystery Arnold brought to the Sembritzki farm almost a century ago. There was a small earthen mound, or slight gradual rise, not far east of the old homeplace. As a child, she and the other children played on the mound. In jumping up and down in one unusual place, they discovered that it had a hollow sound.

The children played there often just to listen to the uncanny hollow ring. No one ever investigated the mound, Verne is sure, for by then her father had lost all interest in pursuing phantoms.[46] Strangely enough, the small mound lay a mere quarter of a mile northeast of Dave Arnold's diggings, and perhaps half that far from their house.

The evidence that the Spaniards were present in the nearby region continued to mount over the last century. In the general area where the mysterious silver medallion and Mexican gun were found about fourteen miles southeast of Baird in 1879, other Spanish artifacts continued to turn up. Swords and pieces of armor were discovered on Burnt Creek twelve miles southwest of Baird.

At the base of four small peaks about ten miles south of Baird, ranchers recall a Mexican stranger who appeared in the early part of the century seeking something buried. Even today one can hear stories of local ranchers bringing pieces of what appear to be an iron mesh to town, all of which have later been identified as chain mail—the protective armor vest of a Spanish soldier.[47]

5

The Curse of Dave Arnold's Map

No one knows how superstitious Dave Arnold may have been, or whether he placed much credence in any of the Mexicans' warnings that the treasure he pursued was cursed and would imperil all who became involved with it. Arnold, better than anyone, was aware of the peculiar events associated with the mysterious sheepskin he carried and the artifacts it led him to. But somehow the ancient Spanish curse seemed to follow in his footsteps.

There was yet an unsolved murder on the Double Mountain Fork—the skeleton of the presumed sheepherder who had led Arnold to the Spider Rock. Family troubles, divorce, financial ruin, even death seemed to plague Arnold's quest from beginning to end. Early in 1906, after disassociating himself from those who had defied him at the Sembritzki farm, Arnold again returned to the diggings on the Salt Fork where he had unearthed the Spider Rock several years before. He believed there was much yet that he had failed to find. Somehow the discovery of those things appeared to be based on what he had found at the Sembritzki farm.

Little is known about Arnold's whereabouts and actions between 1906 and 1909. Much of that time, he continued his search at the Spider diggings overlooking the Salt Fork, twenty miles or so northwest of Haskell. For part of that period, he lived with the Joe Allen family north of the forks, and with the Kelly Johnson family west of Munday. He also rode over the country seeking trail markers or landmarks that only he seemed to be able to follow from one to the other.

It is known that by early 1906, word was getting out that Spanish artifacts had been found in the nearby hills. Apparently, few details were known, but reporter A. W. Grant attempted to chronicle some of the discovery and legend in association with recent copper discoveries in his story to the *Fort Worth Telegram* on February 6. The unnamed old man and his secret map must surely have been Dave Arnold. The page-one headline, "Lost Mines Of Spain Found In Texas Hills," set the stage:

Staff Correspondence.

ASPERMONT, Texas, Feb. 5.—Is the secret which the old Spaniards took with them when they fled from the hills of what is now Stonewall county, fully 100 years ago, about to be wrestled from the rocky ledges and forbidding cliffs where they once toiled? Is the mystery of their hidden treasure which has been tradition in this part of Texas for two generations, about to be fathomed by practical, unromantic workmen of the Twentieth century?

These are questions which old settlers of Stonewall county are now asking in view of recent developments in the region lying between the Double Mountain and Salt Forks of the Brazos river.

Into this vicinity, until this year reached only by a single daily mail stage from Stamford, forty miles to the southeast, there have recently come visitors from the north, miners and prospectors, who have tried to keep the purpose of their visit secret, but whose actions were such that those who saw them could easily guess their object. They plainly had been attracted by the stories of the hidden but hitherto unattainable mineral weath of the Stonewall county hills, and came to find out first hand just how much of trust there was in the stories that have been told about Stonewall county for the past fifty years.

It has become known that at least four men who have been prospecting in this vicinity for the past several weeks are from Michigan, and they are also from the greatest copper producing region in the United States. That there is copper in the Stonewall county hills has been known for a century. The Spaniards who mined it knew of it, although they probably were searching for gold when they sunk their deep shafts in what is now known as Copper Hill.

But until this year, when the Kansas City, Mexico and Orient railroad steadily making its way northward through the plains and valleys from Sweetwater, and southward toward its north-projecting rails from Wichita, Kan., offers the immediate prospect of railroad facilities to the copper-producing region, there were no possibiliities, no matter how rich the earth might be in minerals, of working the ore deposites, so long as the ore, or even the crude metal, could not be taken away from the mines except on wagons.

Now, the line of the Orient is nearly opposite the copper-bearing hills, and in a few weeks is expected to pass less than a dozen miles from where the Spaniards built a crude blast-furnace about the time Paul Jones was taking prizes off the coast of France. The ore is in the hills. Building a railroad spur nowadays is as easy as cutting a pack-horse trail a century ago. What could be more simple?

Northern capital might acquire an interest in the ore beds, and an industry greater than even the wildest dreams of the early prospecting Spaniards, spring up among the hills of Stonewall county, which hitherto have yielded nothing but a little timber and only fair grazing ground for the cattle of the ranchmen of the vicinty.

Probably few Texans know that the Spaniards once worked at least three mines in the Stonewall county hills. That they prospected all along the Colorado river in their adventurous marches which finally led them up into what is now New Mexico is well known. But how any of them came to stray so far to the north and east probably always will remain a mystery.

How many went to the Stonewall county region and how long they stayed will also probably always be a mystery.

The only traces they left were the ruins of an ore-reducing furnance, part of a stone house, and three deep shafts. How deep these shafts are is not known by present residents of the region. The shafts are nearly full of water, and are said to have never been sounded.

But while the Spaniards left the shafts, the ruins of their house and furnace, they used most extraordinary precautions to cover up the traces of their work while in the vicinity.

A few years ago a ranchman riding in the region of Copper Hill noticed an opening in a clay bank which had apparently been uncovered by a flood or repeated rains. Investigating, he found that the opening was the mouth of a tunnel which had evidently been covered up. Later investigators found the floor of this tunnel, as far as they entered, covered with furnace slag, evidently from the old furnace of the hills The caution that prompted the Spaniards to haul the slag and refuse away from their furnace and bury it in the earth has been one of the mysteries of the Copper Hill, as yet not satisfactorily accounted for.

Why did the Spaniards wish to preserve secrecy? If they were driven from the region by Indians and left in hasty flight, would they not have left slag and furnace cinders lying in the dump piles where they had been thrown? These are natural questions and the accompanying suggestion made by the questioner always is that the Spaniards in their prospecting found some great vein of mineral wealth, and unable to work it sufficiently with the force at hand, covered up the traces of their endeavors and left for some southern colony of their countrymen to get reinforcements, intending to return at some later late.

Another suggestion, equally popular with Stonewall county oracles, is that being only partly satisfied with their results at the Copper Hill mines, the Spaniards abandoned their workings and pushed on farther north hoping to find some better field, perished while on their journey and that their mines were lost until found again by the Texas pioneer settlers who penetrated the region.

The theory that the Spaniards went south for more help has more friends than the second suggestion. It might be said that it has more possibilities to the imagination of the treasure-hunter theories.

What could be more natural than that the Spaniards, having decided to go south, possibly into Old Mexico, should bury some vast amount of treasure in the hills near where they worked in order that they might travel lighter, or else carry back in its place specimens of copper ore to convince possibly incredulous compatriots?

Why would they not bury both treasure and cover up as far as possible the evidence of their workings in order that others coming into the region would be led to conclude the district had been abandoned after a fruitless search for riches.

The Spaniards are also represented in history as being in an unrelentless search for gold, usually painfully lacking in that precious metal, and willing to enter all sorts of hazardous ventures in order to get it. But in the version of the modern story teller the Spaniards always went round with a carload or two of gold packed on the backs of their burros, to bury at convenient places whenever it became too heavy for the tired mules to pack from camp to camp. Why the Spaniards would carry a vast quantity of gold into the hills of Stonewall county and leave it there is as much of a mystery as why they covered up nearly all traces of their work before leaving, but there are plenty in this vicinity today who believe that they did that very thing, and many is the hole which has been dug in an attempt to prove the theory.

A number of years ago an old man came into the neighborhood, representing himself to have a secret map of the hills from an old Mexican, gotten when the latter was on his deathbed. The stranger roamed about the hills for some time, dug a number of holes, and uncovered a number of relics which the Spaniards had undoubtedly left.

Implements, a hatchet, an old sword, and a few other articles were found. Other searchers at the time dug into the grave of one of the Spanish explorers, evidently an officer of the party, for all of the glittering uniform was not gone and various articles in the grave led to confirm the belief.

Later a mysterious copper plate was found, covered with an infinitely puzzling labyrinth of lines, inscriptions and notations. The finders regarded it as a map to the treasure caches of the region, but none was able to furnish the key. The plate bore the date "1812," and is supposed to have been inscribed just before the Spaniards departed in order to guide them when they should return.

The Spaniards undoubtedly knew of verdigris and how quickly copper becomes coated with its deposits, and why they would bury their map in the ground instead of taking it with them is a question which a matter of fact man would quickly ask, but the believers in the hidden treasure stories are generous and readily overlook such details.

Eighteen or twenty years ago a mining company was organized for the purpose of developing the copper industry in Stonewall county. It was known as the Brazos, Croton Creek Mining Company and its purpose was purely commercial. It took no recognition of the tales of Spanish treasure and accepted only expert assays on the copper in the hills. The company found not only copper ore, but gold and silver as well, but owing to the difficulty of working the mines, inaccesibility and inability to get fuel and other practical restrictions, has not developed its holdings. It still retains about 2,100 acres, including what is known as Copper Hill, and it is believed that if the Orient railroad can provide facilities for either taking away ore or bringing in fuel for an ore-producing plant, it will realize handsomely.

It is understood here that already offers for options have been made to the stockholders in the Brazos, Croton Creek Mining Company by Michigan mining representatives, and something more definite is expected to develop in the next few months.

Copper Hill is located in a picturesque region, even aside from the historical associations of the district.

It is not far from Kiowa peak, named after that Indian tribe which was quartered in that vicinity before the government moved it further north to a territory reservation.

Not far to the southwest is the famous Double mountains which gives a name to a long fork of the Brazos running near its base. This double mountain, so called, because of its being composed of two hills exactly similar in outline, rises from 600 to 1,000 feet above a fairly level, surrounding plain and forms a landmark which can be seen for fifty or sixty miles.

Kiowa peak is in itself a landmark, and from its top it is said the court houses of five neighboring counties can be seen.

Copper Hill is also not far from the now almost deserted town of Rayner, formerly the county seat of Stonewall county. The county built an excellent court house and jail at Rayner, costing about $30,000, but the center of population moved westward and so the county seat was moved to Aspermont. Now the imposing two-story court house is used as a postoffice and dwelling, the jail is also a dwelling, and a country store also completes the homes on what is naturally a beautiful townsite.

The Ten-X pasture runs to the edge of the townsite. It is well known to Texas cattlemen, but it is said that it will soon pass into the hands of the settler and be no longer used for grazing purposes. According to reports here, ten sections or more of the pasture will be surveyed in the spring and placed on the market.

One wonders if the stone dwelling of the Spaniards referred to, with its three mines and smelter, was not the same mysterious stone building south of Kiowa Peak long believed to be a Spanish mission, complete with corner stone bearing the date 1812.

Dave Arnold's relationship with Dr. Terrell and Cabe continued to remain close, as was their own to Bud Jones. Perhaps because of his long-standing interest in the search and financial support of it from the beginning, Dr. Terrell had become custodian of the stone maps—the Spider Rock and its sister stone from the Sembritzki farm, as well as the copper plates and other artifacts.

To safeguard those treasured relics, Dr. Terrell hired Jones to build a masonry vault in the rear of his Haskell drug store. Built in February of 1907, the vault was mounted with a steel door. There everyone felt those antiquities would be safe, protected from both theft and the elements. Also in the vault were important papers, leases, and contracts giving each man an equal share when the Spider Rock treasure was found.[1]

At those diggings about twelve miles northwest of the hamlet of Rule, Arnold and his companions concentrated their efforts. Sometime earlier, Cabe had rejoined his father at his drug store, and once again he spent much of his time on the quest, often going to the diggings with Arnold or Jones. Dr. Terrell himself devoted more of his time to the search and apparently contributed more of his money.

Many were the times that Arnold rode into Haskell to confer with Dr. Terrell or Cabe and spend a warm afternoon seated on the sidewalk in front of the corner drug store. Always Arnold spoke of the Spanish treasure, the long trail he had followed, or the work to be done tomorrow. Many were the times that twelve-year-old Charles listened wide-eyed to Arnold, his father, and older brother ponder the mystery. Then all would go to their home three blocks west of the courthouse at the corner of First Street and Avenue H, and pursue the quest over dinner.

Frances Caroline Terrell and her nineteen-year-old daughter, Frankie, always cooked a hearty meal for their guest. Dr. Terrell always got Arnold a hotel room when he stayed overnight. Caroline was as optimistic as her husband and sons that one day soon the trail would end. So sanguine were they of that impending discovery that they brought R. E. Sherrill into their confidence. Sherrill ran a hardware store and owned a steel vault. When Arnold felt sure they would break into the treasure chamber by day's end, he asked Sherrill's permission to use his private vault. Arnold feared placing it in either Dr. Terrell's vault or that of the local bank, where it might be looted. Sherrill was to be notified a little after midnight—but he was never called upon to open his vault.[2]

The Terrells knew there were clues Arnold had not yet found, such as the twin mulberry trees he believed he must find or, if they were gone, determine where they had grown. The Terrells may or may not have known about the stone map Arnold said was buried between them. Arnold would never find the twin mulberry trees, although only three miles or so north of the Spider diggings, he might have examined the crumbling ruin of a stone wall twenty feet long and shoulder high. The earliest ranchers of Stonewall County all agreed that the stone ruin was there when they entered the country, appearing old even then. The stone wall lay in Beaver Canyon, the mouth of which was only two miles downstream from the forks of the river, and almost opposite the Allen ranch, where Arnold so often stayed.[3]

On the back of an envelope Dr. Terrell kept in his private papers were penciled these words: "Rock wall and other papers." Inside that envelope was the letter Miguel Anhubta of Taos, New Mexico, wrote to M. Dillon of Fort Worth on March 7, 1897, interpreting the meaning of the symbols on a map in Dr. Terrell's possession. The date the Mexican ascribed to the map was December 12, 1783. No one can now say with certainty, but that map may have been the one given to Dr. Terrell by the ailing Mexican before the Terrells moved to Haskell in 1898. The peculiar stone wall disappeared in later years when a nearby rancher found a need for building stone.

Clues were not always found while pursuing them. One day in 1908, perhaps a half-mile east of the Spider Rock hill, Bud Jones was tracking a lame deer he had shot, when he sat down at the edge of a small canyon to rest. He was observing the rock formation around, noting he was near the head of that arroyo, when he discovered next to him a faint drawing on the stone ledge, barely visible to the eye.

He scratched over the curious design, cleaning out the carving with a small stick. He recognized many of the same symbols that appeared on the Spider Rock. There was the arrow that forked at both front and back, a cross, a circle cut in two, several F's, two daggers, and a strange hooklike symbol. Jones knew that they were too similar to those gracing the Spider Rock not to relate to it. And they were not far from where the Spider Rock had been found.

Jones climbed down into the canyon to investigate further, going in the opposite direction from the arrow he had found carved. A few feet to the north he found the symbol of a pot with legs and bail carved on the stone ledge. Next to it was another arrow, also pointing northward farther down the canyon. Jones found nothing more unusual that day, and if Arnold, proficient in following such symbols, offered an explanation for the cryptic signs, it has not been remembered.[4] Among the papers and letters Cabe kept during his lifetime appeared a drawing similar to that carving found by Jones. While similar, it was not the same, and whether it was another carving found—or not found—perhaps cannot now be determined.

No one can say just when Arnold abandoned his search at the Spider diggings. Always it was his belief—and it is the recollection of Charles, who when between seven and fourteen traveled with his father to the diggings—that the Spanish sword, silver epaulets, and other articles actually marked the entrance of the tunnel to the chamber containing the Spanish treasure.

Part of the reason behind that belief was the various colors of clays found in each of the small drilled holes in each square of the angular lane that led from the left side of the Spider Rock about midway down, then turned abruptly into the inner circle. Arnold's men encountered those same soil colors in the holes they dug, but found no tunnel beneath the stone ledge, which was eleven to fourteen feet thick. Arnold concentrated most of his search just below the head of that canyon and followed the various colored clay balls of the supposed angular lane down the edge of the canyon from the top. He then excavated the hill atop the bedrock where the symbols of stone and metal were found, in addition to those carved into its surface.

It is known from a notation by Dr. Terrell that Cabe and Jones went to the diggings as late as August of 1908.[5] Almost obsessed with unraveling the hieroglyphic puzzle, Dr. Terrell continued to devote his time and resources to it. Ominous circumstances transpired in the months ahead that would completely change the lives of every member of the Terrell family—and reinforce once again the belief in the curse of Dave Arnold's map.

A mere two months later, Dr. Terrell filed for bankruptcy on October 2.[6] In the *Haskell Free Press* of October 10 he ran this advertisement: "For Sale, The Terrell Drug Store building, southwest corner of public square, Haskell, Texas. Will exchange for good land."[7] At age fifty-four, Dr. Terrell, a druggist since he was sixteen years old, had depleted his funds. In the spring of 1909, the doctor became ill with fever and was bedridden for three or four weeks.

On the night of May 7, 1909, the Terrell Drug Store burned to the ground. In the masonry vault behind the prescription counter were the Spanish artifacts and stone maps Arnold and Terrell had discovered in their seven-year search. The complete inventory of the vault cannot be known. The following morning of May 8 brought still another tragedy. Dr. Terrell died from a damaged liver without ever knowing of the loss of his business. All was reported lost in that fire, except for a few pieces of silverware belonging to Cabe's wife, Annie Louise, which she retrieved from the ashes.[8]

Their father dead, the business destroyed, the Terrell family suffered both grief and financial loss. The doctor left five children. Cabe was twenty-six. After taking care of family responsibilities, he would leave for a job at a drug store in Snyder. Still living at home were Frankie, twenty-one years old; Charles, fourteen; Barnie, a boy of ten; and Edenia, a girl of six. Dr. Terrell's wife, Caroline, would be forced to make clothes to support herself and the younger children.

Some months before Dr. Terrell's death, Bud Jones moved to Pratt, New Mexico, to seek his fortune in mining. Arnold was living in Munday with members of the Johnson family, preparing to make another dig in his long search. After their family loss and grief, it is not difficult to understand the secret the Terrell family would keep throughout most of their lives.

Although any papers and contracts in Terrell's drug store masonry vault burned that night of May 7, 1909, the fire did not actually destroy the entire contents of the vault, as was reported by every member of that family for more than six decades to come. The beautiful hieroglyphic Spider Rock itself survived but was cracked in two. The stone map from the Sembritzki farm, however, crumbled into pieces. The copper plates and daggers and replicas found with both stones survived, although they were blackened from the fire.

The silver epaulets found with the Spanish saber survived, but what little gold tassel remained on them had turned a silvery gray. The edges of the ornate epaulets showed the effects of severe heat. The saber with hilt apparently did not survive. Only the hand-carved silver overlay remained of the ebony and silver crucifix, its hard black wood having burned away.[9] There may have been other ornaments destroyed in that fire. For lack of an inventory, no one can accurately say. Many are sure that far more articles were uncovered in the grave of the priest and at the Spider diggings. Some of those articles may have been sold to help finance the search. Such is the tragedy of this historic quest.

The artifacts that did survive, along with the papers, letters, and map tracings that had remained in the Terrell home, became the possessions of Cabe. He would guard them and show them to no one outside his family for the remainder of his life. By the time his father died, Cabe had a wife and child of his own. His family obligations, and his father's defeat and possible financial ruin from his involvement, perhaps best explain why he never revealed to Arnold that some of the Spanish discoveries survived the drug store fire.

From Munday, Arnold had Kelly Johnson's brother Moss write the following letter to Cabe on June 21, 1909:

> My Dear Friend: We have got some good information and we aim to make a dig on old Lana Grande just as soon as we get through with thrashing, and of course, we ex-

THE JOHNSON CASH STORE

DEALER IN

HATS, CAPS, BOOTS AND SHOES. — DRY GOODS — NOTIONS AND GENTS' FURNISHING GOODS.

MUNDAY, TEXAS, June 21 1909

Mr Cabe Terell
Haskell Tex

My Dear friend we have got some good information and we aim to make a dig on old Lana Grande just as soon as we get through with thrashing and of coarse we expect you will want to represent your father Interest and we want to know if the contracts and plats got destroyed by fire or not, and if you still have them we will want you to bring them with you, we will notify you either by letter or wire when to meet us let us hear from you at once As ever your friend

D M Arnold
by A M Johnson

On June 21, 1909, from Munday, A. M. "Moss" Johnson penned this letter for Dave Arnold to Cabe Terrell, telling about a forthcoming dig and asking if the stone maps were destroyed. (Courtesy Charles Terrell)

> pect you will want to represent your father's interest, and we want to know if the contracts and plats got destroyed by fire or not, and if you still have them, we will want you to bring them with you. We will notify you either by letter or wire when to meet us. Let us hear from you at once. As ever, your friend.[10]

If Cabe answered that letter at all, he told Arnold that everything had been destroyed—a story that would be repeated many times over the following years and believed by everyone involved in the search. No one knows now where Arnold's "old Lana Grande" may have been. He had two known excavations yet remaining: one on the Brazos, and another on a tributary of the Double Mountain Fork. Arnold would never again contact a member of the Terrell family. So far as they knew, he just disappeared.

None of the original participants with Arnold ever forgot what he had found, what they had seen when those clues were carefully tracked, and then painstakingly unearthed from their long entombment. Everyone knew there was much he had not found, just as they always believed that the underground rooms, tunnels, or chambers they sought harbored a fabulous trove, if only they could find them. Each man had seen more than enough evidence to corroborate that belief. Occasionally one of them would return on his own to try just one more time.

R. R. Davis was one of those participants. From Haskell, he wrote Jones in Pratt, New Mexico, on July 26, 1909:

> I have made a trip over to the works a few days ago and I find that someone has been at work over there a short time ago and they have dug two places and I think that they have taken up something. I think that I have the man that we want or I will

With the death of his father and destruction of the family business, Cabe Terrell left Haskell, later opening his own drug store in Post. Here, Cabe and his younger brother Charles are shown in 1912. (Courtesy Louise Terrell)

> know in a week or two. Please let me know whether you can come soon or not. Mr. Smith, the owner of the land is gone, and I saw Mrs. Terrell in regard to the papers and she has failed to find them. Can you give any information in regard to them? Please let me hear from you soon.[11]

Jones, in turn, wrote Cabe: "Cabe, it will be impossible for me to come as I have not made a dollar since I left Haskell. I want you to be sure to keep your eyes open and don't let any of that outfit get hold of anything you have. Be sure and keep those lease papers that your Pa and I drew up on the land with Hoy Smith. I was sure grieved to hear of your Pa's death and also the loss in the burn."[12]

Jones would always be haunted by the aura of the Spider Rock, but it would be fifteen years before he could return to those diggings. Like the Terrells, Jones would never know what became of Dave Arnold, but the bizarre search he led would be imprinted in Jones's mind for the remainder of his days.

In 1910 young Charlie Terrell joined his brother at his drug store in Post City, a town built by multimillionaire Charles William Post, a longtime friend of the Terrell family. C. W. Post met Dr. Terrell when the two were living in Fort Worth, Post having gone there from Battle Creek, Michigan, in the 1880s because of failing health.

It is an old family story that Dr. Terrell treated Post for tuberculosis, and because of their friendship and penchant for experimenting, together they developed the formula for Postum, a coffee substitute, which Post began producing in 1894. Later he added Post Toasties and Post Bran.[13] In 1906 Post bought a 200,000-acre ranch in Garza and Lynn counties, where he founded Post City and carried out agricultural and rainmaking experiments. It is interesting to ponder what might have developed had Dr. Terrell interested the food manufacturer in his West Texas treasure hunt. His own health failing, Post committed suicide on May 9, 1914.[14]

The death of Dr. Terrell ended the treasure quest for the Terrell family, which may have begun in Fort Worth as early as 1897. Cabe would never return to the Spider diggings or those at the Sembritzki farm. Nor would he ever discuss that pursuit, except to his immediate family, and even then very little.

Cabe's oldest daughter, Louise, born in Haskell the fall before her grandfather died, recalls that her first knowledge of the Spanish artifacts came while she was in high school in Waco, where the family moved in 1920. Occasionally Cabe would spread the copper plates, daggers, sun replicas, and map tracings on the table, and his wife and three daughters would watch as he pondered out loud their meaning, convinced that he and his father surely must have come close to finding the colossal treasure that each man believed was there. Always he concluded two possibilities: either the "key" needed to find the treasure was missing, preventing anyone from finding it, or it had already been removed when they unearthed their many clues after the turn of the century.[15]

There may have been other reasons Cabe revealed so little of that search. He knew all too well the heartache it had brought his family. He knew all too well the story of the curse, and the failure and anguish of those who had become obsessed with finding the Spanish gold. To his dying day in June 1970, the artifacts that survived the drug store fire were kept carefully hidden. With them was an envelope marked "Important." Inside the envelope was a small leather pouch, and in it, wrapped in cloth, were dried cauls—the membranes once encompassing the head of a newborn child. Cauls were always thought to be a good omen, and whoever possessed them would be fortunate and escape danger.

Dave Arnold was a man obsessed with finding Spanish treasure. Just as he had disappeared forever from the diggings on the Sembritzki farm, he disappeared, too, from those he so long conducted on the banks of the Salt Fork. The summer of 1909 he was making a dig "on old Lana Grande." Within the next year or so he would make at least two new digs, both within thirty miles of the Spider diggings. Each site would be in the opposite direction from it. He had yet one more stone map to unearth in the enigma that had led him thus far.

6

Inca Treasure, Aztec Gold: The Stone from Double Mountain

Only Dave Arnold knew how far the tentacles spread from the center of the Spider Rock's web. Only he fully understood how to follow the surface signs that marked those radial lines, and when to dig for the stone maps that lay hidden beneath. Only he could have known what one stone map meant to the other, or how they related to the symbol-laden sheepskin that always led him. It was as if the carefully guarded sheepskin took him just so far on that trail, and then the search depended solely on finding the stone maps and following their cryptic symbols.

It was late in 1909 or perhaps early in 1910 that Arnold followed the proverbial cairns, "rock piles" as he called them, over the countryside, having now decided to concentrate his next search on the banks of Gyp Creek, about five miles from where it ran into the Double Mountain Fork of the Brazos. The site turned out to be near the farm of Bob Hayes, who lived six miles east and two miles north of Rotan.[1]

A historic landmark—Double Mountain—lay perhaps ten or eleven miles distant, a few degrees west of north, much like Kiowa Peak in its direction from the Spider Rock. Interestingly, too, the Gyp Creek search lay some twenty-five miles southwest of the Spider diggings. From both those sites, it was roughly sixty miles southeastward to the Sembritzki farm near Clyde. Since time immemorial, Double Mountain has served as a landmark. That it now became important to Arnold's quest seems only natural.

Other quests actually preceded Arnold's. The fact that the legends long existed may have in part led Arnold in the direction he chose. No one can say when the legend of lost Inca treasure, or that of the Aztecs, crept into the Spider Rock mystery. Treasure attributed to both of those ancient peoples once conquered by the Spanish conquistadors has been said to be part of the vast trove so carefully concealed by the weblike network of intersecting lines and circles—the spider web that Arnold followed on his sheepskin map.

According to the legend that preceded Arnold, a sacred, golden Inca sun-god bedecked with jewels was buried on the Double Mountain Fork of the Brazos somewhere in present southern Stonewall County, close to a smelter works the Spaniards built to reduce

The Double Mountain, a historic landmark to Spanish explorers of centuries past. Comanche legends tell of men dressed in shiny armor being buried there. A few miles almost due south, Dave Arnold unearthed another of his cryptic stone maps. (Photos by the author)

many of those priceless ornaments into ingots. The story is interlaced with subterfuge and intrigue, but it enraptured seekers of past generations. At least one man living in recent years glimpsed a small portion of a treasure unearthed in this region in 1913, and he was just as sure in later years that what he found was meager compared to what one day would be discovered.

When the Spanish conquistador Francisco Pizarro crushed the ancient Incan civilization and captured the fabled riches of Peru in November of 1532, he demanded enough gold "to fill a room twenty-two *varas* by seventeen and as high as he could reach." Historians have estimated that ransom to be worth $20 million. But not even that vast store of treasure freed the Inca ruler Atahualpa, whom Pizarro later ordered strangled.

Gold crazes men's minds. Pizarro and his fellow captain Almagro began to quarrel, and Almagro lost his head to a sword. To avenge his father's death, Almagro's son assassinated Pizarro, and still later, a vengeful friend of Pizarro slew Almagro's son. It was during that fighting among the Spanish armies that much of the vast Inca treasure was smuggled out of Peru northward into Mexico. Among the contraband was the golden Inca sun-god, adorned with jewels from the mountain streams of the once-vast Inca empire. No one knows how long the golden idol remained hidden in Mexico, or just how it later came to be removed to the northern regions of New Spain, but that it was secreted out of Mexico at a time the Spaniards were mining on Los Brazos de Dios, where a smelter had been built, is a belief accepted by many.[2]

It is believed the Spanish custodians of the golden sun-god intended to reduce it into ingots at the great smelter on the Double Mountain Fork. Indian troubles already plagued the mysterious Spaniards who were carrying out the secretive mining activities in the uncharted wilderness of northern New Spain. Because abandonment of those operations was imminent, it was agreed to bury the golden sun-god and other spoils of a conquered race.

Twenty-one holes were dug seven *varas* deep, and into one was lowered the Inca sun-god. Finding that burial site would depend upon finding each of the other twenty, and then following those to the concealed treasure. The legend deals with Aztec treasure almost as often as it does Inca. Either presents a strange twist to the Spider Rock story, because neither was ever mentioned by Arnold himself, although on numerous occasions he would speak of a lost city that somehow fit into the Spanish puzzle.

Tradition does not name the seeker who first became aware of this story and purchased a large piece of property alongside the Double Mountain Fork within sight of the looming Double Mountain. He began his search for the twenty-one holes, and found and cleaned out ten of them to their original depth of seven *varas*, or about nineteen feet, where he found trinkets of ancient design. Nothing more was unearthed alongside the Double Mountain Fork, and the story of Spanish treasure seemed to be forgotten until sometime prior to the turn of the century, when a descendant of one of the first settlers on the river found what appeared to be the remains of a primitive smelter. A clay crucible containing small amounts of gold was also found.

Mrs. Ivy La Madrid, who once lived on the upper Brazos, remembered that while the discovery of the primitive furnace was yet fresh in mind, an aging Spanish aristocrat made his presence known to the ranchers along the river. He spoke proper English, wore fine clothes, and possessed his own camp outfit. The story the Spaniard told made sense of the smelter ruins found earlier, and he now sought an agreement with the landowners to help him find a mine in which he knew had been hidden a great treasure in gold bullion.[3]

Don Español was what he was called, probably because no one could pronounce his Spanish name. He revealed that his ancestors had smelted large amounts of gold ore into bullion while working a rich mine along the river. An Indian attack ended those operations, but one ancestor had made a chart to the gold, the map that Don Español now possessed. The Spaniard was emphatic in his belief that no American could understand or follow the chart, regardless of how long or hard he might try. For one-half the gold, the landowners agreed to assist him in his search.

Don Español consulted his map often and directed the diggings. His instructions always hinged on the signs he found carved on stones. The only symbol that resembled anything familiar to the landowners was the carving of a muleshoe, looking like a U, which only Don Español knew how to interpret. Several days into the search, the workmen unearthed the grisly remains of four skeletons laid head to feet in the form of a quadrangle. One skeleton faced east, one faced west, one north, and one south. Not far east from the skeleton pointing in that direction, the workmen uncovered a stone perhaps two feet square that had been hollowed out into a box, and it was sealed with a stone slab. The curious stone box was found to be full of white river sand.

At this juncture, Don Español predicted that the mine would be opened in three days. It was rich and had never been worked out, he said, but he would claim no part of it if the ranchers agreed to let him have the bullion he knew would be found inside. That was not the original understanding, the spokesman retorted. Each man was to have an equal share of whatever was found, and that went for bullion as well as the mine. If there was as much gold as he claimed, they demanded, why should he be so greedy?

Don Español angrily interrupted that it was not greedy for a man to claim what rightfully belonged to him. They saw him old and alone, but in Spain, poor kinsfolk had denied themselves to gather up enough money to send him to claim their ancestral inheritance. His family were once hidalgos, Don Español lamented, but were ruined generations ago. The map he possessed was their only hope of regaining some of the prominence they had once known. The mine was worth far more than the bullion, but he could not take it home to Spain. The gold must be his.

There was heated talk among the workmen. Finally they decided that no gold would be taken anywhere unless they received their equal share as they had first agreed.

"That will never be!" declared Don Español. "You have the power, but I have the knowledge. Without me, you will never find the gold. I am not strong enough to kill you, and you would still not find the bullion if you killed me. So, my greedy ones, I am going."

The Spaniard wheeled around in a fit of rage. After a few steps, he paused, pulled the big gold watch from his pocket, and dashed it against a rock, shattering it as a timepiece, but only denting its heavy case. He cast it on the ground and, after a moment, turned and shouted his final words.

"Pigs! You can look for the bullion and the mine until your eyes go blind and your arms wither, but you will find neither of them!"

With that, Don Español walked away, taking both the knowledge and the map with him. His ruined gold watch was kept for years by one of the men who later searched on his own. Finally, both it and the heavy stone box containing white river sand disappeared. Don Español's prophecy has remained true to this day.[4]

It is not known whether Dave Arnold was familiar with the foregoing events, but chances are that he was. He left few stones unturned in his own search, and if he felt any of the oldest settlers of the canyon breaks might know something of value, he usually questioned them.

Strangely, about the same time that Arnold worked at the Spider diggings, a similar search was occurring about sixteen miles across country to the southwest on the Double Mountain Fork, or about nine miles south of Aspermont and some distance upstream. In 1908, Charley William Sanders homesteaded his farm on the Double Mountain Fork and worked the land with his brother-in-law, Bud Alston. Neither Sanders nor Alston knew anything about Arnold or the search he was then conducting on the Salt Fork. Nor did they know anything about lost Spanish gold.[5]

Not long after they began clearing their land, Alston was digging out a stump on a high bluff above the river when he struck a stone slab perhaps twenty inches square. Upon removing it from the roots that entangled it, he saw that the stone was no typical rock but had been buried many years before. Its face bore an intricately carved map composed of strange signs and symbols.

A Mexican sheepherder worked on the farm nearby, and Sanders and Alston asked him to examine the stone carving. The Mexican interpreted the symbols to indicate an enormous Spanish treasure of gold, diamonds, and jewels. "Enough to blind the eye," he cautioned, and urged them to return the stone to the soil from whence it came. When asked to guide them in the search for the treasure, the Mexican became almost terrified, refusing to be involved any further. He would have no part in disturbing sacred ground.

Charles Sanders and Bud Alston were not superstitious, and they began the search on their own, enlisting the aid of nine other families between the river and Aspermont who all furnished teams, plows, and fresnos. For two or three months, the farmers dug blindly, guessing at what the stone map might mean. The search was not totally unsuccessful, for other surface signs were found atop the bluff, along with what were believed to be the walls of a mission.

With their teams and fresnos, they cleared away the soil where Alston had dug out the stone map. At a depth of seven feet, they uncovered a turtlelike pattern carved into the bedrock, its deeply chiseled grooves filled with charcoal. That season nearly every farmer in the search party came close to losing his crops, including Sanders and Alston. One by one, the families returned to their own farms to harvest their fields.

No one ever quite understood the turtlelike or circular pattern discovered on the bluff, remembers Sanders's son, Marvin, who lives in New Mexico. His father and uncle always believed the Spaniards had gone down the side of the bluff overlooking the river and tunneled back under the bedrock. At the same time, they must have dug down to the bedrock from the surface and carved out the circular pattern of the map, filling its deep grooves with the charcoal.

Marvin was not born until the year after the discovery on the Double Mountain Fork, and never saw the stone map his uncle Bud Alston first found. He always believed, though, that something of value must have been found later, farther out from the strange pattern carved on the bedrock, for his father had spoken of seven or perhaps nine lines that led into the center of the charcoal-filled design. Two groups later dug on those lines leading into the corner of the circular carving. The evidence of a casket or box of some kind was later seen in a hole dug by a man and his two sons who lived nearby. They moved away soon afterward, seemingly not without funds.

The next year, in 1909, Sanders and Alston sold their farm and moved to Oklahoma.

Before leaving Aspermont, they turned the stone map over to officials at the Stonewall County Courthouse, only to learn later that the sandstone slab bearing the Azteclike-drawing had been destroyed in a fire.[6] The terms "Aztec drawing" or "Aztec burial" were almost always used when Sanders spoke of the stone map and the circular pattern of carvings. The term *Aztec* is understandable, for the untrained eye might easily associate such a cryptographic design with Aztec glyphs, or even the Aztec Calendar Stone of ancient Mexico.

While the story of the discovery on the Sanders farm may or may not have been known to Dave Arnold, around a year or two later he would unearth his own stone map on Gyp Creek, the mouth of which must not have been far from the Sanders farm. Were the discoveries on the Sanders farm, the story of the Inca sun-god, and Don Español's search near the ruins of a smelter—all of which occurred on the Double Mountain Fork—related to one another? Certainly the stone map found on the Sanders farm, and the subsequent discovery of the cryptic symbols and their deep carvings filled with charcoal, are an all-too-familiar part of the Dave Arnold mystery. Surely it must have been a site he was then seeking. Unfortunately, today those sites cannot now be pinpointed, even though all are yet embedded in the memories of those who participated in the searches early in the century.

Such stories may have led Arnold to the farm of Bob Hayes on Gyp Creek, although it is known that Arnold followed more tangible evidence than just stories to that location six miles east of Rotan. Hayes settled his farm in 1907. Arnold lived with the Hayes family for some months while he sought the treasure, and on their farm, once again, he had followed piles of stone on a direct north-south line that at that time were still visible. Hayes's grandson, also named Bob, recalls little of his grandfather's story of that search, except that Arnold encountered considerable trouble and was once placed in jail.[7]

George T. McBeth of Rotan was eighteen when he was hired by an old gentleman whom he believes must have been Arnold. It would have been in either 1909 or 1910, McBeth is sure, when his uncle, George McBeth, was persuaded by the stranger to enlist the help of several local residents in digging for a treasure on the banks of Gyp Creek. George T. and his cousin dug one of those holes on the west side of the creek, while three other parties dug within a few hundred yards of one another.[8]

McBeth, at eighty-four, remembered that two groups dug south of the hole he was instructed to dig, while another party searched in a cave not far to the north, farther down Gyp Creek on what used to be the Prue Ranch. The stranger planned to give the landowner one-quarter and the workmen one-quarter, and retain one-half for himself, but no one found anything that day.

Area resident Jess Lee Kiker, born in 1900, remembers from her early childhood the interest in one party digging for treasure beside Gyp Creek at a site just north of the present highway.[9] She said she never heard of anyone digging there in later years. From where McBeth and his co-workers dug that day, Double Mountain looms in the distance, a few degrees west of north.

Arnold appears to have worked on Gyp Creek the least of any of his excavations, and the consequence is that almost nothing is known about his search there. The fact that the stone map he unearthed there survives today, and the story of how it came to be in the hands of its present custodians, is as bizarre as any of the searches Arnold conducted. No one now living knows precisely where he found the third stone map, which bears many of the same symbols carved into the stones found on the Salt Fork and the Sembritzki farm. That so little is known about Arnold's Gyp Creek search may in part be explained by one who knew about that quest and pursued it.

No one could tell the story of Double Mountain better than the man who found part of the treasure that Arnold missed. That was Walter Leach, who until his death lived just west of Rotan. A stubby-bearded, white-haired, big-boned man, Leach once made his living hunting lobo wolves on the West Texas plains.[10] When he first began his search in 1912, the memory of Arnold was still fresh in the minds of many local ranchers, both those who liked Arnold and those who had plotted against him, hoping to grab a share of the gold that haunted him. Leach seemed sure that Arnold's companion at Double Mountain was Dr. Terrell of Haskell. But if that was true, Arnold began his search on Gyp Creek before the doctor's death in May of 1909.

Leach himself never met Arnold but was well acquainted with those who had known him. At this time Arnold almost always drove a buggy hitched to two gray mules with which he combed the country, much of that time living with the Bob Hayes family, who seemed to have had little interest in what he was seeking. Arnold's search on Gyp Creek was similar in many ways to his others, from the sketchy details that are now known. A snake carved into a huge mesquite tree was a sign, as were shallow holes filled with the ever-present charcoal. As in his former discoveries, Arnold found a human grave, and near those remains, he unearthed a single slab of white stone some thirteen or fourteen inches long, seven or eight inches wide, and perhaps two inches thick.

On each side appeared cryptic markings apparently carved by the same mystery mapmaker who crafted the earlier stone maps. Many of the symbols on the first two maps were identical, yet the third obviously told a different story. The white, alabasterlike stone lacked many numerals that formed so much of the other stone maps, but even though numbers were lacking, puzzling symbols were not.

On one side appeared the ever-present concentric circles found on the Spider Rock and the stone from the Sembritzki farm. Interestingly, each stone bore half as many circles as the other: the Spider Rock had eight, the Sembritzki stone had four, and the Gyp Creek stone had only two. Like the pattern on the other stone maps, where carved lines intersected the circles, a gouge or small hole appeared.

On the same side were carved what appeared to be two streams intersecting near one corner of the stone. Opposite the wavy stream line, and carved into the edge of the stone, were nine slashes. A straight slash ran down the center of the stone from one end to the other, dissecting the center of the concentric circles and a larger oval-shaped circle surrounding them. At one end appeared an N, perhaps for north. Eight stars were cut outside the circles. Might they have stood for fixed stars? Other ciphers were *DL, VROE, XII,* and *29 F.*[11]

Arnold noted that *29 F* also appeared on the Sembritzki stone map. At one side of the stone appeared a crude symbol, perhaps indicating a rising sun, and within the large oval, another *29 F,* a rectangular figure or box, the ciphers *11.00000,* and below, the word *ORO,* Spanish for "gold." The stone map Arnold found on the Sembritzki farm, the Spider Rock he unearthed on the Salt Fork, and the stone he uncovered on Gyp Creek all bore unmistakable resemblances, yet each one revealed a different topography, a different code of directions.[12]

If the mystery cryptographer who carved the Spider Rock was not the same who made the other stone charts, cartographers—with a common knowledge of those ancient symbols and their meanings—surely must have carved the stones and buried them with their myriad clues. What incredible Spanish mystery awaits revelation in the hieroglyphic stones? How many such stones were part of the web? How many more such stones yet wait to be found?

Arnold's trail had been riddled with deceit and chicanery, and already at Gyp Creek, there were those who were plotting to take the treasure from him when it was found.

One day soon after Arnold unearthed the plat rock with its mystifying symbols, he was attempting to match those ciphers with the surrounding topography when he spied a gnarled mesquite that seemed to be a good place to stop. He had already had heated words

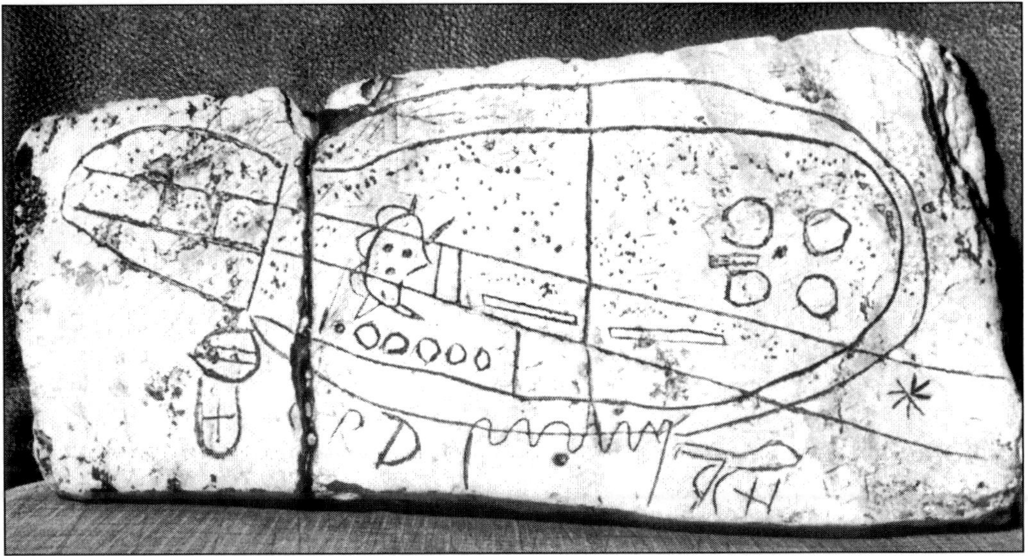

Sometime in 1909–10, Arnold unearthed his third stone map on Gyp Creek, sixty miles northwest of the Sembritzki farm. The stone appeared in Waco in 1914 and served as a doorstop for many years. About fourteen inches long, eight inches wide, and two inches thick, it is the only known stone remaining from Arnold's discoveries. One edge bears the carved figures 994. (Courtesy Dock Henderson)

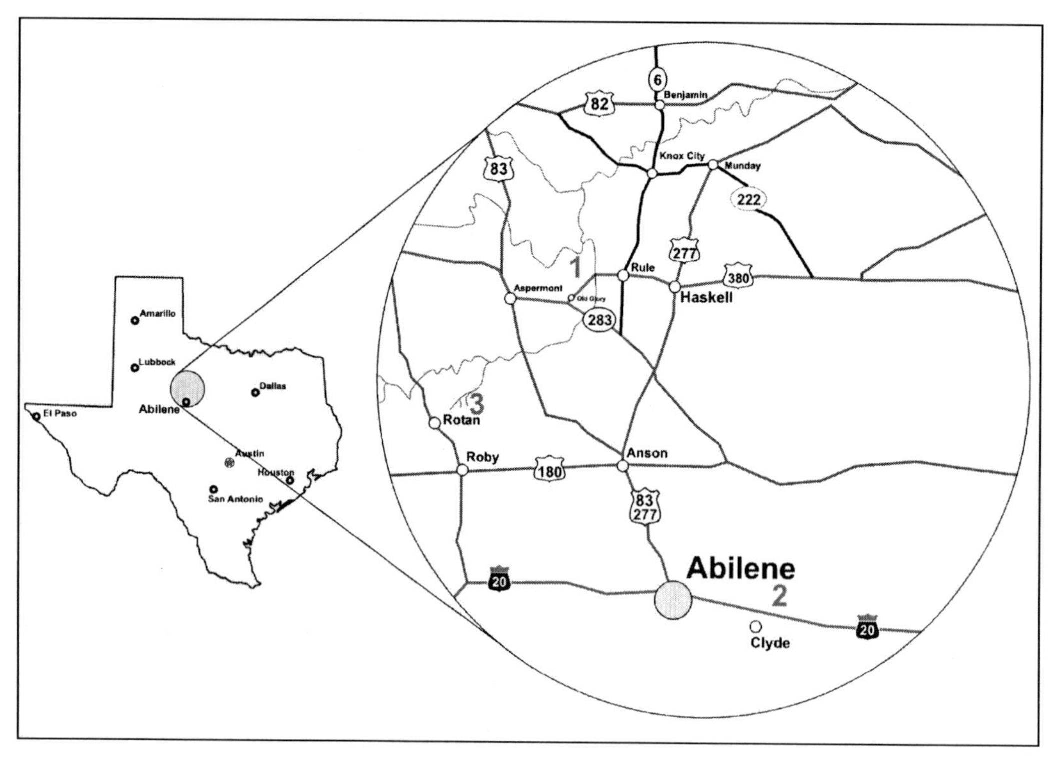

Map shows the location of the three hieroglyphic stones unearthed by Dave Arnold, the first just southwest of the Salt and Double Mountain forks, the second northeast of Clyde, and the third northeast of Rotan. (1. Spider Rock Discovery, 2. Sembritzki Stone, 3. Gyp Creek Stone.) Map by Raymond Watkins.

with some ranchers, and, weary and growing short on patience, he suspected treachery. He may have known he was being watched. Perhaps to test that suspicion, he whittled a stake from a small mesquite limb, and with the heel of his boot, stomped the stake into the ground at the base of the tree.

The story goes that that night, the ranchers had Arnold arrested on a trumped-up charge of horse stealing, and he was lodged in the Roby jail. With Arnold temporarily out of the way, the ranchers conducted their own search, and the mesquite where he had driven the stake was grubbed out, and a hole sunk deep enough to reveal nothing was to be found. According to Walter Leach, Dr. Terrell visited Arnold during his search and on one occasion, he, too, found himself the victim of ill deeds.

Prior to meeting with Arnold, Dr. Terrell had delivered a baby just inside Fisher County. There seemed to be some question about whether the doctor's license permitted practice outside Haskell County, and on this pretense, the ranchers managed to have the doctor incarcerated in the Roby jail long enough to prevent him from interfering with their search. After discovering their chicanery was getting them nowhere, the ranchers propositioned Arnold that they would drop the charges against him and the doctor if he would cut them in on half the treasure. Arnold agreed and both men were set free. It was then that Arnold disappeared from Gyp Creek.

Although the foregoing story may be true, the Terrell family never knew of such an episode concerning the doctor and had no knowledge of Arnold in the Double Mountain area. Certainly, if Arnold and Dr. Terrell hunted together on Gyp Creek prior to the doctor's death, Arnold returned afterward when he discovered the stone map buried there—a map that was not among those items in the masonry vault when the Terrell drug store burned on the night of May 7, 1909.

It is sad that so few details are known of Arnold's apparently brief quest on Gyp Creek, and that the exact site where the third stone map was uncovered is today unknown. The Hayes family never forgot Arnold, and Bob Hayes talked about his visit for many years afterward, remembers his grandson. But the details of that memorable visit—like the trail that Arnold followed—have dimmed with time.[13]

Arnold had yet one more location to dig, a site a mere mile or so upstream from the mouth of Wild Horse Creek on the Brazos where a few years before he had guided Kelly and John Johnson to the grave of a priest from which came the ebony and silver crucifix kept in Dr. Terrell's vault. While Arnold worked that site on the Brazos, headquartering with members of the Johnson family, Walter Leach joined a party seeking the treasure they believed Arnold had failed to find on Gyp Creek.

It was sometime in 1912 that Leach became a member of a party of twenty-three, who made up the search at a time when many of the clues Arnold found were still fresh in mind and others were yet plain to see.[14] The snake carved on the gnarled mesquite was one such marking, as well as the shallow holes that had contained pockets of charcoal, similar to those at the Spider diggings and the Sembritzki farm.

Leach recalls that the search lasted intermittently for more than a year when one day, by a streak of luck, they unearthed a single gold ingot in the bed of an old buffalo wallow. That gold bar, somehow overlooked by Arnold, was split twenty-three ways and was the sole result of their search. Each man's share amounted to $73, as gold was bringing $18 an ounce. The small ingot weighed just over seven and three-quarter pounds, and its markings—a cross for the church and a V for the viceroy—showed it to be of Spanish origin.

One clue that was never found during that search, Leach recounted, was the subject of much speculation. A huge stone, some fifteen feet long by eight feet wide, was said to be buried somewhere on the south side of Double Mountain. On the face of the stone was carved another, much larger Spanish directional map. But that stone remained unfound over the years.

Double Mountain, rising some five hundred feet above the arroyo-ridden land it surrounds, presents many puzzles of Spanish origin not yet explained. One of Arnold's coworkers was Jack Freeman of Abilene, a former stage driver when he met Arnold. Freeman continued his own search in later years at Double Mountain.[15] In about 1928 he found the foundation ruins of what appeared to be an ancient building on the saddle of the peaks. Freeman unearthed large clay balls that had been buried about a hundred yards apart, running east-west across the saddle.

That search yielded unmistakable evidence that it had once been a Spanish occupation, Freeman was sure, for he unearthed several human skeletons, pieces of chain mail, and other antiquated artifacts. What link Double Mountain holds in the Spider Rock mystery can only be conjectured. An old Comanche Indian legend states that horsemen in shining armor lie buried on Double Mountain.[16] Was it their bones and armor that Jack Freeman found, with knowledge once shared by Dave Arnold?

As Walter Leach sat in his trailer home west of Rotan within sight of Double Mountain to the north, surrounded by books on surveying and engineering, he recalled his own quest of six decades before and pondered what might yet be found in the old buffalo wallow after all these years. Inca treasure? Aztec gold? Spanish ingots? Seemingly, only Dave Arnold possessed that knowledge. Leach remembered one other thing about Arnold: he had dug at two other sites not far away. One was eight miles west of Rotan; the other was eight miles south of Snyder on Deep Run Creek.

Arnold made other quests before he was to disappear forever. One of those was what he had referred to as "old Lana Grande" in his letter to Cabe. And there may have been other sites Arnold dug, and clues he found, about which nothing is now known. Many members of the Johnson family yet recall Arnold and his second wife, whom they knew affectionately as Uncle Dave and Aunt Susie. They were all children then, and the Johnsons never forgot the old man from Mexico with his Spanish waybill, and the many excursions that their fathers and uncles made with him, always seeking signs and markers on the banks of the Brazos in western Knox County.

Edwin Johnson, who lives on the farm three miles west of Munday where Arnold so often headquartered and apparently lived during his final days of his quest, remembers his father, Kelly, saying that the final search was for a colossal $18 million in gold. Edwin was only a youngster then but remembers seeing Arnold.[17]

Kelly, his brothers, John, Moss, and A. J. V., and other members of the Johnson family participated in Arnold's search at the Spider diggings twenty-five miles or so up the Brazos from where he was now to dig, a mere mile from the mouth of Wild Horse Creek. Edwin recalls, too, how his father would talk long into the night about Arnold and all he found, until the children had long fallen asleep. But as children, Edwin laments, no one thought of writing down the details, all of which were lost with the death of Kelly Johnson in 1963 at age eighty-nine.

Arnold had found markings on the south bank of the Brazos some five miles or so north of Knox City, on land owned by a man named Covington. Most of Arnold's search was concentrated just east of what is now State Highway 6, where his method of digging was similar to that of his former work. Perhaps his use of teams and scrapers to tear up that strip of land, or Covington's own distrust of Arnold, caused the landowner to ask him to leave. A story was later told that Covington himself had discovered markings a mile farther south that Arnold was not aware of, and with that discovery and his knowledge of Arnold's search, he believed he could find what Arnold apparently had not.

Arnold may have abandoned that quest at his own satisfaction, for the story says that he left those diggings with $65,000 in gold. Sad again that so few details of his final search are known. Edwin Johnson recalls only that "human bones and the proverbial charcoal" were found at that Brazos River site.[18]

Mrs. Blanche Nelson of Munday recalls that she was fourteen or fifteen years old when she last saw "Uncle" Dave, then in his late sixties. It was 1914 or 1915. Her father, Tom Tompkins, a brother-in-law of Kelly Johnson, participated in a search with the Johnson brothers and Arnold. One place they examined was Blanche's uncle Bud Johnson's farm, a mile north of Knox City.[19] At that time Arnold sported a full head of graying hair and, mustache, and of course, everyone knew him by his "Santa Claus belly." He wore his usual overalls or work pants held up by suspenders. Blanche remembers a small gold ring mounted with a blue stone that Arnold had found and always enjoyed showing to others.

Ed Johnson and his wife, Mary, of Munday remember "Uncle" Dave and "Aunt" Susie from their childhood days, when they were seven or eight years old. Susan was younger than her husband, had long black hair, and played the piano and organ. Arnold always delighted in entertaining the children wherever he went, and Ed and Mary remember his ability as a ventriloquist.[20]

The Johnsons remember that Arnold and his wife would be gone for a short time, then reappear for a week or so while the Johnson brothers hunted the river canyons with him. Ed's father, A. J. V., often participated in the search with his brothers Kelly, John, and Moss. Arnold seems to have spent as much time living with one family as another. By this time, Arnold and his wife seemed to live a gypsy-styled life. He and Susan traveled over the country in a covered wagon pulled by two horses while leading another one behind. They had their chuck box in the back of the wagon, and Ed remembers a shotgun Arnold carried with him. Both Ed and his wife Mary recall the "Spanish maps" Arnold carried, one of which must have been the ever-present sheepskin.

It was always Ed's impression that Arnold made his living at this time by witching for water. He seemed to have a knack for it and was called on by many area farmers for that purpose. He seems, too, to have now carried a divining rod, which he used while seeking the Spanish treasure. It was a six- or eight-inch-long brass tube, Ed remembers, filled with a heavy substance. Attached to it was a gold ring, and the ring to a gold chain from which he dangled it. Arnold and his wife always helped with the family chores whenever they stayed with the Johnsons. He would mend the fence, and she would pitch in with the washing or other work to be done. Both attended the Primitive Baptist Church while they stayed with the Johnson families.

One other site Ed recalls his father and uncles working with Arnold for days at a time was on the north side of the Brazos, northwest of Knox City near the community of Brock. No one remembers just what all was found there, but along with the many Spanish markings Arnold was accustomed to finding, the Johnsons recall pieces of Spanish armor among other similar artifacts. Interestingly, the site appears to have been not many miles distant from Kiowa Peak, lying to the south. Neither Ed nor Mary remembers seeing "Uncle" Dave or "Aunt" Susie after 1913 or 1914. Ed and Mary went to school in 1913 when they were seven, and recall Arnold and his wife coming only once or twice after that. But neither would ever forget the memories they left behind.[21]

Dave and Susan Arnold left the Brazos River bottoms, never to be seen or heard from again by anyone who had known them there. Their disappearance is as much a mystery as the man himself and the incredible search he led for over a decade. We may never know how far his trail stretched over West Texas or for how long a time. We know from the Johnson family that before he appeared in Haskell in 1902, he said he had found $12,500 in Spanish gold in Comanche County, a location not far southeast of the Sembritzki farm.[22]

Yet, still farther southeastward, Amos Sheppard of Gatesville, in Coryell County, remembers Arnold appearing there sometime in 1896, seeking something six or seven miles west of town on the Leon River.[23] Sheppard believes, too, that Arnold then went under an assumed name. Might he have been seeking the ruins of the Spanish settlement—and mines—which Colonel Jacob Snively found in 1844? It may not be merely coincidental that Arnold lived near Evant in Hamilton County in 1897, bordered on one side by Comanche County and the other by Coryell County.

No one knows—or has yet come forth with the information—about what became of Arnold and his sheepskin map. Some believe he may have returned to his former home near San Angelo. Joe Woods of Abilene, who began his own quests when Arnold had long abandoned his, believes he last saw Arnold in 1927 or '28 in Eastland.[24] Jack Freeman, who once worked with Arnold, told John Smith of Abilene he last saw Arnold in Weatherford about 1930 but heard later he had been murdered. If so, Arnold would have been in his mid-eighties.[25] Walter Leach and others heard Arnold had gone to Kansas, where he fell victim to the curse of the treasure he so long pursued, for rumor had it that he had been murdered for the sheepskin map.[26]

And then there is the strange search that Gurney Ward led in the Sacramento Mountains of New Mexico. Ward was known to have often followed in the footsteps of Dave Arnold. Had Ward followed him to Alamo Canyon as well? Arnold's death remains a mystery.

When Arnold vanished from West Texas, he did not know that at least a part of the Spanish treasure he had found at three separate locations actually survived the Terrell drug store fire. The Terrell family still possessed the magnificent Spider Rock, although broken in two from that fire, and Cabe possessed the copper plates and replicas from both the Spider diggings and the Sembritzki farm, as well as the silver crucifix, map tracings, and various letters. Each of those he would carry with him first to Snyder, then Post City, Baird, Corpus Christi, and finally, Waco, where he settled in 1920.[27]

Neither memory nor legend has explained the disposition of the third stone map Arnold unearthed on Gyp Creek in 1909 or 1910. How it came to leave Arnold's possession is also a mystery that may never be solved. The fact that it exists at all today is as incredible as its discovery. That stone map, too, found its way to Waco, but by a much different route. The family that came to inherit the stone in about 1914, only four years or so after its discovery, would know nothing about who had found it, where it had been found, or the mystery surrounding it. They knew only that it had come from near Double Mountain and that it could lead the person able to read it to "a treasure of silver bricks."

James Roberts was somehow chosen for the inheritance of a cryptic stone map about which he knew nothing. He moved to Waco from Austin in 1914, and that year his son, Jesse Augustus, married. Jesse's wife, Uda, who was twenty years old that year, recalls the story of the stone that came to be known in the Roberts family as simply "the treasure rock" and for years served as a doorstop and conversation piece.[28]

When her father-in-law was given the stone, Uda remembers, James Roberts was told that a Mexican sheepherder had died not long before at the county farm in Waco. His sole possession was the stone map, about which he revealed a story to the farm manager, a man named Bull, before he died. Bull, in turn, told the story to Roberts and gave him the stone. The Mexican sheepherder perhaps did not tell how he came by the strange stone or who had found it. The details of his story are sketchy at best after so many years, but he told Bull that "a great treasure in silver bricks would be found somewhere near Double Mountain."

James Roberts did not find time to hunt the treasure until some years later. Whether he ever knew just where the stone was found is to be conjectured. With his son, Jess, he searched the region about Double Mountain during the 1920s. James and Jess believed, Uda recalls, that the stone map was somehow the key to a mine. Her husband and father-in-law searched off and on for several years. All they found was a fellow who said he had discovered a "large iron pot of Spanish money" under a huge stone, and he showed them where. When James died in 1925 in his seventies, his son Jess inherited the cryptic stone.

Jess and Uda's daughter, Mrs. Naomi Roberts Cleghorn, born in 1921, remembers hearing as a youngster the many conversations spawned by the stone that for years served as a doorstop in their home. "The treasure rock" was the center of attention at every party they had, Naomi remembers.[29] When her father died, her son, John Ray Terrell, inherited the stone. Of no relation to the Dr. C. L. Terrell family, neither the John Terrell nor Roberts families knew of Cabe Terrell, then living in Waco, or his search early in the century with the very man who had discovered the stone that James and Jess Roberts long puzzled over. How ironic it was that both families were living in the same city and harbored the Spanish clues all found by Dave Arnold, yet neither knew anything about the other.

John Terrell, who had traveled with his grandfather Roberts to Double Mountain as a youngster, returned to the West Texas cedar brakes in 1964 and intermittently for several years afterward. But he came no closer to deciphering the stone map than had his great grandfather, James Roberts, who had fallen heir to it a half-century before.[30]

But who was the Mexican sheepherder? And how did he retrieve the stone from Dave Arnold? Those answers we may never know. We do know that Arnold consulted several Mexicans in an effort to decipher the stone maps when he had failed. We know, too, that a Mexican sheepherder helped lead him to the Spider Rock and guided much of the subsequent digging there. We know that many of the original participants believed the sheepherder misled Arnold and retrieved the two copper vessels. And they believed he was murdered.

What neither Arnold nor any of his search party ever knew was that before the sheepherder vanished, he scrawled a letter and gave it, along with a map, to the family he was living with. Might it be that the Mexican sheepherder was not murdered after all but died at the county farm in Waco some years later, whispering his final secrets about a stone map that Arnold had actually found? If so, whose skeleton was found that day with the two empty copper vessels?

The cryptic letter the Mexican scrawled late one night would spawn yet another search by the family entrusted with it.

7

The Mexican Sheepherder's Letter

Neither Dave Arnold nor any of his followers knew of the existence of the Mexican sheepherder's letter, which was scrawled late one night before he disappeared forever. The recipient of that letter and the map that accompanied it would guard that secret for fifteen years before finally seeking help in translating the letter, which appeared to be in Spanish.

Mrs. Pauline Edwards Tabor was a high schooler in Pauls Valley, Oklahoma, when she was pulled into the Spider Rock mystery in 1923. Pauline knew nothing about the Spider Rock or the story of the Mexican sheepherder and his part in that quest. When the sheepherder mysteriously entered the search with Arnold, then some months later vanished just as quickly, he had lived with the Stuart family, who had a dugout east of the forks of the river, a couple of miles northeast of the Spider diggings. The Stuarts left the cedar brakes years later to resettle in Pauls Valley.[1]

William Stuart was in his seventies or eighties when Pauline met him. He had met the Edwards family and learned that Pauline was studying Spanish. One day as she was on her way to school, Stuart approached Pauline and asked her to translate an old letter that he carried. Pauline did not have the time to look at it then, but several days later the old man appeared at her home with the letter.

At first, Stuart explained nothing of its story, saying only that the letter had been given him many years before and he had found no one who could translate it. The letter had been scrawled on a brown paper sack, and portions of it were almost illegible from the creases caused from its being folded and unfolded over the years. Pauline could readily tell that although portions of the message were in Spanish, that language was mixed with another, and it would take time to decipher what appeared to be instructions.

Over the weeks that followed, Pauline pieced together the strange directions to finding a Spanish treasure buried centuries before. As she deciphered the message, Stuart revealed the story behind the letter and its writer. Stuart said he had gotten to know the Mexican sheepherder well over the months that he guided Arnold, first helping find the Spider Rock and its copper plates, then the canyon with the personal effects of a Spanish cavalry officer, and finally, the hillside fronting the canyon where more symbols of stone and metal had been placed atop the bedrock, called the "spider circle."

Beneath the bedrock and in that canyon side, Arnold and every man in his party believed that the discovery of the treasure chamber was imminent. The guns each man packed and the secrecy that bound their search testified to that belief. That Arnold himself was suspicious of the sheepherder caused several of that party to carefully watch the Mexican's movements.

Because of the imminence of finding the treasure, Stuart said, the men dug late one night at the excavation. A member of the search party approached the sheepherder and warned him that if he valued his life, he should leave before the treasure was found, for he was convinced that afterward he would not have that opportunity. The Mexican slipped into the darkness, walking as fast as his legs would carry him along the riverbank, and crossed to the east side of the forks, where the Stuart family lived in a small dugout.

The Mexican arrived at the Stuarts' home exhausted, trembling, and fearing for his life. He asked them to immediately snuff out their lanterns, except one in a far corner, where they huddled. He recounted what had occurred and stated that he must leave that night. Should he not return, he wished to leave a letter of instructions on how to reach the treasure that he knew would be found. Those directions, until now, he had kept only in his mind for fear they might otherwise be stolen from him.

Without revealing where he had first read the secret message and memorized it, he reached for the nearest thing at hand and scrawled, often trembling, that message on a brown paper sack as he now remembered it. In addition to that two-hundred-word document, he gave the Stuarts a copy of a map that he said would be necessary to follow the instructions.

With that, his final words were that if he should not return in a reasonable amount of time, the map and letter were theirs to keep, for he wished them to have the treasure for having been so kind to him. Despite the Stuarts' efforts to persuade him otherwise, the Mexican then disappeared into the darkness. The story of his final visit to their dugout late that night, and the hurried instructions and map he left with them, would remain a secret with the Stuart family until the story was shared with Pauline Edwards that day in 1923.

It was some time later, Stuart told, that the human skeleton was found in a pasture along the Double Mountain Fork a mere few miles south of his dugout. Of course, whoever it was, everyone believed he had found a small part of the treasure because of the two empty copper pots.[2] Although no one could say with certainty, Stuart did not believe the sheepherder had been killed, even though that story was circulated. But the Mexican had indeed vanished.

Stuart kept the map and letter of instructions, and when he left his farm in the Brazos River bottom and moved to Oklahoma some years later, he had honored the wishes of the Mexican who so hurriedly shared his knowledge before disappearing forever. Stuart had tried to obtain a translation of the Mexican's letter but without any success, for the Spanish words were mixed with the words of another language.

Pauline soon discovered the reason for Stuart's difficulty. The letter was a mixture of archaic Spanish and Portuguese, a dialect common to Occidental Spain, or the southwestern region from which had come most of the *conquistadores* of Spain's Gilded Age. Southwestern Spain had been the birthplace of the original letter writer, and the Mexican sheepherder, perhaps only semiliterate, had memorized the instructions and written them as best he could under stress late one night. That letter, as the sheepherder scrawled it on the night of his departure, was this:

> Protecion de certo cadabares serto documentos que astestigan la beram figura con que se senal. Ela fecto de certo. A grado para. Definar en el articulo: el lugar es peceno donde esta el efeco deciado pero se aguardo sin recelo que pueda tropezar dificultita a el lugar donde esta guardado el tesoro. Esta a una embocadura definida. La contabilidad principia de la cabeza a 150 metros en una concabidad de la fosa primera que existe entre dos fosas, ambos en la segunda existe algo de barros, escrupulosos articulos de gran valor presuntoso. Encontrado esta marca N, 3 metros esta el toresoro de 66860 todo sellado, 18 barros de oro, 22 de plata. Al sellarce con el sello de los eum, esta fue quitado a los conductos que traneitaban para K. C. en 1671. Cofre son en forma de pato que contiene los effectos llapa. Existe un komp se abre esa camera con una llave secreta que nadie la puede sino por de cignos la pierda gaspiada de signos. Hinserto el sentro principiano encha se ubicado cado en cierta pocisiou que contro citio umbicada en una possession origanario ILP que tien domino p——— no con la humanidad ninguna oppero ay un medio el saber los para. No tropezar con difficultabes.[3]

Pauline translated that mysterious message of antiquated Spanish and Portuguese as well as she could, and while doing so, she made copies of both the letter and map without telling Stuart. Her intellectual curiosity aroused, more than any interest in the treasure, Pauline wanted the letter and map to study later.

A translation of the sheepherder's memorized instructions reveals something of the Spanish treasure trove Arnold and his Mexican counterpart sought, but it also adds to the mystery of who the Spaniards were, or the purpose of their intense secrecy. Two translations are offered here, the first by Dr. E. Michael Gerli, a Spanish linguistic scholar at Georgetown University, Washington, D.C., who pinpointed the dialect of the Spanish-Portuguese wording to southwestern Spain. That translation, complete with words that appear untranslatable because of their spelling or abbreviation, is this:

> Protection is certain. The bodies are hinterland documents that attest to the true markings. This is for sure. The steps to find the articles: the place where the desired effects (objects) are is dark, but I do not think you will have any difficulty finding the spot where the treasure is. It is at a well-defined opening (aperture). The count begins here: 150 meters from the head there is a concavity covered by brush (leaves) in the pit. In the second one there is some pottery in which I found beautiful articles of great wealth. The sealed treasure of 66860 is three meters to the North: 18 bars of gold, 22 of silver. It is sealed with the seal of the *eum* that was taken from the travelers headed for K. C. in 1671. The strongbox that holds the effects is in the form of a duck [perhaps trunk]. Next to it there is a *komp*. The room can only be opened by a secret combination that can only be deciphered from the petroglyphs. Once you decipher them and apply the combination and go in, it gets wider as you go. They are in the original position. ILP that has mastery *p*———. There is no one alive who can, but there is a way of knowing (deciphering) them. You should not have any trouble.[4]

Dr. Clevy Strout, professor of Spanish at the University of Tulsa and a leading authority on the Coronado Expedition, offers this translation, somewhat different, and equally puzzling:

> Protection of certain cadavers, certain documents which testify you will see a figure with which it is pointed out. The fact is certain (true). I am pleased to define (explain) in the article: the place is small where the item (effect) is left, but it was kept without fear (distrust). One can come upon (find) with little difficulty the place where the treasure is kept (hidden). It is at a definite opening (narrow passage). The counting begins from the head at 150 meters in a concavity from the first flat stone (pit, or hole) which exists (is) between two flat stones (pits, or both). In the second there is some thing (pieces) of jars (clay or earthenware), things scrupulously looked at of great presumed value. Having found this mark N, three meters (at three meters) is the treasure of 66860, all sealed (stamped, or covered), 18 bars of gold, 22 of silver. When sealed with the seal of the *eum*. This was removed by the leaders (conductors) who were on their way to K. C. in 1671. Coffers are in the form of a duck which contains the effects (items) *llapa* (in addition?). There exists a *komp* (key? combination?). That room is opened with a secret key and no one can (know?) it except by the signs, the stone scratched (or scraped) with signs. Inserted, in the center it fills up. Each is placed in a certain position which is opposite the place located in the original position. ILP (which or who?) has the control (key?) *p*———. Will not be able with mere humanity (human wisdom?), but there is a way to find them out. One will not (should not) have any difficulties.[5]

In 1923 Pauline translated enough of the sheepherder's message to send Stuart back to the Salt Fork. The map the Mexican had given Stuart meant nothing to Pauline, although he had obviously intended that it be used in conjunction with the written directions. The map may have meant nothing to Stuart either, for it was not a copy of the Spider Rock that the Mexican had handed him, but a copy of the stone map Arnold was to unearth, or perhaps had unearthed, on the Sembritzki farm. It is doubtful that Stuart was ever aware of that discovery. Pauline would not learn of it until many years later.

Stuart returned to Arnold's diggings of fifteen years before, and, with Crockett Scribner of Pauls Valley, made several attempts to follow the directions left him late one night. He believed the starting point of the search was the very canyon in which the sheepherder had led Arnold to the Spanish sword and silver epaulets. But Stuart dug blindly, and neither the map he possessed nor the mysterious directions did him any good.

Not many years later, Stuart died. His daughter and son must have inherited the map and letter. The son attempted a short-lived search of his own, but finally he, too, returned no more. During one of those brief visits to the Spider diggings, the son revealed a story that, if true, explains in part Arnold's suspicion of the Mexican sheepherder's treachery and compounds the enigma of the map he handed the Stuart family along with the hurried letter.

The younger Stuart explained that while the sheepherder guided Arnold to the Spider Rock and the subsequent discoveries, the Mexican knew that Arnold also sought a map cut on a bluff near the forks of the river. Perhaps only the Mexican knew the relationship of one map to the other. With the Mexican's guidance, it was that carving that the Stuarts sought, and they found it cut into a canyon wall just west of the forks, perhaps two miles north-northeast from where the Spider Rock was found.

The details are not clear at to whether the sheepherder, or the Stuarts, destroyed that majestic stone carving, but once copied, it was hacked from the face of the bluff to prevent Arnold from finding it. That stone tracing was the map the Mexican gave the Stuarts upon his departure, strangely believed to be the same map Arnold would discover carved on stone and embedded in the roots of the huge oak on the Sembritzki farm almost sixty miles away.

The chronology of the Mexican sheepherder's relationship with Arnold is an important factor, for it cannot now be determined just when in that search he disappeared. It is equally difficult to say exactly when the sheepherder entered Arnold's search near the forks, partly because other Mexicans were involved in that quest at one time or another.

It is almost certain that Arnold discovered the Spider Rock atop the red-clay hill on the Salt Fork between the fall of 1902 and late 1904, for during the winter months of early 1905, he temporarily abandoned that quest to seek the second of the stone maps he was to find at the Sembritzki farm.

Later in 1906, and at least through the fall of 1908, Arnold and his followers continued work at the Spider diggings. If in fact the Mexican sheepherder guided Arnold to the Spider Rock, as the story has come to be handed down, he must have known far more about Arnold's search and the things he sought than anyone realized.

At least once, the sheepherder warned that the Mexican government was aware of the Spanish treasure and that certain priests in Mexico possessed the knowledge to find the treasure. To have made those statements and to have led Arnold to the Spider Rock, and then to the Spanish saber and silver epaulets, would have required considerable knowledge of the stone maps and the Spaniards who made them.

Such knowledge was available only to the one who found, and could read, the maps and documents revealing that story. Arnold had come by the sheepskin chart that described many of those things to him. The sheepherder's source of information must have come from the custodians of the original records. Whatever that source, the sheepherder appears to have possessed knowledge that Arnold knew he lacked.

It is uncertain whether the Mexican sheepherder disappeared before or after Arnold's year-long search at the Sembritzki farm, for more than once he called upon Mexicans to assist him there. And no one can explain how a Mexican sheepherder obtained the third stone map that Arnold unearthed on Gyp Creek around 1910. If in fact the sheepherder disappeared prior to Arnold's work at the Sembritzki farm in early 1905, then the mystery is even more bizarre, because the message he scrawled from memory, and the map he gave the Stuart family, were of the stone map Arnold came to unearth from the roots of the huge oak tree.

If that is so, then the sheepherder knew beforehand what Arnold would find at the Sembritzki farm, and what symbols and diagram that stone would bear. If his disappearance came after that discovery, and the map he gave the Stuart family was but a tracing of that stone, then he still carried in his mind the instructions he had memorized—a message that bore the same date as the stone that Arnold found. That date, carved in archaic script which resembled 1671, was read by Arnold as 1731. Might Arnold have been wrong? Might the correct date have indeed been 1671? And the "*ILP*" that "has the control," as it was worded in the sheepherder's message, those same letters appear twice on the stone map from the Sembritzki farm, as they also appear incised on one of the three copper daggers found there.

"... One can come upon (find) with little difficulty the place the treasure is kept (hidden).... The counting begins from the first flat stone ... from the head at 150 meters in a concavity, the treasure of 66860, all sealed ... removed by the leaders (conductors) who were on their way to K. C. in 1671 [1731?].... That room is opened with a secret key ... the stone scratched with signs.... Each is placed in a certain position which is opposite the place located in the original position...."

What centuries-old document had the Mexican sheepherder found? How accurate was his memory when he scrawled that secret message while in fear of his life? Who were the travelers of 1671 (or 1731)? Where was the room that could be opened with a secret key—that key being the stone of signs? Was this the lost city Arnold spoke about?

Pauline recounts that in the years immediately after she translated the sheepherder's letter for William Stuart, Crockett Scribner, who assisted him, sought other translations, thinking perhaps she had interpreted the letter incorrectly. He finally found a Mexican woman in El Paso who offered help, but upon reading that puzzling message written by someone from antiquity, she threw her hands up in great anguish and pleaded with Scribner to abandon his search. The treasure was sacred, she wailed, sacred to the church, and should not be touched, for surely great peril would come to that person. The woman could not have known that others had warned Dave Arnold in almost those exact words decades before when he showed them the stone.

Pauline and her brother, Burt, were not stopped by what appeared to be a curse hovering over the treasure. They waited fifteen years, until long after Stuart had died and his son had stopped looking, before they pursued the trail on their own. That was in 1938. During that year and the trips that followed for the next two or three, they, just as had Stuart before them, returned to the grassed-over Spider diggings where the Mexican sheepherder first led Arnold more than three decades before.[6]

Although their own intermittent quests spanned four decades, Pauline and Burt Edwards never gave up hope that one more trip would provide the final clue to unraveling the mystery letter first written perhaps centuries before.

8

The Treasure Dave Arnold Missed: Dock Henderson's Fifty-Year Search

Only a few persons living today can say they knew Dave Arnold and recount some fragment of the bizarre search he led in the first decade after the turn of the century. Of all those who became involved in that search or were affected by it, only one man has lived the story throughout most of his life. Without his vast store of knowledge, much of this story could never have been written. His life is inseparable from the Spider Rock treasure.

He was born William Bunkley Henderson, named for the doctor who delivered him. The name Dock stuck throughout his life. Dock never knew Arnold, for in the year of Dock's birth, 1903, Arnold was at least two years into his decade-long quest. But no man—perhaps not even Arnold himself—has seen the overwhelming evidence that Dock glimpsed in the more than fifty years that he looked for the Spider Rock treasure. In that half-century, Dock saw more clues to this puzzling lost Spanish treasure than Edgar Allan Poe could have invented had he spent an equal time creating the story—clues Arnold surely must have sought yet somehow missed.[1]

If it were not for the incredible amount of tangible evidence Dock found over those many years, he might have long ago shrugged it all off as simply a fanciful tale. But silver statuettes do not lie, nor do silver crosses, nor crudely smelted nuggets of gold. And large chunks of slag and accompanying charcoal and ash from antiquated smelter pits cannot be ignored. And then there are always the signs—those cryptic Spanish symbols carved into stone, found by happenstance over the rugged landscape since the country was first settled. Only someone who has lived a lifetime in this land could amass the knowledge and evidence that Dock has in the many years since he first stepped into the mystery.

Dock's father, Preston Alex Henderson, moved his family to Haskell County in 1912. Dock was a tousle-haired youth, and in the many years that followed, he came to know this land as perhaps no one has before or since. The Spider Rock has been as much a part of his life as the land in which its story unfolded. As farmer, cowhand, hunter, rock hound, he has always been close to the soil, always seeking its every beauty, story, or clue to those who came before.

Weather-beaten from those years, his calloused hands and lined face reveal his closeness to the land, but his roughhewn exterior is no indication of the man himself. He can shoot a rattler with quick aim, or adopt an abandoned bobcat cub and raise it for a pet. His home is full of the centuries-old treasures he has found while riding horseback or walking over this land—treasures in the form of projectile points or other stone artifacts of early man here before or since Spanish colonial times.

Dock's mind is imprinted with the discoveries of more than a half-century: historic sites of nomadic inhabitants, remains of extinct animals, ancient hearths of long-forgotten tribes, nuggets and veins of rich copper and lead sought by the earliest explorers, and the long-abandoned crude smelters of armor-clad conquerors who came for heavy metal and left an incredible trail of clues of their own.

The cedar brakes, the canyon country about the headwaters of the Brazos River, is such a land, where men have been murdered for its secrets. Like gold flakes in a stream, enough clues and enough treasure have been discovered over the years to tantalize the seeker forever onward, another day, another month, another year, hoping he will one day find the mother lode. No man could tell the story of the Spider Rock like Dock.

"It gets so quiet down here I can almost hear the sun go down," Dock drawled, sitting in the shade of a large mesquite at the ranch he managed on the Double Mountain Fork, fifteen miles from the nearest paved road south of Aspermont. Fate brought Dock into the Spider Rock legend, even some years before he became personally involved in that quest.

While Arnold worked at the Spider Rock site between 1902 and 1908, he leased the land from Hoy Smith. Some years later an oldster named Dane bought the river land to run a few hogs. Sometime in the late teens, Dane was unable to pay his note, and Dock's father, Preston, and his friend Sprout Robinson, helped the old man by paying the note. Dane later paid Robinson back, but he gave Henderson the deed to about 300 acres along the Salt Fork. Preston Henderson ran a few head of cattle on the land, then later sold it to the Rochester bank. About 1920 the Hendersons bought a farm east of Hamlin and moved there.[2]

Meanwhile, one of the original Spider Rock participants, who had left in 1908 before its conclusion, never put out of his mind all that had been found at those diggings or what Arnold was sure would be found. That was W. J. "Bud" Jones, whose family had settled the land north of the Spider diggings across the Salt Fork and on whose very farm had been found a copper plate bearing mysterious tracery. Jones had worked closely with Arnold, Dr. Terrell, and his son Cabe. In 1924 Jones was living in Bisbee, Arizona, and was then in his late fifties or early sixties. He possessed one of the few blueprints remaining of the Spider Rock, which he had helped uncover more than twenty years before. During those years, the stone map continued to haunt him.[3]

It was Jones who in 1907 built the masonry vault in Dr. Terrell's drug store in which to place his artifacts. Perhaps more than anyone else, Jones knew just what had been found and what each item revealed to Arnold. Finally, in 1924, he returned to those overgrown diggings to renew the search.

With Jones came Andy N. Moss and Walter Urion from California. They would assist whenever possible, and for their grubstake would receive an interest in anything found. It was one of those strange quirks of fate that associated the Hendersons with the Spider Rock treasure. Preston Henderson was doing business in Hamlin that day when he ran into Jones and learned of his purpose. Henderson told Jones he had once owned that very piece of land on the Salt Fork, had sold it to the Rochester bank, and could probably buy it back. The four formed a partnership and pooled their resources.

Once the land was repurchased, Jones set up his camp just south of the large excavation that he had helped dig to bedrock, beneath which Arnold had believed the treasure chamber would be found. Preston offered to help as much as he could, but it was his son, Dock, who came to spend much of his time with Jones, helping him follow every lead that had crossed his mind in the sixteen years since he had last set foot on that ground. Dock was twenty-one that year, in 1924.

Jones possessed little more than an iron cook stove and a tent, but his obsession with finding the Spanish treasure was no less than it had been when he worked side by side with Arnold and the Mexican sheepherder. Often he would pull out his blueprint of the Spider Rock and explain how they had proceeded once the stone was uncovered. Always he believed, as each man had so many years before, that the treasure lay beneath the bedrock on top of which was found the same symbols as those etched into the Spider Rock found atop the hill two hundred feet or so to the east. When Arnold began his search at the three red hills, a mile and a half south-southwest of the confluence of the Salt Fork and Double Mountain Fork, there was no town of Rule ten miles west of Haskell. That hamlet arose in about 1905 with the coming of the railroad and made replenishing supplies much easier.

About four miles west of Rule, an unimproved road winds its way northward, hugging that stream, then turns westward before the river merges with the Salt Fork. About two miles west from that turn, or twelve miles out from Rule, a huge mesquite tree stands at the corner of a barbed-wire gate and trail leading another half-mile northward to the old diggings.

Over that road one day in 1925 drove Charley Terrell, coming from the oil fields at Ranger, where he was working. Jones had written the doctor's son and asked him to drive out for consultation. As a youngster, Charley had visited those diggings with his father with horse and buggy. He went now only as a favor to Jones, who had been a family friend since those earlier days.[4]

Charles could offer little advice to Jones. He recalled visiting the diggings about 1902, when he was only seven. He was fourteen when his father died. He reiterated the fact that it was always his father's belief, as it was Arnold's, that the treasure chamber was a round room (indicated by the inner circle on the Spider Rock), and that a tunnel led to it (indicated by the angular lane leading into that circle). Always they believed that the Spanish sword, silver epaulets, and personal effects of a Spanish officer marked the location of that tunnel. If that reasoning was correct, it would appear that the tunnel would lead into the canyon from beneath the bedrock, much of which had been exposed in the earlier excavation, for many of the same symbols appearing on the Spider Rock were also found placed or carved on the bedrock.

Charles suggested that Jones drill through the bedrock in an attempt to find the chamber beneath it, and offered to send him the necessary drill bits. He told him, too, that his brother Cabe, who had worked almost daily with Arnold and Jones, was now living in Waco. Charles never again returned to the diggings that Arnold had named Mount Lama Vista early in the century, when every man in that party believed the treasure was within his grasp. But Charles kept his word and sent Jones a one-and-a-half-inch oil field bit in three- to four-foot sections.

Dock was present the day Charles visited the site for the last time. Before the drill bits

Dock Henderson, left, was drawn into the quest when W. J. "Bud" Jones, right, returned to the site in 1924 in a final attempt to find the elusive treasure. This photograph, made that year, shows their catch of rattlesnakes near the old diggings. (Courtesy Dock Henderson)

arrived, Dock and his father furnished a team and slip and began to clear out the acre-square excavation dug almost two decades before. The excavation, which had been dug between three and eleven feet, was deepest toward the west end as the hill led upward from the edge of the canyon. Along the canyon's edge, near where the sword, silver epaulets, beads, and gold buttons were found, Jones recalled, they had followed the angular lane of red, black, and blue clay balls northward for about forty feet when they turned abruptly inward.

Using several teams of horses pulling slips and fresnos, Jones remembered they had leveled much of the hillside to the bedrock and dumped that overburden into the canyon. The angular lane led about forty feet more to the center of the eight concentric circles, the outer circle being about twenty-one feet in diameter. Each of those circles was formed from red, black, and blue clay balls about five or six inches in diameter. Because Arnold had believed the hidden room holding the treasure would be found beneath the bedrock, he took little care in exposing the symbols that had been placed there. Many of those symbols were buried with the overburden they removed. What soil was not dumped into the canyon was piled up in corners or on the sides of the large excavation, roughly 115 feet wide by 150 feet long.

Dock Henderson, cowman, horseman, outdoorsman, knew the West Texas cedar brakes like no other man. He rode over, walked over, and hunted the canyons on the Salt and Double Mountain forks of the Brazos, finding his own clues to past explorers. (Photo by the author)

The oval-shaped stone, depicted by the same sign as on the Spider Rock and located where the angular lane turned inward, was the first stone they found, Jones remembered. It was pushed off into the canyon. Sometime later, after that stone had itself been reburied under tons of debris, the story was told that the stone itself may have been hollow and may even have concealed a map. The strange symbol on the south edge of the outer circle, between the two sets of Roman numerals, was found carved into the bedrock. The stopper rock design, as it appeared on the Spider Rock, was not found on the west side, as many other symbols were not. In the center of the inner circle, Arnold had directed that they dig through the bedrock, thinking there they would strike the treasure chamber. That shaft led to nothing but clay.

Jones always lamented that everything had been destroyed at "the spider circle," as he called it, by the hasty excavation and by dumping the overburden into the canyon. He clearly remembered the oval rock, some eighteen inches high, being pushed over the rim. Whenever Jones found any kind of a marker or symbol, he left it in place so that all the pieces could be fitted together for a picture they might tell. He often wished later that they had left each object in place just as it was found.

That all the symbolic objects had not been found was verified when Dock dug out the southeast corner of the old excavation, a portion that had gone almost untouched previously. Perhaps two or three feet below the surface, Dock unearthed three or four stones that had been placed in an upright position. One elongated stone, about two feet high, had a hole drilled through it. Just west of those stones Dock found what proved to be a mammoth tusk, about seven feet long, pointing north. On the opposite side of the formation of stones, appearing much like the symbol shown in that same corner of the Spider Rock, Dock cleaned out a depression two feet deep filled with slick cobblestones. Those same objects also appeared as etched symbols on the Spider Rock, but apart from that, no one knew their significance.

When the drill bits arrived, Dock and his father rigged up a kind of sawhorse drop auger, and with ropes and two pulleys, they had a seven-foot drill bit mounted on a windlass. As Jones turned the bit and added water, Dock and Andy Moss pulled the ropes, pounding the one-and-a-half-inch bit into the bedrock. By that method they could drill three or four holes a day through the bedrock, penetrating the eleven- to fourteen-foot-thick stone. They drilled from the edge of the canyon to the center of the old diggings, well below the bedrock level, in their latest attempt to find the chamber Arnold so patiently sought, or a tunnel that led in that direction from the side of the canyon. But the months passed, and they had nothing new to show for their efforts.

Other than Arnold himself, there was now only one man Jones could turn to for the pieces to reconstruct their search of sixteen years before. That was Cabe Terrell. Cabe had worked with Arnold for some time after Jones left for New Mexico, the year prior to the doctor's death. When Jones saw him again for the first time since they had last worked together with Arnold, Cabe was employed at the Praetorian Drugstore in Waco.

No one knows whether Cabe and Arnold saw each other after Dr. Terrell's death, before Arnold vanished forever. Cabe may well never have answered Arnold's letter from Munday on June 21, 1909, inquiring about what was destroyed in the drug store fire and suggesting Cabe represent his father's interest in a forthcoming search. Cabe had remained silent about the survival of the Spider Rock and the copper and silver artifacts in the masonry vault when Arnold sought that information, and he remained silent when he again met Jones in 1925.[5]

Cabe's silence is not so difficult to understand. His father and Arnold's quest had ended in failure, a handful of artifacts, loss of the family business, and, finally, the doctor's death. The curse—whether real or not—had too often touched Cabe's life.

Cabe recounted almost nothing of that search even to his family years later. If he ever even mentioned Arnold's name, they did not remember it, just as they had no idea of the origin of the box full of artifacts he kept out of sight. Only on rare occasions would he spread them out on the kitchen table with a tracing of the Spider Rock he had made himself and ponder them.

Cabe's oldest daughter, Louise, was born in 1908 when Cabe, Jones, and Arnold were still working at the Spider diggings. Cabe was at the diggings during her birth. She remembers Jones's visits in 1925. She never met him but recalls that her father "was always delighted to see him."[6] It is doubtful that Cabe showed Jones the silver epaulets, crucifix, and copper plates found with the Spider Rock and the stone map from the Sembritzki farm. Jones never mentioned it, believing as everyone else did that everything had been destroyed in the fire. Perhaps Cabe thought it best to let the Spanish relics so remain. Other than one of long-standing friendship, he had no interest in Jones's renewed search at the diggings now.

Somehow Jones met a newcomer to the search named Jack Childress from San Angelo, who, with Andy Moss and Walter Urion, joined in helping grubstake Jones in his final search. Childress was an engineer on the Frisco railroad, which ran through West Texas between San Angelo and Oklahoma. Periodically, he stopped off at the diggings northwest of Rule. Once, Childress and Jones took the blueprint of the Spider Rock to a Mexican in South Texas, hoping to obtain a new translation. What transpired showed Jones's overwhelming belief that the treasure had to be somewhere near the discovery of the Spider Rock.[7]

The Mexican studied the blueprint anxiously, offering possible explanations for the enigmatic symbols. Finally, he directed them to look for a mountain somewhere to the northwest, where the treasure should be found. Jones retorted that the treasure had to be near the diggings, not miles away from it. At that, the Mexican shoved the blueprint back at him, telling him to interpret the map himself if he did not wish to listen.

Bud Jones returned to renew his search sixteen years after he helped Dave Arnold and the Mexican sheepherder. He built his own dugout just south of the large excavation he helped dig to bedrock. The ruins of his dugout remained four decades after Jones left a final time. (Photo by the author)

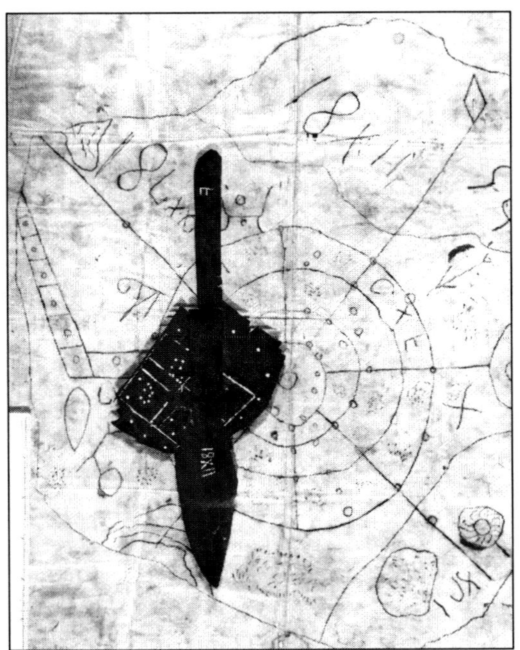
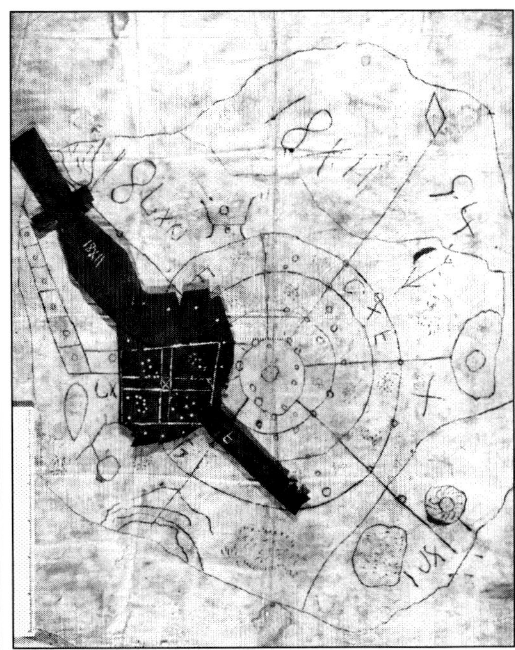

Controversy always surrounded just how the copper dagger, leaf, and key were found lying atop the Spider Rock. A paper pattern kept by Cabe Terrell revealed this connection, while Bud Jones's memory of how the artifacts were placed was quite different. Here the actual copper replicas are placed on the tracing of the Spider Rock as indicated by the two versions. (Courtesy Charles Terrell)

Dock continued to work with Jones whenever he could, and when Jones later dug himself a half-dugout into the hillside just beyond the diggings, Dock would often stay overnight. Over the many months that followed, Jones shared what he knew and what had been found while working at those diggings with Arnold and the Mexican who guided him and, Jones believed, also misled him. Jones never knew, nor did Dock then, that before the sheepherder disappeared, he left a map and letter of instructions.

Jones wished now, like every other man in that party, that he had more carefully observed Arnold and the sheepherder, and questioned them more closely. In the intervening years, those questions came to his mind many times, as did the many clues they found. Jones knew that many things had gone unfound and somehow fit into the cryptographic puzzle. But after two years at the old diggings on the Salt Fork, Jones abandoned his quest a final time, taking only the memories of those searches with him.

For Dock Henderson, the search had just begun. Seldom a year went by that he did not discover something new that Jones had never seen or suspected might exist. The evidence that there were many things Arnold never found, or at least never talked about, slowly mounted as Dock explored the rugged canyon country on his own, theorizing possibilities for many of the symbols on the Spider Rock, or many others that turned up elsewhere along the banks of the rivers or some secluded side canyon. And there were yet other signs of past Spanish mining activity scattered over the country.

For many years in the early part of the century, people appeared from various parts of the country, even as far away as New York, seeking a hidden mine in the rugged region northwest of the forks. A nester and his son who lived nearby had heard the story of the mine from several who sought it, and in their spare time they began looking for it. They

Dock Henderson points to grassed-over depression on hilltop where Dave Arnold unearthed the legendary Spider Rock, the first of many tantalizing clues to a fabled Spanish treasure. (Photos by the author)

found the ruins of a stone building about six miles due south of Kiowa Peak. Its walls were made of large, flat stones much too heavy for one man to carry. The stones formed four rooms and were about waist high. The structure's occupants had erected it at the base of two high hills, one on the north and the other on the west.

Some believed the stone ruins marked the site of a Spanish mission, and many who viewed the structure witnessed the stone at one corner bearing the date 1812, which was visible for some years to come. The site seemed meaningful to Dock, for it lay only about three miles north-northwest of the Spider diggings, and the date 1812, which he also observed, seemed to match that possible date I8XII carved on the Spider Rock.[8]

One discovery led to another, and once the stone ruins were found, the nester and his son easily found the tunnel located around the hill to the northeast a few hundred yards away. Its entrance had long before caved in or had been sealed, but signs of the old diggings were yet apparent enough to disclose it. Whether a mission for a priest or a dwelling for Spanish miners, the stone building was well located, for beds of copper-bearing ore are readily apparent in the surrounding arroyos. Nuggets of bluish-green copper heavy with lead remain visible on the dry arroyo beds or in veins exposed in the banks.

Once the nester and his son had dug a few feet through the debris, they crawled into the tunnel and could stand up inside it. They followed it into the mountain for perhaps seventy-five feet before reaching a point where it had caved in. For that distance, it had been shored with cottonwood and hackberry timbers. The tunnel had been dug at the eastern base of a high hill. A small knoll to its front bore indications of a primitive smelter, and small pieces of slag around its base showed that the miners had crudely refined some of the ore they dug from the mine.

No attempt was ever made to clean out the tunnel, but Dock knew that sometime in the late teens or early twenties, Joe Allen Jr., and neighboring rancher Tommy Greer were hunting near the mine with their dogs. The entrance then was large enough only for a small animal to enter, and the dogs, good hunting hounds, chased a rabbit into it. Somehow they must have become trapped, or fallen into a shaft beyond the cave-in, because Allen and Greer never saw the dogs again.

About 1928 Dock opened the old tunnel a few feet to determine the extent of the cave-ins but found the cottonwood and hackberry timbers too decayed to chance further digging without proper reshoring. There is nothing today to show there had ever been a tunnel into the hillside, nineteen miles northeast of Aspermont on the road toward Kiowa Peak. Only the small pieces of slag found nearby might lead someone to those conclusions. A careful eye can yet detect the pieces of smelted residue exposed on the surface of the small knoll beside the mine, whose entrance today has totally blended with its surroundings.

Dock remembers that Jones often told the story that Arnold more than once maintained that if he could find "the twin mulberry trees," the Spanish treasure would not be far away. Arnold had come closer to finding that clue than he must have ever realized, for those gnarled trees grew in Beaver Canyon, a mere few miles north of the Spider diggings. Emptying into the Brazos perhaps two miles north of the forks of the river, the mouth of the canyon was just across the river from the Allen F-2 Ranch, ironically where Arnold lived much of the time he searched for the Spider Rock treasure.

Dock learned about the twin mulberry trees too late to have gained the knowledge they offered the cipher breaker careful enough to follow the cryptic signs they guarded. Joe Allen and his son Crawford knew about the twin mulberry trees from their long acquain-

Dock Henderson points to the stone ledge beneath which Arnold's party discovered the Spanish sword and silver epaulets shortly after the turn of the century. (Photo by the author)

Henderson stands at west end of Arnold's massive excavation, where his co-workers uncovered symbols made from stone, metal artifacts, clay balls, and even carvings made on the bedrock. In 1935 Jim Suggs unearthed a small lead arrow in the old diggings. (Photo by the author)

(Above) Henderson stands on edge of canyon where Arnold's party followed clues into the hillside they excavated to bedrock. The Spider Rock hill appears behind him. (Below) The canyon between the excavation and Spider Rock hill widens as it leads to the Salt Fork at upper left. Top center shows one of the red promontories on the edge of the river. (Photos by the author)

From atop the promontory on the Salt Fork of the Brazos, one can view the Spider Rock hill at top left and Arnold's large excavation across the canyon at top center. (Photo by the author)

tance with Arnold. Joe's daughter Mattie married Bill Males. He was familiar with the story when, sometime about 1924, he heard that Dean Lelton's boys were cutting firewood across the river in Beaver Canyon and found a pair of large mulberry trees. Males and a companion named Buck Bridges later found the stumps of the trees where Beaver Canyon forked. They were unusually large stumps, and they must have been abnormally old trees when they were chopped down. If they were the trees Arnold had so long sought, Males knew that his instructions were to dig exactly thirty-three *varas* out from the center of the two trees, to the north of them.[9]

Males and Bridges carefully measured that distance and had dug to a depth of nine feet when they struck a beautifully carved square stone that bore symbols similar to those on the Spider Rock and its proverbial concentric circles. At each corner at the top of the stone was carved an F, and at each corner toward the bottom appeared a 4, made in the fashion of that same number carved on the Spider Rock. Below the stone lay a much larger, elongated stone, and below it was a forked mesquite limb that had once been sharpened. The point of the limb pointed directly to Kiowa Peak about four miles distant.

In their excitement that day, Males and Bridges left the stones and mesquite limb just as they had found them and filled in the hole, with the intention of returning when they had time to investigate further with a more thorough reconnaissance. So that no one else would remove their chance discovery, they dug up the mulberry stumps and carried them down the canyon.

Males would later curse the day he abandoned the stone Arnold so badly wanted, for the days dragged on into weeks, and those weeks to years, until the country was so changed that it was impossible for him or Bridges to find that site again. In Rule, within a few miles of that eventful discovery, Males recalls vividly the details of his mistake. He cannot, however, recall the details of the strange design and symbols he glimpsed momentarily.

The gnarled twin mulberry trees that were forever removed from Beaver Canyon, and the stone map that must yet lie buried just where it was discovered, may in some way relate to a most curious stone wall that was twenty feet long and five feet high when Dock first observed it. Simply a single wall of stone that ran east-west, it never appeared to have been part of a building but instead seemed more like a breastwork. The earliest settlers knew nothing about the wall, other than that it was found near the head of Beaver Canyon when they first came into the brakes.

Interestingly, the stone wall lay only a quarter of a mile northwest of a fork in Beaver Canyon that Males believes may have been the location of the twin mulberry trees. In later years, the single wall became too handy for ranchers looking for building stone, and it appeared to have no historical significance. By 1934, the wall, too, had disappeared. When Dock first observed it, he thought it strange that the breastwork appeared on a perfect line with the Spider diggings lying to the south-southeast, and Kiowa Peak, to the north-northwest.

About midway between Beaver Canyon and Kiowa Peak lies Panther Canyon, another tributary emptying into the Brazos from the west. On more than one occasion, unexplainable discoveries have been made there. A nester named "Uncle" Wash Lindsay lived on the south side of Panther Canyon in a mesquite flat only about two miles southeast of Kiowa Peak. He had a small frame house and decided to dig a cistern at one corner of it. When he reached a depth of twelve feet, he discovered he was not the first to occupy the land, for he uncovered the remains of a human skeleton. Lindsay decided he did not need a cistern, after all.[10]

In that same mesquite flat, Lindsay found five large piles of copper nuggets when he and other settlers came in. No one ever knew who had gathered the mounds of nuggets, but three lay on an east-west line, while two on the west end lay on a north-south line toward Kiowa Peak. The mounds of nuggets all disappeared when the bottomland was broken.

Not far up Panther Canyon toward the west, another old mine was found during the late twenties or early thirties. It lay on the south side of the canyon, south of Kiowa Peak and some distance west. A prospector seeking copper found it, and although the mine was filled, he could tell that it had been an old shaft. He discovered just how old when he cleaned out the mine to a depth of eighty feet and found drill holes in the west wall. In the holes were short mulberry poles used to climb into and out of the shaft. The prospector abandoned his discovery before following it to its end, according to Crawford Allen and his brother-in-law, Tom Epply, who both saw the pile of decayed mulberry poles that had been pitched to one side at the top of the shaft.

Kiowa Peak has long been the center of interest for copper mining, and considerable activity occurred there in the late 1870s and early 1880s. General George B. McClellan became interested in the copper deposits in 1877 and reported that the copper found between Kiowa Peak and Medicine Mound, in Hardeman County to the north, ran as high as eighty percent.[11] The general formed the Grand Belt Copper Company to work the deposits. It was probably McClellan's company that built a smelter about three miles southwest of Kiowa Peak in what was later dubbed Smelter Canyon. The large ironworks was salvaged for scrap metal during World War II, although Dock managed to save one large iron flywheel that he found.

It is not so surprising that the copper here attracted early prospectors. Some years ago, Dock discovered a small tree metamorphosed into copper lying about a mile west of the peak. Its trunk was fifteen feet long and seven or eight inches across when Dock dug it out. Even though it was broken every eighteen inches or so, it was one of the most singular specimens Dock ever found. Nearby, he found large quantities of broken glass long turned purple, no doubt left by earlier prospectors. It is said Dave Arnold once sought a Spanish mine in the hills near Kiowa Peak. An old tradition holds that a mysterious tunnel was once found in one of the three peaks that appear on the horizon southwestward from Kiowa Peak.

Perhaps ten years after Jones concluded he could find no more than Arnold had, still another tantalizing clue was revealed, one that had defied all previous seekers. Dock's uncle, Jim Suggs, had long searched for someone adept at reading Spanish symbols or who knew something about ancient cartography. Suggs finally found a priest in Blackwell, Texas, and interested him in the Spider Rock. One day in 1935 they visited the old diggings on the Salt Fork.

Suggs showed the priest where Arnold and his party had leveled the hillside to the bedrock. No one had ever completely cleaned off the bedrock; instead, the soil had been shifted from one side to the other. After some random digging while measuring from the center of the concentric circles found in that excavation, Suggs and the priest uncovered a small lead arrow some four inches long and not more than two feet deep. It unmistakably matched the same arrow shown on the Spider Rock and was similarly located in its relation to the other symbols.

Toward the west end of the excavation, where less work had been done, further digging at about the same depth to the bedrock turned up a diamond-shaped stone which again matched the same symbol shown on the Spider Rock. On that stone, the diamond was a plate of copper cut and fitted into it. The diamond-shaped stone now unearthed from the southwest corner of Arnold's old excavation was similar, for inlaid with equally careful craftsmanship was a diamond-shaped nugget of almost pure copper.

What was the meaning of the "spider circle," its symbols of metal and stone matching those same symbols carved into the Spider Rock found across the canyon a few hundred feet to the east? What cryptographic message had the Spanish mapmaker left for future pursuers to puzzle over? Those questions remain as unanswered today as they were when Arnold must have pondered them so many years before. Suggs and the priest found nothing more, but their discoveries verified Bud Jones's memory of his earlier search with Arnold, as well as the apparent mathematical calculations that seemed to be ever-present throughout the mystery of the Spider Rock and all that was found in the hillside excavation.

Dock never flagged in his belief that the mystery could be solved. That persistence led him closer to the Spider Rock treasure than perhaps any other man. Over the years, Dock returned time after time to the small red hill south by southwest of the forks of the river, the hill that marked the apex of an imaginary acute triangle where the Spider Rock was found.

Someone once said that the treasure would be found buried among the bones of prehistoric animals. Dock did not know the reasoning behind that statement. Certainly, archaeologists would cringe at the thought of destroying such prehistoric deathbeds without careful excavation. But that the wily Spaniards used such bones for markers is evident from the original quest. This portion of the Salt Fork has been the scene of such discoveries many times since the turn of the century. The tailings from a shaft sunk at one side of the western red promontory overlooking the Salt Fork reveal such fossilized remains, undoubtedly a mammoth. In recent years, Dock discovered the five-foot-long tusk of one in an arroyo nearby where a clay bank had eroded away.

Dock did not know or observe the party of men who sometime in the early 1930s unearthed a truckload of such prehistoric bones in a canyon a half-mile west of the old Spider diggings. No one thought much about it at the time, for the excavators claimed to be archaeologists from the state university. Not until later was it discovered that many of those bones of antiquity had been carelessly discarded in the canyon, something no reputable archaeologist would do.

The only unusual thing discovered near that unorthodox digging—and it may have been known to the excavators—was a badly weathered carving that has since entirely disappeared. When Dock discovered it, the petroglyph appeared on the face of a stone ledge on the east side of the canyon. It was a large diamond-shaped symbol, pointing skyward, and measured about nine inches from tip to tip. On either side of the upper portion of the diamond were similar but smaller designs, while inside the large diamond were carved curved arrows, X's, a WX, and a circle. At the apex of the diamond appeared a V. The arrows all appeared to point toward the northwest.

Perhaps a half-mile west of that carving was a natural spring. A strange formation of stones was found placed around it. A story dating from before the turn of the century told that antiquated weapons had been found near the stones. No one seemed to recall what the weapons were, only that they were old and decayed. The landowner was aware of Arnold's search only a mile downstream, and to prevent him or his party from examining the strange formation of stones, he removed them one by one, forever destroying whatever purpose they may have served.

Similar discoveries have been found within a few miles' radius of the Spider diggings. It must have been during the thirties, when the road was built between Rule and Aspermont, that construction workers found a large, round stone a mile west of Rule. Carved on its surface were arrows and symbols that were completely foreign to the road graders. Dock was tied down to his own job at the time and could not investigate. The stone was soon buried in the roadbed. It would have been located south by southeast of the Spider diggings.

Similar discoveries have been made on the opposite side of the Salt Fork. A half-mile northwest of the diggings, a canyon empties into the fork. Bud Jones remembered that numerous carvings were found in that canyon. Some were of snakes, turtles, and arrows, but they all had disappeared by the 1920s. One of those markers, however, was intended to survive the others, for it was carved an inch or more into the stone face. Dock discovered the marker, a long, curved arrow, near the mouth of the canyon. Similar to other such arrows he had seen, it bore the point and forked tail, and it curved so that it pointed north after stretching across the face of the stone twelve or fourteen inches. Where it pointed, no one knew, unless it indicated to proceed downstream around the bend toward the forks.

Dock Henderson stands on edge of canyon east of the Spider Rock hill where Bud Jones found a cryptic stone carving. The arrow etched into the stone pointed to a primitive smelter at the top of the hill, where slag and charcoal could still be found. (Photo by the author)

Dock does not believe the Spider Rock itself was as difficult to find as some might believe. It is probable that Dr. Terrell was seeking the Spider Rock, or something closely related to it, when Dave Arnold appeared. Whether Terrell would have found it without Arnold's help is conjecture. It is definite that the Mexican sheepherder was seeking the Spider Rock at the same time Arnold was. It is probable that he would have found the Spider Rock without Arnold's knowledge but decided it wiser to work together than to work alone. How long the sheepherder had been looking when Arnold met him cannot be known. It would seem that perhaps separate sources led Dr. Terrell, Arnold, and the sheepherder all to the Salt Fork—near its junction with the Double Mountain Fork.

To someone familiar with the land and the canyons leading into the rivers at the forks, the trail of markers found there at the turn of the century would all have led to the red clay hill where the Spider Rock was buried, three hundred yards south from the center of the two red promontories on the bank of the Salt Fork.

Jones told Dock, who later observed most of it for himself, that the cairns and trail markers carved on stones, and still others formed on the surface from mussel shells, could all be followed on a horse riding at a lope. Arnold had followed such trail markers to the forks. The Mexican sheepherder must have known this, for he led Arnold's party to the hill, where rocks and mussel shells formed the same pattern of concentric circles as the engraved stone hidden there. Lines of mussel shells radiated outward from the concentric circles for several hundred feet. In the center of that surface pattern, the Mexican directed Arnold to dig for the "stone of signs" they would call the Spider Rock. One line of such rock piles, which survived most others when the country was settled, led south from Croton Creek near Kiowa Peak and up the west bank of the Brazos to the forks.

When the country was settled, numerous large piles of rich copper nuggets lay scattered along both sides of the forks, collected from the canyon breaks and placed in mounds to be removed later and refined in a nearby primitive smelter. Such evidence supports the belief that the Spanish miners had not completed their work when they disappeared, leaving their testimonials etched in stone and planning to return at a later time—a time that never came.

Henderson kept the beautiful carving covered with other stones. (Photo by the author)

After Dock began his own search, he chanced upon other evidence that the Spaniards had indeed smelted those piles of copper nuggets scattered over the region or other ore they had mined. They attempted to conceal that fact from anyone else who might happen upon the copper and lead deposits found on the surface for miles around. Dock had long thought it strange that the slag left from those crude operations had been found only in negligible quantities. Surely something should remain from the crude refineries, which were often dug into a hillside for proper venting and cleaning, once the molten metal had been collected. Such crude wood-burners, in which the crushed ore was placed in alternating layers with limestone and wood (or perhaps mesquite roots for fuel), had not yet been discovered in the cedar brakes.[12]

That they had once existed near the site of the Spider Rock was evident, however, for just north of the large excavation made by Arnold and later reworked by Jones, and midway across the bed of the Salt Fork, a long pile of slag had been dumped and was periodically exposed by the river and again hidden. Large black clinkers of slag stretched for considerable distance across the riverbed, showing that the smelted residue had been dumped over considerable time. What better place to dispose of the telltale evidence of that nearby furnace?

Although Dock had found the slag from that crude furnace, no surface evidence re-

Bearing the familliar F's and other symbols found on the Spider Rock, the stone carving as it appeared in 1963. (Photos by the author)

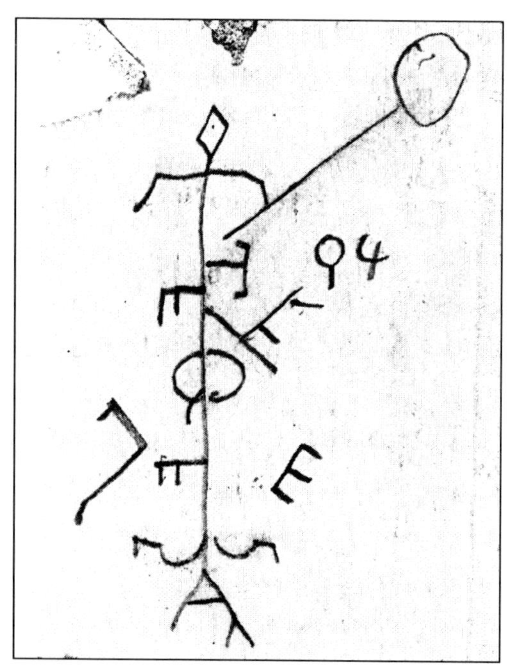

Among Cabe Terrell's papers remaining from his association with Dave Arnold was this drawing of symbols, similar to but not exactly like any other found near the diggings. (Courtesy Charles Terrell)

Years before, Henderson had made this photograph of the carving. (Courtesy Dock Henderson)

mained to show its location. Such a furnace might have been dug into the side of any one of a hundred small canyons leading into the Salt Fork near the Spider diggings. Dock verified that one lay nearby many years after he was shown the stone carving that led him to the long-buried remains.

Just a quarter-mile or so east of the Spider diggings, Jones had found a strange carving on the face of a large, flat stone at the edge of a small canyon when he was tracking a lame deer. Arnold seemed to be as puzzled by the carving as anyone. Bud showed it to Dock in 1924. Its majestic pattern, bearing symbols that also appeared on the Spider Rock, had weathered badly since the Spanish cryptographer chiseled its message into the face of the stone. The cryptogram showed many F's, symbols, and grooved depressions connected by arcs and lines. Outside that pattern were a hooklike figure similar to a J, an inverted F, a small cross, two daggers, and an arrow of the same design as all the others found associated with the Spider Rock. The arrow pointed westward up a small hill.[13]

No one ever deciphered the petroglyph, but it required no special knowledge to follow the arrow. Even so, it was not until many years later that Dock discovered what the arrow pointed to, about two hundred feet westward up the hill overgrown with brush and scrub cedar. Little visible evidence remained except a few small pieces of slag and burned rocks covering an area that was six or eight feet in diameter and sunken in the center. Dock

South of Kiowa Peak stand the stone ruins of a four-room construction. A stone in a corner once bore the date 1812. Nearby, a tunnel was found leading into the mountainside. (Photo by the author)

seemed sure that it was one of the primitive smelters the Spaniards had dug to refine copper, lead, gold, and silver into crude bars or ingots.

The verification of that discovery lay only about eighteen inches below the surface. After it was last used, the smelter had not been cleaned out, for Dock could bury the handle of a long-handled shovel in the ash and charcoal and estimated it to be six to ten feet deep. Fist-sized chunks of clinkers were among the charred contents, some showing the color of copper, others only the blackened residue. The primitive smelter was as good a proof as any yellowed documents that the Spaniards had mined in the hills nearby and refined the ore only a quarter-mile away from the Spider Rock.

Henderson uses his pistol to point to the entrance of the hidden tunnel he believes was dug and shored by Spanish miners. Nothing remains today to mark the tunnel except a few pieces of slag found nearby. (Photo by the author)

The search almost always started at the forks, two miles or so northeast of the Spider diggings. When Dock concentrated his search there, several things of interest came to light. He learned that it was west of the forks that the Mexican sheepherder had directed the Stuarts to destroy the stone carving that appeared to be a duplicate of the stone map that Arnold unearthed on the Sembritzki farm.

One day while Dock was prowling the west bank of the river just downstream, or north, from the forks, he spied fist-sized pieces of slag at the base of a small hill a few feet from the river's edge. Much of the slag residue was speckled with the predominant green copper. Other chunks showed that while the slag was still hot it had been channeled onto the ground. The red clay was baked into the slag as it hardened.

When Dock found the site, he dug beneath a large, flat stone that appeared unnatural in its precarious position on the hillside. About eighteen inches beneath the surface, he unearthed an antiquated, rust-eaten square shovel and, below it, what appeared to be a rust-pitted piece of the iron core to the hub of a cartwheel. No doubt those broken items had been pitched into the hearth and covered when the smelter was abandoned forever.

Today a seasoned eye might detect the few clinkers yet remaining on the bald hillside. Much like the smelter near the Spider diggings two miles southwestward, this site showed that care had been taken to dispose of the residue.[14] Unlike the other smelter, this riverbank furnace necessitated no hauling to dump its unwanted evidence of mining nearby.

Just north of the forks of the Brazos on the west bank, Henderson discovered the remains of another primitive smelter, complete with chunks of slag heavy in copper and lead. Note slag in his hand and pieces atop flat stone. (Photos by the author)

Henderson stands in the bed of the Brazos River just north of the forks, near the site of a primitive smelter behind him. Here he holds bag of slag and rusted core of iron found at the site. More stone carvings were found nearby. (Photo by the author)

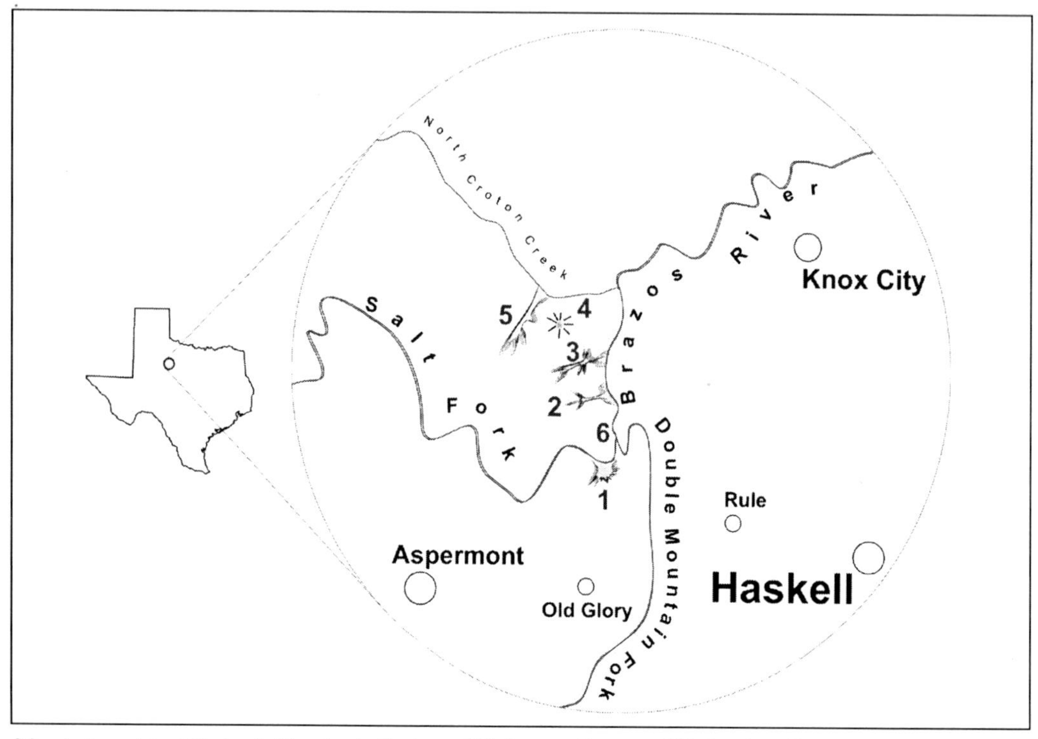

Map is keyed to (1) the Spider Rock diggings; (2) Beaver Canyon; (3) Panther Canyon; (4) Kiowa Peak; (5) Smelter Canyon; and (6) the junction of the Salt and Double Mountain forks. Map by Raymond Watkins.

One can stand on the barren hillside and imagine Spanish horsemen, clad in helmet and chain mail with muskets in hand, guarding the pack train hauling precious ore to the primitive but effective riverside hearth. It requires no imagination to make out the beaten path of what may have been that trail winding its way down the canyon side to the riverbank. If only the relics of yore could tell their tale!

The smelter site at the forks yielded nothing more, but Dock remembered that the site he had found near the Spider diggings was also accompanied by a rock carving nearby that eventually led him to the site. About four hundred yards downstream and some distance west up a canyon, he found a carving that may or may not have related to the river smelter. Carved on a flat limestone rock was the same hooklike symbol—similar to a J—that had also appeared near the smelter on the Salt Fork. The J was carved on one side of what appeared to be an arrow with a long shaft, while on the opposite side appeared a circle. Those symbols were placed below the letters BC and to the right of the numbers 14. What was the meaning of the trail marker?

Not far downstream, perhaps a half-mile below the forks, Dock later found by happenstance a small lead star lying in the dry riverbed and exposed by the blowing sand. Seemingly formed from the same impure lead that was used to mold the lead arrow that his uncle Jim Suggs had found at the Spider diggings, the five-pointed star bore a hole through its center, as if it had once been nailed to some object.

Had the metal star served as a trail marker? Was it indicative of measurement, using the ancient method by celestial bodies, perhaps representing the North Star itself? How long it lay buried in the river sand, or where it had washed into the river, could not be determined. But for Dock, the evidence continued to mount, leading him over an enigmatic trail every bit as spellbinding as any Egyptian pharaoh's lost tomb riddled with ancient hieroglyphics.

9

Silver Arrows, Crosses, and Statuettes: The Uncanny Luck of Bill Reid

Two years after Jim Suggs and the priest found the lead arrow and diamond-shaped stone that Arnold and his men had overlooked, a stranger presented himself to Suggs and offered his assistance in finding the Spider Rock treasure. Bill Reid was the name he gave, and he said he worked for the federal government. In what capacity no one knew, but they soon learned that, much like Dave Arnold, Reid had spent a large part of his life pursuing phantoms in unlikely places.

It is known that Reid conducted such quests near Bront, Blackwell, Robert Lee, and Sweetwater. He was a light-complexioned, husky, tall fellow with dark brown hair, in his mid- or late thirties. Later, his Indian wife and five young girls joined him, and much of the time they lived south of the hamlet of Jud. Reid was never eager to share his knowledge or relate its origin, but no one could deny that he was able to follow the clues where others had failed.

In the spring of 1937 he devoted part of his time to the old diggings on the Salt Fork, dawdling with the Spider Rock blueprint in one hand and pencil and paper in the other, always figuring, calculating, and estimating, seeking distances, angles, and degrees while attempting to decipher the map. Like Arnold, he sought the assistance of a clairvoyant from Sweetwater, who joined in the search. Then one day Reid unearthed a single object that Arnold and his party once again had overlooked.

Farther down the canyon that had yielded the Spanish sword and silver epaulets, Reid probed along the base of the same stone ledge, digging it out gently. Of course, above him at the top of the canyon was the huge excavation dug by Arnold and his men, where, only two years before, Suggs and the priest had found the lead arrow. Just down the canyon from where Arnold's party had dumped tons of earth from that excavation, Reid continued digging carefully beneath the stone ledge.[1]

After some time, his small shovel struck something small and metallic. Anxiously, he wiped away the red clay that clung to the object to find a small metal arrow much like the one Suggs and the priest had found, but this one did not fork at the tail. And instead of lead, it was formed of almost pure silver, about as wide as Reid's index finger and four inches long or so. Reid was careful to note that it pointed northwest—in the direction of the red promontory on the riverbank and Kiowa Peak beyond.

Reid's ability at finding clues was uncanny. It was almost as if he had taken up where Arnold left off. Reid subsequently moved his search four miles northeast of the Spider diggings to the east side of the Brazos, a location not more than a mile from the Allen homestead, where Arnold had lived intermittently. The forks of the river lay three miles west by southwest of the single store in the village of Jud, eight miles northwest of Rule. About two miles northwest of Jud, Jake Scoggins showed Reid a place on his farm that always struck him as strange, where the soil was discolored and nothing would grow

Nearby, Reid found a small slab of sandstone lodged in the forks of a large mulberry tree that had barely escaped the farmer's ax and plow, for a wheat field lay only a few feet away. That embedded stone pointed downward, facing north, at the edge of the plowed field. Reid made a visual sighting from the lodged stone, and, as he suspected, the imaginary line struck the patch of earth in which nothing would grow. There he and Scoggins began shoveling.

Not more than two feet beneath the surface, they struck a metallic object. Reid threw his shovel to one side and, dropping to his knees, scooped away the soil with his bare hands. Soon he pulled out the object his shovel had struck—a small silver statuette little more than two fingers wide and seven or eight inches high, impure, with yellow streaks of gold. With the silver figurine were two small chunks of crudely melted gold and a single musket ball.

That same evening, Dock, his older brother Harry, and their uncle Jim Suggs all viewed and pondered Reid's discovery, a beautiful piece of craftsmanship. Each man thought it ironic that Arnold had lived so close to that treasured object and must have passed within a few feet of it a hundred times on his way to the Allen ranch. Yet he never saw the small stone embedded in the forks of the mulberry tree. What clue did the statuette offer to the Spider Rock mystery? Reid offered no explanation but suggested more would be found not far distant.

No one knew the source Reid drew from in choosing the topography he somehow sensed would lead to those things. It was almost as if he knew exactly where Arnold had failed and knew where the clues would be discovered, even though no known map guided him there. That knowledge, too accurate to be happenstance, must have come from a source on which Arnold or the Mexican had relied, or perhaps someone close to that knowledge.

After the statuette was found, Scoggins's father, Jean, remembered that many years before, he had found a strange-looking dagger in the turnrow as he was plowing his field not far south of the statuette's discovery location. Scoggins showed Reid about where it was turned up. That day, Dock was committed to farming chores of his own, but his brother Harry and Jake joined Reid in his search. After clearing an area of several square feet to a depth that had yielded the silver figurine, Reid's hunch once again paid dividends. Here he found a tall metal container, perhaps a silver drinking cup, although the top had been crumpled.

Once the top of the metal cup was straightened and its contents emptied, Reid and his companions pondered two small nuggets of refined gold the size of the end of a little finger, and two small silver crosses seemingly made to be worn as collar pins. The largest

Henderson found this prehistoric mammoth tusk exposed near Dave Arnold's diggings of almost a century before. (Photos by the author)

of the five objects was a figure made of silver resembling the letter V; each side was about five inches long.

Later that day, Reid and his two companions stepped the distance between that cache and the site where he had found the silver statuette to the north. Their paces measured exactly 475.

Dock never pretended to possess any special knowledge about the Spider Rock or its cryptic symbols. He relied on observation and discovery, and an eagle-eye familiarity with the land. The distance of 475 steps interested Dock, and some time later he reexamined the site and Scoggins's plowed field. He learned that whatever other clues that site had held probably had been plowed up when the sod was broken before the turn of the century. At almost 475 steps farther south from the metal container Reid had unearthed, Dock found broken pieces of glass, once a clear ceramic now bleached purple from long exposure to the sun.

Whatever else that turning plow may have surfaced, at least one single piece of gold almost as large as Dock's thumb remained below plow-point level, where he found it while sifting through the soil. The nugget of gold itself may have been sheared by a plow, for it appeared to have been separated from a longer, more perfect narrow slab or ingot. It was also interesting for another reason, Dock remembers, for the piece of gold lay on an imaginary line. Not far distant toward the southwest lay the forks of the river, and not far beyond the forks, the hill on which the Spider Rock was once buried.

At the time Reid centered his search near the forks, Dock farmed a piece of land about a mile southwest of Jud, not far northeast of the confluence of the rivers. Some months before, he had found a large hackberry tree with an oval-shaped stone wedged in the forks of its trunk, similar to what Reid had found little more than a mile to the north and which had led to the buried statuette. The embedded stone pointed to a large, flat, partially buried slab of limestone not far to the northeast. Equally interesting were the iron braces and strips Dock found, which had been part of a wagon bed or cart and were partially buried at the base of the large hackberry, as if the vehicle might have burned or decayed there.

The limestone slab lay almost hidden in the mesquite brakes. It did not appear natural in its location, alone, partially buried, and near no other stones. No one person could have placed the stone, perhaps three feet long by two feet wide, in its peculiar position, its north side almost sunken while the south side was somewhat raised. It was the raised side that attracted Dock, for barely visible were the tops of what appeared to be carved letters. Dock examined it more closely, cleaning away the grass and soil.

Plain to see were carefully carved letters no more than an inch high—another of the trail markers Arnold surely must have hunted. At one side appeared the small Roman numerals IVXX, a carving of a pot with four legs, and a gouge or small hole in the center of the kettle, three 4's strung out, then a rectangular box, and a long twisted arrow, one portion of which formed the shape of a diamond. Each end of the arrow was forked, and at the point of each fork was a gouge or small hole.

The meaning of that symbolic message was obvious to Dock. The rock was much too heavy for one man to move, and Dock planned to return the following weekend with his brother. He had no reason to believe his discovery would not be safe for a few days longer. He knew of no one who was aware of that carving. He had no way of knowing the landowner was hiring some Mexicans to grub out the mesquites that partially hid the stone. The weekend he returned to that chanced discovery, the mesquites were gone and

Don Smith stands above the ledge at the edge of Arnold's massive excavation where the "spider circle" was found. Years later, Jim Suggs unearthed the small lead arrow matching that same symbol on the Spider Rock. (Photo by the author)

(Below) Henderson stands at the base of the western promontory overlooking the Salt Fork. Crawford Allen, who worked with Arnold, once sunk a hundred-foot shaft here seeking the Spanish treasure. (Photo by the author)

the large stone was turned over. The hole that had been dug beneath it was of sufficient size to contain the kettle that Dock believed would be found there.

Not long after that lamented incident, Reid unearthed the silver statuette little more than a mile to the north. Dock remembered something else he had found near his discovery and led Reid back to the site. The Roman numerals IVXX interested Reid the most, and he read them from right to left, indicating twenty-six steps. That was the exact number of paces to a small, flat stone no wider than a man's hand with a square hole cut through it. Dock had found it earlier, northeast of the large stone. He had dug up the rock to examine it but then placed it back in its impression. The square hole indicated one more step to Reid.

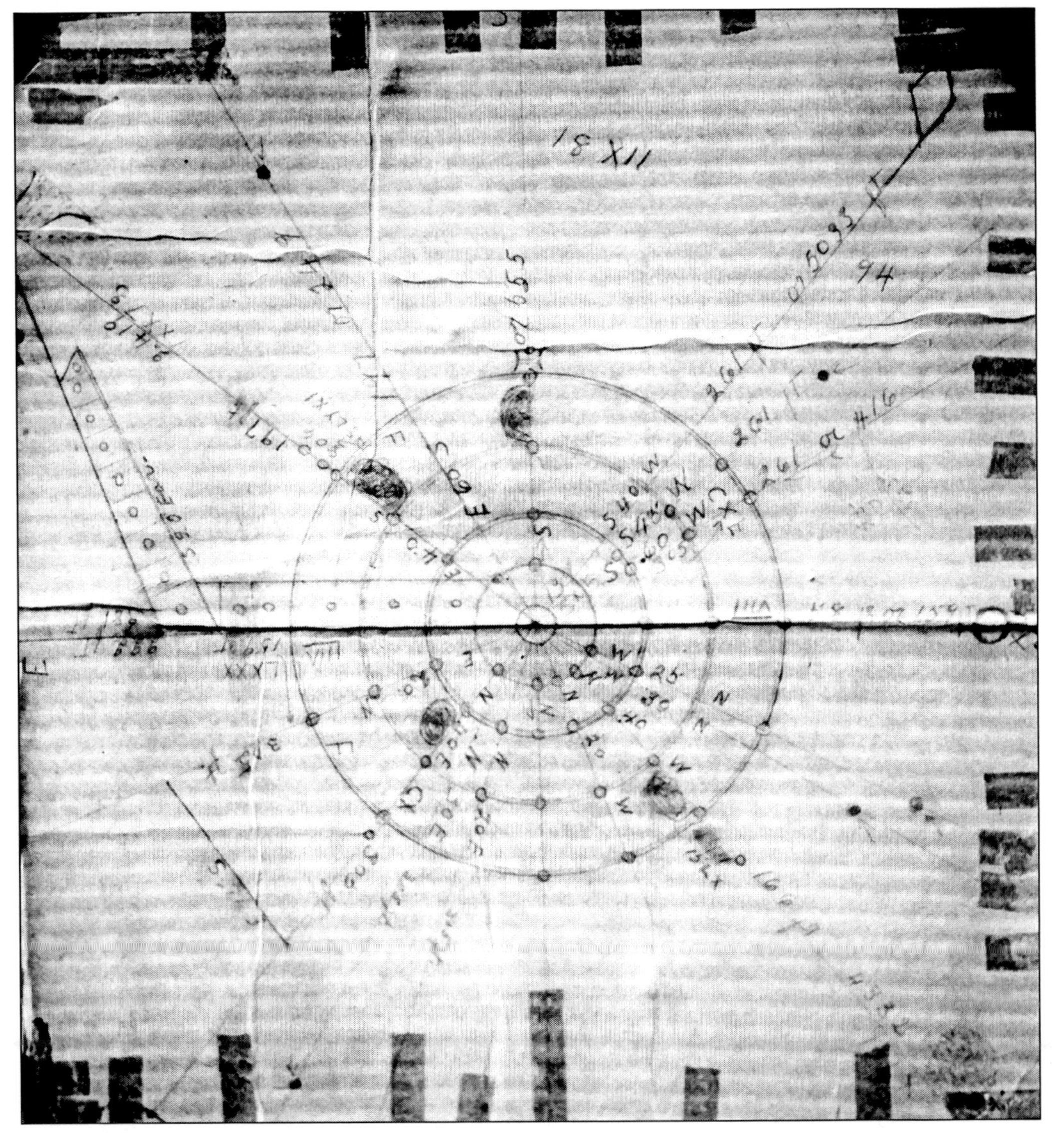

A rough drawing on the back of the Spider Rock blueprint shows numerous possible computations for distances and degrees in various directions from the small hill that yielded the hieroglyphic stone carving. (Courtesy Dock Henderson)

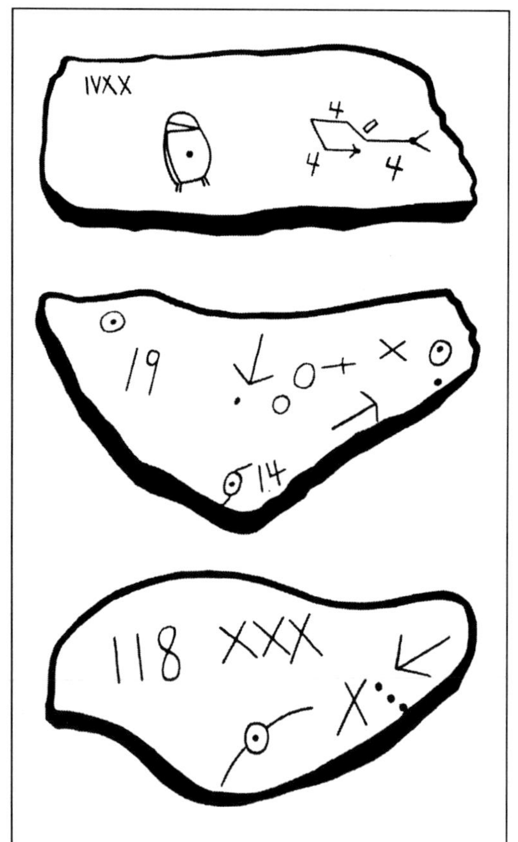

(Left) Henderson discovered the top symbols carved on a stone he found below the forks on the east side of the Brazos. Twenty steps away, he and Bill Reid unearthed the second of the two silver statuettes. Bottom figures show symbols carved on stones found southeast of the forks. (Drawings by the author)

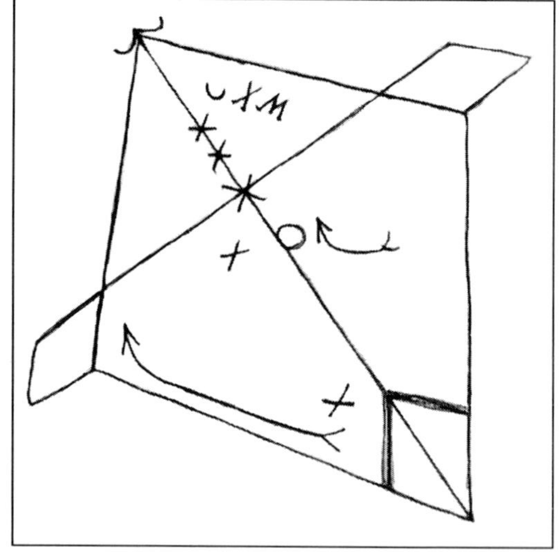

(Above) A half-mile west of the Spider diggings, Henderson discovered this strange carving on a canyon wall. The diamond figure appears often among the symbols associated with the Spider Rock. This carving, like so many others over the years, has since disappeared. (Courtesy Dock Henderson)

(Left) In 1935 Jim Suggs unearthed the small lead arrow from the bed of Arnold's massive excavation, showing that some of the symbols of the "spider circle" had been overlooked. Dock Henderson found the lead star in the riverbed below the forks. The droplet of silver was found in a hollowed mesquite tree. The engraved stones were found southeast of the forks. (Courtesy Dock Henderson)

With shovels in hand, each man began digging where the stone lay. At perhaps eighteen inches, Dock's shovel struck something solid. He knelt down to pull it from the pocket of gravel in which it was buried and, clenching the object with both hands, lifted out a second silver statuette. Much like the first Reid had found, it, too, exhibited streaks of gold running through it.

However, there was a distinguishable difference between the two, for the legs of this one spread apart or forked almost to the width of a man's hand. On the back side of the silver figurine was incised a cryptic message. The single Spanish word *norte* appeared across the shoulders. Below that directional indication appeared a drawing depicting what must have been the forks of the river where they bend shortly before joining as one. Above each bend in the river was drawn a small circle. As with the first figurine Reid found, this one was buried with two nuggets of refined gold.

The silver statuette was clearly a trail marker that had eluded Arnold and the Mexican sheepherder. It was uncanny how accurately the drawing on the figure depicted the forks, for it clearly showed the bend of the Salt Fork, where it turned from its eastward course abruptly north-northwestward, and the bend of the Double Mountain Fork, where it turned from its southwestward course to northwest and met the Salt Fork to form one stream. The pattern from each of those final bends to the confluence of the rivers forms a large imaginary V, with perhaps three-quarters of a mile between the rivers from bend to bend, gradually narrowing until they merge.

What was the riddle of the statuette? Why the circles at the bend of the rivers above the forks? Dock thought it interesting that the statuette had been buried beneath the stone with a square hole through it. He was already aware of a similar stone with such a square hole that he had found at the edge of an adjacent plowed field. It had no doubt been plowed up and later pitched to the fence row.

Reid believed something more might be found toward the northwest. He stepped exactly six hundred paces from where the statuette was found to discover yet another of the trail markers. Four corner stones formed an area fifty feet square. Three of the stones were shaped square, while the fourth was hewn in the form of a man's hand, with the forefinger pointing downstream or northward. In the center of the square, a tree had once grown, but now only a charred stump remained.

The fact that the tree had burned in a prairie fire did not discourage Reid. He easily removed the decayed stump with his shovel. After some probing, he dropped to his knees and dug away the soil with his hands, carefully, as if knowing he would surely find something. Finally, at six or eight inches deep, he did find something, and he gently cleaned the soil from around it, careful not to disturb it. It proved to be a silver arrow about eight inches long, and matched that carving on the Spider Rock and the one made of lead unearthed at the old diggings by Jim Suggs and the priest.

The direction of the arrow was of utmost interest to Reid. It pointed southwest, toward the forks of the river. Of course, two miles beyond was the red clay hill that had so long guarded its stone map. The significance of the silver arrow, or the stone hewn into a pointing hand, Reid did not appear to know. Dock believed the stone hand had pointed to the first statuette, found a mile to the north.

What seemed to interest Reid most were the two circles drawn on the back of the second statuette, one each above the bend of the rivers before they intersected. Reid and Dock made a reconnaissance up the south bank of the Double Mountain Fork a half-mile from the confluence of the rivers. Up a ravine they found a long-dead and somewhat hollow mesquite tree, and Reid was somehow satisfied that it was the marker he sought. Five or six feet up the trunk of the dead tree was a knothole.

Dock never knew whether it was prior knowledge of that knothole or a hunch that led Reid to chop out the base of the trunk. But once Reid had chopped into the tree, it was obviously hollow enough to conceal something small. That object turned out to be a single droplet of pure silver the size of a small pebble. Seemingly, it was all that remained of what Reid believed had been a much larger cache. Anything that small could have been easily overlooked that day, as was evidenced when Dock later returned to the dead mesquite to find that it had been chopped down for firewood. But shining in a crevice made by the axman, Dock found a second, similar droplet of silver, which he cherishes.[2]

Dock knew that Reid pursued one other area in the spring and summer of 1937. For some time he had attempted to follow a line of trail markers leading northwest of Kiowa Peak up Croton Creek. He told Dock he had found the grave of a Spanish priest on that line, and Dock saw a stone studded with gold nuggets that Reid said he had taken from it. Whatever else the canyon tomb may have held, no one Dock knew was allowed to glimpse it.

It was at this juncture that Reid—like Arnold a quarter-century before—suddenly disappeared, taking with him everything he and his associates had found.[3] Where he had come from and where he now went, no one would ever learn. But the fact that he took all the artifacts that were discovered over the months that Dock and others assisted him was regrettable and unforgivable to each man who shared his knowledge with him. Reid's search and subsequent discoveries compounded the mystery of the Spider Rock, and when he vanished, so did those treasures of a former time.

Even so, Dock never stopped looking or believing that the Spider Rock and all its sister cryptoglyphs could one day be explained. What he found in the intervening years never equaled what he and Reid found, but neither has his search gone unrewarded. In this strange land of hill and canyon remain clues yet unfound, waiting to be pieced together in a logical fashion. The secret signs of that web somehow dovetail to reveal the events of a past age, of a people's ingenious ability to mystify all who dared to follow. Perhaps more than anything else, Dock learned that when he was sure all the signs had been found—all the trail markers, all the cryptic symbols—still another one would appear.

Later, Dock again investigated the bend of the rivers just upstream, or south from the forks, following the drawing on the back of the silver statuette. At the bend of the Double Mountain Fork not far above the arroyo where the hollowed mesquite was found, Dock came across a stone perhaps three feet long by eighteen inches wide, one end of which had been chiseled to a point. Dock sighted his rifle in the direction of the stone, which led him farther up the riverbank, where he dug out a rounded, elongated stone. The buried end of the stone bore a drill hole though it. The exposed portion seemed to point to a high red bluff on the west side of the Brazos just below the forks.

At the bend of the Salt Fork on its south bank, Dock found a curious circle of stones, but nothing more. From the bend of each river to their junction downstream is three-quarters of a mile. On the Salt Fork almost directly south of where the two rivers merge, Dock found still other stone carvings that surely must have been a part of the tantalizing web, for so much of what was found was discovered within a mile or two of the forks. On a large, flat stone the size of a tabletop was carved a flying arrow. In one corner of the stone was a drill hole. The arrow might have served as a directional sign had the stone not been moved

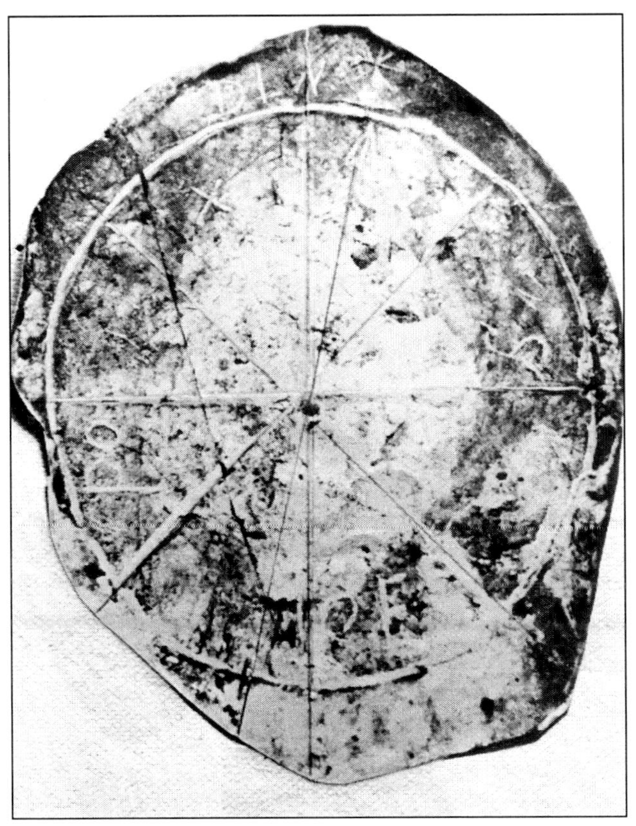

from its original position when a farm pond was dug nearby.

Not far west of the stone, Joe Cauble made an intriguing discovery that Dave Arnold surely must have hunted, for many of its symbols matched those on each of the three stone maps Arnold found. Cauble happened upon a cairn of slick cobblestones barely visible at the surface, but as he dug into them, he found they filled a hole two or three feet deep. At the base of the cairn was another small stone map. One side bore a single circle sectioned off into eight portions, each of which contained symbols.

The stone bears several of the same symbols as the one Arnold unearthed east of Rotan. The PO, OF, S, and DLN and star are obvious on one side with an arrow and sectional lines, drawn almost like a compass. The opposite side bore a dozen triangles circuling the inner portion of the stone. It also showed *11.000* (two zeros fewer than the stone near Rotan), *AD, 40711*, and other symbols and perhaps numerals. One more of the sister stones to the Spider Rock? It would appear so, from its many similar markings. Exactly where it was found is the mystery now. That was Cauble's only discovery near the old Spider diggings.[4]

Joe Cauble said he found this stone. Note the dozen triangles, 11.000, three crosses, and half-moon, similar to the Gyp Creek stone. The opposite side shows what some interpret as the compass, the directional symbols PO, and the DLN that also appears on the stone from Gyp Creek. (Courtesy Joe Cauble)

Local historian, librarian, and self-proclaimed sleuth Allen McDaniel of Abilene offers another possibility about the stone. There is no doubt in his mind that it is authentic, and he believes that whoever carved the Gyp Creek stone also carved the stone Joe Cauble harbored. Furthermore, McDaniel believes it also came from Gyp Creek, probably near the very stone Dave Arnold found in 1909-10. Long before McDaniel became aware of the Spider Rock story, he was aware of two Gyp Creek events in Fisher County.

Years ago, McDaniel was told a story that an elderly Mexican traveled from Mexico to Rotan in 1902 and spent some time on Gyp Creek scouting the landscape. He was seeking hidden treasure and either carried a map with him or had memorized landmarks. After spending some time in his search and finding nothing, the Mexican was given a ride to Snyder by a landowner who put him on the train back to Mexico. No one ever knew how the Mexican came to possess the information he had, but it would be seven years more before Dave Arnold would appear at that same location and unearth the stone map at Gyp Creek.

In 1961 a nearby landowner who was familiar with the above stories began a search of his own and unearthed a grave with a skull. McDaniel did not see the skull but knew the landowner's family and heard the story many times. Some years later, McDaniel learned about Dave Arnold's discovery on Gyp Creek, and he believes the stone which Cauble acquired most likely came from there. "I took a look at it and said that stone was carved at Gyp Creek by the same Spaniard who carved the one Arnold found," McDaniel explained.[5] Too many of the symbols on each stone were the same, and one surely related to the other.

Over the years, other, similar stones with equally curious markings were found. Matt Greer plowed up such a stone about a half-mile east of the forks, as did the Pete Hilton family still farther eastward. Those stones, like the sites from which they came, have long disappeared, as have the stories they might have told.

A year or so after Reid disappeared, Jack Childress reappeared at the old Spider diggings and soon afterward came no more. Childress, who had met Bud Jones and helped finance his search in 1924 and 1925, may have even known Dave Arnold, because he lived in San Angelo near where Arnold's family had once lived. One day in 1938, Childress phoned Dock that he was coming to the diggings. He had come by some information, he said, that he wanted to check out, and he asked Dock to meet him at the diggings one afternoon. Dock rode over early on horseback and waited several hours. When Childress did not show, he returned home. Dock learned later that Childress had come later that day and dug a large hole just west of the head of the canyon that originally yielded the Spanish saber and silver epaulets.

Dock did not view what may have been found that afternoon, nor did he ever see Childress again. He did talk with Raymond Woolridge, a farmer who lived nearby, who said he glimpsed what Childress found that day. In the back seat of his car rested a small silver casket, no more than two and a half to three feet long. The silver coffer appeared old, Woolridge said, and the red clay clinging to it showed it had just been removed from the ground. The farmer did not view its contents. Childress never reappeared at the diggings. Such is the mystery of the Spider Rock.[6]

That mystery grows with each discovery of a new clue that must somehow fit into a puzzle so complex and so extensive that it is difficult to believe so many pieces could exist, or once did. It must have been about 1950 that the children of Fritz Lawton were playing near the farm road leading south of Jud a mile or so, a half-mile east of the Double Mountain Fork. The site would have been almost two and a half miles east of the forks and not far east of the site where the second silver statuette was found by Dock and Reid a dozen years before.

As youngsters do, the children were playing just off the road, not far from their house in a secluded area, and stopping occasionally to pick up some pretty or unusual rock. Something shiny on the small bald hilltop caught their attention, and they discovered that the object was not a typical piece of glittering quartz found there, but a dark bronze-colored metal ingot, perhaps two fingers wide and three or four inches long, that had probably been exposed by recent rains.

Dock soon learned about the discovery, and Lawson showed him the ingot. It appeared to have been broken off from a longer piece of what seemed to be copper. When shown where it had been found by the children, Dock carefully shoveled away a grid on the barren hilltop, seeking anything that might have been buried with the metal.[7] A few inches below the surface, he struck a small cobblestone with a flat side that lay buried face down. He was not surprised when he found the smooth side bearing ciphers similar to others he had found in the cedar brakes. Incised on the stone were the numerals 118, XXX, a circle with a punch mark, and curved lines extending out from either side of the circle. On the right appeared a single X, three punch marks, and an arrow pointing southeast.

Dock followed that arrow perhaps 150 feet southeastward before he found what was unmistakably a human eye carved into the nodule of a large cobblestone, resting at the top of a small hill. The eye looked westward, "as straight as an arrow," Dock said, to the Spanish smelter just below the forks of the river two and a half miles away.

About fifty feet west of the first cobblestone, Dock found a small cairn, now almost level with the surface. The top stone, a flat, almost triangular stone no more than four or five inches in length, again bore the symbols of the age-old mystery. The number 19 appeared near a circle with a punch mark in its center, and 14 appeared near a similar circle with lines extending from either end. There were two arrows, one pointing northwest, the other southeast, three additional circles, one bearing a punch mark, and a cross with an X on one side. Lying directly beneath the stone was a stone arrowpoint, not of Spanish manufacture, but one typical of earlier, native inhabitants.

Westward to within a half-mile of the river, Dock found another, similar cairn. In it were buried three stone war clubs or tomahawks. Nearer the river were three smaller cairns on an east-west line and two more going north, but nothing more was found in the trail markers. Dock knew that this was the farthest east of the forks that any of the trail markers had been found, about four miles northeast of the Spider diggings.

No one knew how far the pattern of the spider web spread. If a ratio existed in the form of feet, *varas*, chain links, or even Spanish leagues—a ratio that matched the pattern of the Spider Rock and its cryptic numerical system—that ratio was not yet apparent, although the evidence thus far lent itself to such a conversion system. Such a system may have been known by Arnold, for he was known to have followed such trail markers, often a lone petroglyph or cairn, as many witnesses observed.

Dock later had a piece of the crudely molded ingot analyzed. Instead of copper, the bronze-colored metal proved to be predominately niccolite, a valuable ore of nickel associated with veins of silver, copper, and nickel. No one knew how long the sculptured human eye had weathered in the cedar brakes, ever watchful over the primitive river

In 1958 Crawford Allen, left, Henderson, and Riddle from Albuquerque returned to Dave Arnold's diggings of a half-century before when Allen participated in that search. (Courtesy Dock Henderson)

foundry. Might the broken ingot have been the Spanish way of indicating that smelter, where the ore was melted and poured into crude clay molds? Every object, every carving, every rock pile seemingly was a piece of the cryptogram.

Other strangers have entered the cedar brakes seeking clues, following knowledge that somehow came into their possession. One such stranger was a fellow named Riddle from Albuquerque. He came in 1954 with a rough sketch of a map that had been deposited in a bank vault. Although the map showed no similarity to the Spider Rock, some of its symbols and numbers were curiously the same.

Two wagon wheels were drawn on either side of the top of the map. Between them was a star. Between the star and each wheel was a tree. Pointing downward from each tree was an arrow, drawn like the arrow on the Spider Rock. Each arrow led to a large V, at the point of which was a circle with the words "Hole filled with rocks 90 feet deep." Between the star and hole was the number 94. Another 94 was indicated from one wheel to the other.[8]

Riddle sought information for some days before locating Crawford Allen, who was long retired as the sheriff of Haskell County and as a young man had worked with Arnold. Allen and Riddle visited Dock that day, and Riddle imparted his story. The map in the Albuquerque bank vault had been placed there by an old Indian who had died some years before at 114 years of age. When he was fourteen, the Indian had helped bury a large treasure in chests in a ninety-foot shaft somewhere just south of the forks of the river. The above markings and distances were all that he remembered. Neither Allen nor Dock had found those markings, but both recognized the similarity of those symbols with those on the Spider Rock, the 94, for example. Riddle did not say how the Indian happened to escape with that knowledge.

The lost treasure shaft which Riddle hunted might well be connected to Dave

Arnold's own quest, for a story told in later years concerned such a shaft which Arnold sought—and is said to have found—just downstream on the Brazos in Knox County from where he is last known to have hunted. The quest, as related many years later, took place in an area known as the Narrows, where the Brazos and Wichita rivers run about five miles apart not far east of Benjamin. Interesting, too, the story centers around Dr. Terrell, even though he was unnamed. It was about 1948 that a prospector began looking for the legendary gold mine of the Narrows. The story dated back to the California gold rush of 1849. Wilson Gilbert, noted Indian fighter of Cooke County and brother of Mabel Gilbert, the first settler of Wichita County, was heading for the gold fields when somewhere in the Narrows region, he found nuggets that he later learned were gold. Alas, he was never able

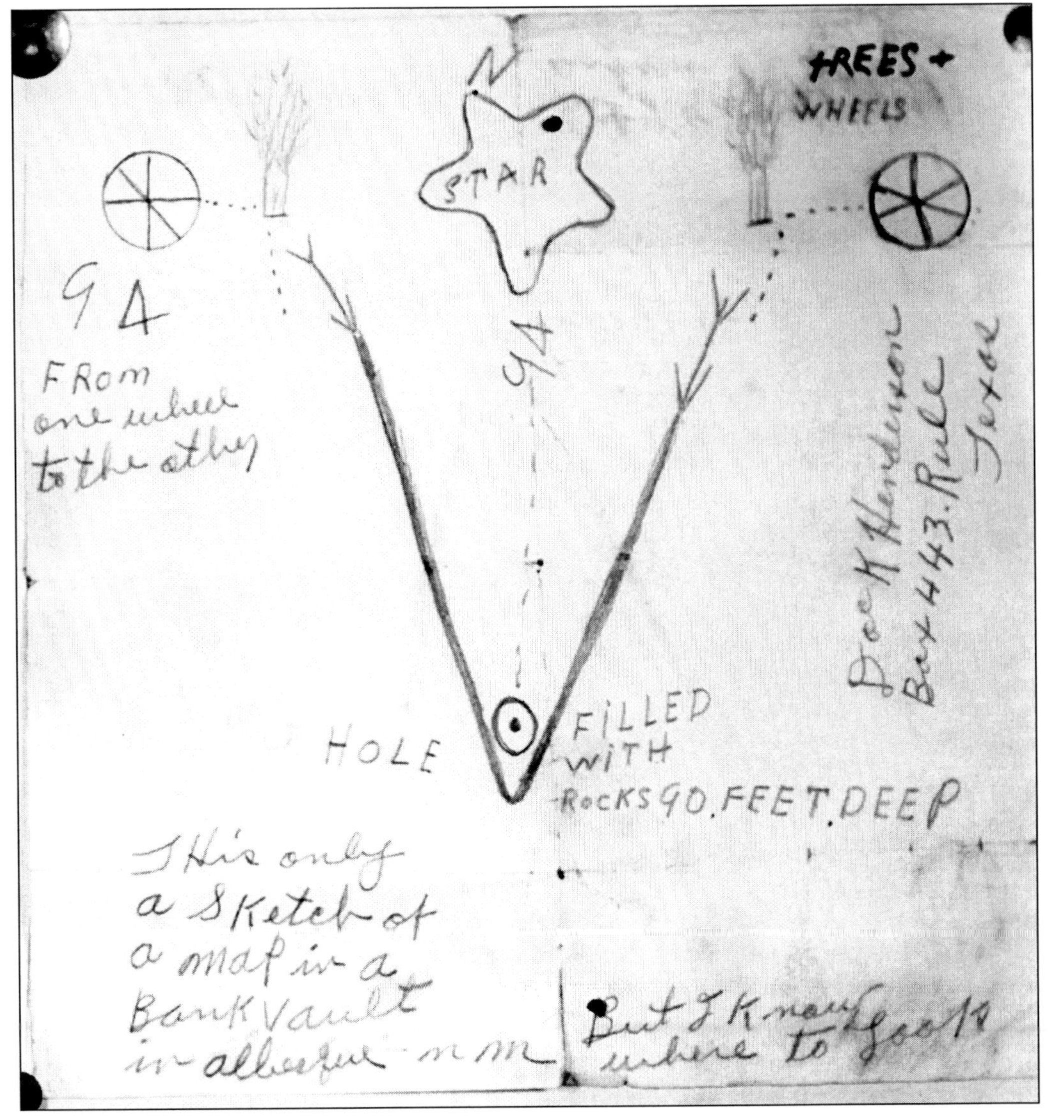

Riddle brought this sketch of a map in a bank vault in Albuquerque made by a 114-year-old Indian who said he helped bury the treasure in a ninety-foot-deep shaft. Note the 94, arrows, and cartwheels, all similarities to the Spider Rock. (Courtesy Mrs. Noah Gillentine)

to relocate the site when he returned some years later, and he completely disappeared during a final attempt in the fall of 1873.[9]

W. B. "Noah" Gillentine of Benjamin long believed there was to be found in the Narrows a rich silver mine which had been worked by the Spaniards, and he believed he had found a number of carved symbols in the region to prove it. The prospector in 1948 might well have been led to the Narrows by Gillentine, a treasure hunter who spent much of his life in that quest.[10] The prospector, who remains unnamed, discovered what he believed was a mine shaft which had been filled with stones. Removing several feet of those stones convinced him of what he had found. It was not long afterward that he met—perhaps through Gillentine—a nearly hundred-year-old man who years before had been employed by a "treasure hunter" in Knox County who was "removing a fabulous Spanish treasure from the bottom of a mine shaft," he told the prospector.[11]

The hundred-year-old resident may or may not have told that he was employed by Dr. C. L. Terrell, but the facts of his story, even though somewhat forgotten and confused in later years, could have concerned only Dr. Terrell of Haskell. If Dave Arnold were mentioned, and certainly he must have been there, he was not remembered now. The oldster recalled they had found "three large vaults at the bottom of the shaft, and they were full of gold, silver, jewels, and copper."

They removed a part of the treasure when the employer became sick and he was taken to the Haskell hospital. The ancient shaft, which had just been dug to the eighty-foot level, was filled back in to protect their discovery. His employer was hospitalized, and the recovered treasure was placed in the local bank, the old man remembered. Soon afterward the employer died, "and on the same night the bank burned and the treasure was lost."

Interestingly, on May 26, 1911, a fire did heavily damage the two-story building on the northeast corner of the courthouse square in Haskell which housed the Haskell State Bank, but the unidentified man who died must surely have been Dr. Terrell, and the building that burned, his own drug store. Unfortunately, the centenarian was never named. The prospector in 1948 was sure he had found the same shaft, which according to the oldster held three million dollars in its three vaults, somewhere in the wastelands of the Narrows. Why he never returned to the mysterious shaft himself could never be determined.[12]

There have been other unexplainable discoveries in the canyon brakes. There may be others of which nothing now is known. Not many miles up the Salt Fork westward from the old diggings lies one hill of gypsum known to be honeycombed with tunnels extending well over two hundred feet into the hillside. Sometimes it has been referred to as the Spider Cave. The hill is located at the junction of Rock Creek and a canyon tributary five miles north of Aspermont and two miles eastward.[13]

Found three miles up Rock Creek on a straight line from its confluence with the Salt Fork, the tunnels were never known to have been discovered by Dave Arnold, even though he prospected the Salt Fork and lived for a brief time with the John Metcalf family a few miles away. No one now can recall who found the tunnels, but Dock remembers that when he worked with Jones in 1924 and 1925, two men named Smith and Coles were then digging them out.

A flat rock covered the entrance on the northeast side of the hill opposite the canyon to its front. The original discoverers found an antelope skeleton just behind that rock. Strangely, the grave of a Spanish priest was sought far back into the tunnels, only large enough to crawl into. In recent years Jack Gore of Rule visited the old tunnels and, far into one, found recent diggings. At the end of the excavation, Gore picked up a large black button about the size of a quarter. The button, with one side flat and the other bearing a rose-cut design, appeared to be obsidian but was not. Molded into its flat side was what appeared to be a gold hook. Whatever its composition, the button was hard enough to cut glass. It presents the appearance and feel of antiquity.[14]

The discovery of the tunnels might well have been attributed to the crude drawing cut into a stone ledge that was once evident on the north side of the hill, which, until it completely eroded away some years ago, bore the date 1764. In recent years a driller, who believed he could find anything of value by drilling from the hilltop, is said to have flooded some of the tunnels. However, one large shaft at the surface can yet been seen where an attempt was made to enter a chamber. Any relation the tunnels may have to the Spider Rock is still unknown.

There are other such mysteries. Dock's uncle John Henderson found a token of those earlier miners who worked the Brazos River brakes. Up the Double Mountain Fork west of the Old Glory-to-Hamlin road, John was cowboying for the Swenson Ranch right after the turn of the century when he found a copper ingot on the riverbank. Dock's father, Preston, and John later staked out a copper deposit and worked a claim for a time, but they never found the mine from which the copper ingot must have come.

About twelve miles farther up the river, west of the road south of Aspermont, a cave was found whose ceiling bore a carving of concentric circles and radiating lines similar to that of the Spider Rock. Many years ago, Dock was to meet Burt Cochran and Joe Cauble on the river to search for the cave, but obligations of one kind or another always prevented that reconnaissance. No one today knows the whereabouts of the cave, but many have heard of its discovery.[15] It must lie in the same region in which Charley Sanders and Bud Alston found a stone map in the roots of a stump on the Double Mountain Fork one day in 1908. This was only a couple of years before Arnold unearthed his third stone map on Gyp Creek, a few miles upstream. If only the stone maps could talk . . .

Time and again the mystery appears to lead to Kiowa Peak, that lone landmark eight miles distant and three degrees west of north from the red clay hill that yielded the Spider Rock. Early in his own search, Dock examined Kiowa Peak, a historic landmark for travelers for centuries. As late as 1872, the C. W. Holt surveying party observed an estimated 50,000 buffalo here.[16] Dock found circles of stones placed around the peak, beginning at its base. The peak rises two hundred feet above the surrounding terrain. At the top of the lone butte, he found three final circles formed of stones.

Might it be that the Spaniards used Kiowa Peak as the landmark of orientation while reading degrees of direction from the Spider Rock? No one yet has determined the geographical center of the Spider Rock, and its sister stone carvings are known to have been found over a wide expanse of West Texas. What secrets might Kiowa Peak hold?

In recent years, two articles of note have been stumbled upon here. The first and most intriguing was found near the east side of Kiowa Peak. Dan Ferris of Rotan was hunting the day he found a copper disc, old and pitted, apparently dug out of the rocks by rodents or washed out of the hillside.[17] The disc did not appear unusual until Ferris rubbed away the embedded clay to find that each side was incised with what he later learned were miniature replicas of the Spider Rock and the stone map from the Sembritzki farm.

Neither etching on the copper disc is a duplicate of the stone maps, but they are similar enough to cause one to ponder its purpose. Whoever carved the replicas on the one-eighth-inch-thick disc, a mere one and three-quarters inches in diameter, obviously was familiar with both maps. C. O. Duke of Rotan, who later procured the copper disc, believes it to be authentic but has no explanation for its intent.[18]

Twelve miles northeast of Kiowa Peak in southwestern Knox County, rancher B. B. Hendrix was examining an outcropping of copper on his land when he found a copper medallion similar in size to the disc Ferris chanced upon. Obviously a religious article, one side of the medallion bore an imprint of Saint Peter reading an open Bible. On the opposite side appeared an angel, and the Latin words "*S. PATER BENEDICTVS. SILVESTCON SILF*." Below was stamped the date 1647.[19] Perhaps the possession of a Spanish priest, the medal posed more questions about its origin.

It must have been in the Kiowa Peak region that Thomas Longest took shelter in a cave during a storm and found a rusty pick and shovel. That was in 1887, and neither of those relics interested Longest as much as the ledge of ore at the back of the cave, which he believed to be silver. He broke off perhaps five pounds and later sent it to New York to be assayed. It was identified as lead, but seventy percent pure.

Longest was a horse buyer from Georgia. He later told L. D. Bertillion about this discovery. He said he was riding on the east side of the Brazos near the confluence of the forks when he saw a steer with a set of horns he wanted. A cowboy riding with Longest told him that better specimens could be found a day's ride northwest, showed him a crossing safe from quicksand, and directed him toward Croton Creek. After Longest had ridden several hours, a storm came up and he took shelter in the cave. Bertillion knew that Longest planned on returning to the lead mine, but tuberculosis took his life before those plans materialized.[20]

The story is also told that in the Croton brakes still farther northwestward, two government trappers were working on the Four Sixes Ranch at the turn of the century when they were caught in a dust storm and took refuge in a cave. At the back of the shelter they found chunks of rich lead ore. Resting on a stone ledge were a Spanish spur of probable eighteenth-century vintage and a cloth military sash that disintegrated when touched.[21]

To anyone familiar with the Spider Rock—its history, its romance, its spellbinding hold on anyone who dares to reveal its secrets, to follow its beckoning trail—it is not difficult to understand how one can become trapped in the spider's web. To follow the trail of the Spider Rock—to witness the cryptic signs carved into stone, to handle the charcoal and slag remaining centuries after the Spanish miners fired those furnaces to melt precious metals, to talk with those who knew Arnold and witnessed the clues as he found them, who believed they were on the verge of finding something wondrous—is to be caught in the magnetic pull as great as that which beckoned Coronado and his conquistadors in quest of the Golden Cities of Quivira.

Other counties surrounding Stonewall and Haskell also have spawned strange discoveries. A few miles southeast of Clairemont in Kent County, adjacent to Stonewall on the west, lies what has come to be known as Treasure Butte. It seems that about 1903 a surveyor and his son were running lines through the county and were working near the mound. Instead of using a tripod, the surveyor's son improvised with a "Jacob's staff," which he would drive into the sand. When the staff hit something unusually solid one day, curiosity enticed the surveyor and his son to remove the object. Only a few inches below the surface, it turned out to be a stone, but no ordinary stone. It was a flat white stone, perhaps eighteen or twenty inches long by half that wide. Cleaning it revealed a crude map carved into one side, and five circles on the other.[22]

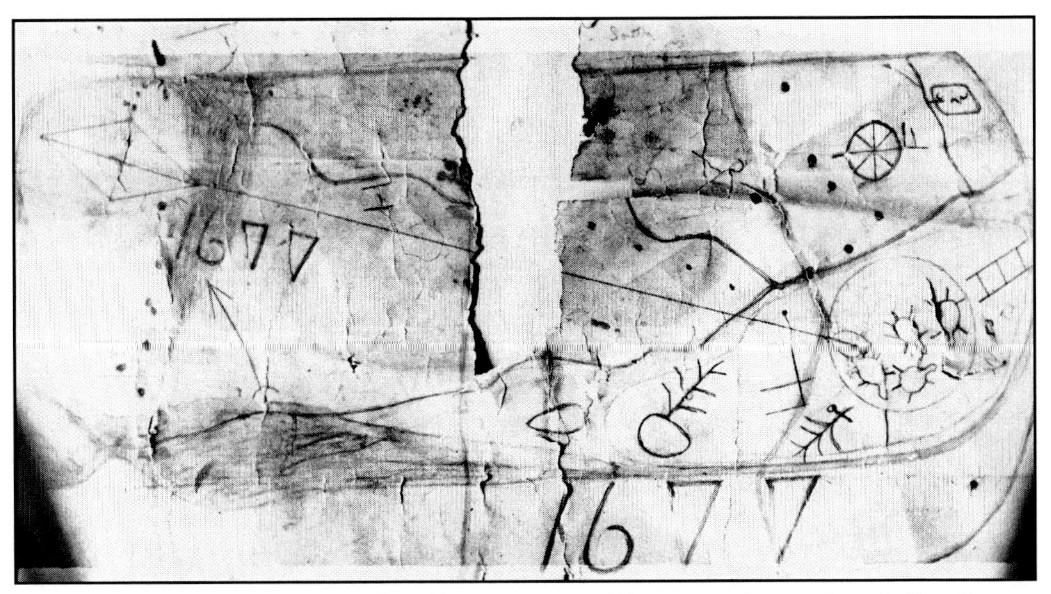

The Cartwheel stone was accidentally found by a surveyor and his son near Treasure Butte in Kent County. This copy appeared in the 1930s. Note the diamond figure, five turtles within a circle, ladder, compass, and F's. Not shown in the torn portion is the CXF, found on all the stones associated with the Spider Rock. (Courtesy Jack Brown)

Beautifully carved into the top side of the stone were the numbers or date 1677, shown twice. Below one date was an arrow pointing to a large diamond figure. A line led from the diamond diagonally across the stone to a circle with five turtles in it. To the right of the turtles appeared to be a ladder and the symbol N. At least two F's appeared on the stone, one beside a circle carved into eight parts. One carving appeared to represent the forks of a stream. Near the stream appeared the letters CXF, with the F inverted. On the opposite side of the stone were five circles.[23]

The discovery of the stone attracted considerable attention. Not long after the discovery, a stranger appeared at the search who might easily have been Dave Arnold, although that is not the name he gave. A brief description of the stranger curiously smacks of Arnold.

"This old treasure hunter had found several buried treasure-troves, and was a typical gold hunter, mysterious, uncommunicative, and unfriendly," remembered one who observed him. "But when he learned of the findings of these people, he became more friendly and told his story, which soon convinced the people that their stone map and findings would lead to the buried treasure."[24]

If in fact the stranger was Dave Arnold, he must have recognized immediately that the father-son team had found one more stone map in the Spider Rock puzzle, undoubtedly shown on his ever-present sheepskin map. The diamond figure was also shown on the Spider Rock. The CXF, with the F inverted, appeared on both stones and would be found on the stone from John Sembritzki's farm. The oval-shaped cipher was another similarity, as well as the separate F's carved over it. If Arnold was the stranger, he knew there could be no doubt about the stone's connection to the Spider Rock.

The stranger explained there were diamond-shaped graves depicted on the stone. One contained three bodies, another held two, and the third held one. The circle enclosing the

Dock Henderson shows off a few of the many arrowpoints he found over the years while prowling the cedar brakes. (Photo by the author)

five turtles indicated "a round hole with five terrapins attempting to climb out of it," he said. Many of the symbols were later found, such as the diamond-shaped grave containing the five skeletons. Even a partially decayed lone cart wheel was uncovered.

The stranger explained that they would find seven oxcart loads of gold bullion which had been buried by Spanish travelers. The stone map would lead them to three springs. One spring was found on top of the butte. Another spring, found nearby, was walled up with stones and discovered in that condition by the earliest pioneers, showing it had been done at a time prior to the first settlers of the region. The third spring was never found, and eventually the search was abandoned. If in fact the stranger was Arnold, he did not tarry at Treasure Butte, nor did he take the stone with him.

The story is told that the surveyor who found the stone was the uncle of Joe Cauble. If that is true, the Cartwheel stone was probably the site that first attracted Cauble to Arnold's trail. Unfortunately, many of the details of this early story are unknown, but what is known is that Joe Cauble possessed the Cartwheel stone sometime in the teens and appeared at the ranch of Bilbe Wallace, owner of the 75,000-acre O Bar O. Wallace knew that various symbols on the stone had been found over his ranch, and he had found what he believed was a "kiln" on the eastern part of the ranch.

The Cartwheel stone location might well have been the first of Arnold's sites that enticed Joe Woods, for soon Cauble and Woods were working together. Whether Cauble related what he found, or what he knew the surveyor and his son found, is questionable. Cauble said he found the five skeletons buried together with one pointing, but it led only to an empty stone vault. Cauble said he worked from the compass as well as the North Star. The diamond figure shown on the stone map was in fact "lined out in rocks eighteeen feet across and twenty-six feet long." Cauble believed the stone map also bore symbols representing the Big Dipper and the North Star. The five skeletons he found were six miles west-northwest from the large diamond outlined in the surface. Cauble worked on the Treasure Butte site intermittently for years. He was sure he had found the remains of a Spanish smelter on the west side of Cooper Mountain between Clairemont and Snyder, the slag of which contained silver.

It is known that in the 1930s, interest was renewed in the site and more human bones were found. It was then that the wall of stones was found, forming what appeared to have been a vault. But alas, the chamber was empty of the contents it must have once guarded. Joe Cauble or Joe Woods, which one is unsure, gave the Cartwheel stone away. Although the stone has not been seen for thirty or forty years, the chances are good that it still survives. Allen McDaniel of Abilene does not question the 1677 on the stone standing for *varas*, but also believes those numbers represent the year the stone was carved, just as he believes the stone from Sembritzki farm was in fact dated 1671. If McDaniel is corrrect, the Spider Rock and its sister stones may be older than even Dave Arnold believed. Interestingly, the Cartwheel stone would have been found forty miles or so west-southwest from where Arnold unearthed the Spider Rock. One wonders if the Cartwheel stone is not somehow connected to Don Español's quest and discovery on the Double Mountain Fork early in the century.

Duane Hale inspects the ruins of a stone building south of Kiowa Peak long believed to have been a Spanish mission. A stone once bore the date 1812. (Photo by the author)

No other Spanish mystery even similar to the Spider Rock is known to exist in the Southwest, or even Mexico. No known books or documents hint about its existence—or they are so well guarded they have not yet become known. Those who are familiar with the Spider Rock mystery and have not become trapped in its web are few indeed. The desire to unravel the mystery, to decipher the stones, to follow the trail to whatever was hidden under such secrecy and complexity is an obsession not easily overcome.

It is incredible that after more than a half-century of

The author examines the copper artifacts found with the Spider Rock at the site where the stone was found a century ago. (Photo by Dale Durham)

Historian Dale Durham examines the topography on the Salt Fork with the key and leaf in hand, two of the copper replicas originally found with the Spider Rock. (Photo by the author)

searching and pondering, Dock can speak today with such calmness about the age-old mystery. Not everyone who has pursued this Spanish enigma has possessed that sobriety. Early in his search, Arnold was warned the treasure was cursed, and he was cautioned by many who viewed the stone maps to deny its vicelike grip on mind and soul. Arnold did not deny himself one of the most bizarre treasure quests of the twentieth century. We know about many of the things he found in the presence of others. Of course, we know nothing about what he may have found while alone.

Others have come and gone under mysterious circumstances, not solving mysteries, but adding to them. As recently as the spring of 1971, several Mexican hunters appeared at the antique shop of John Smith in Abilene with a hoard of gold ingots and large nuggets to sell. They had followed an arrow carved on a stone, they told Smith, to what area settlers had always supposed was a grave over which stones were piled.

That cairn was known to exist a mile or so north of Old Glory, not far south of the Salt Fork, and perhaps less than a mile from the old Spider diggings. Two of the gold ingots were stamped with the names SALAS and CRUZ. Below SALAS appeared the date 1631. Nothing is known about Cruz, but it is well documented that Fray Juan de Salas was a missionary to native tribes in West Texas in 1629 and again in 1632. Little survives about Juan de Salas and his activities, and the site of his mission has never been found.

John Smith was aghast at what he saw before him but managed to hold the owners' attention long enough to snap several photographs. They were ready to sell their discovery, but Smith was ill-prepared to barter for such a purchase.[25] Smith did not tell them he had once been close to the Spider Rock legend and had known several of those who had

The author, Duane Hale, and Don Smith found this stone in 1976 in a cow trail adjacent to the primitive smelter near the old Spider diggings. Note arrow, N, and other indiscernible marks. (Photo by the author)

pursued its trail with Dave Arnold. Ironically, he now felt that the trail pursued him. The Mexicans soon left, taking their discovery with them.

Smith himself does not intend to pursue the Spider Rock treasure. Not long after the Mexicans departed, Smith began having a recurring dream. In the dream a Spaniard dressed for battle came to him and warned him of the peril that he would encounter should he pursue the treasure, a treasure cursed with the blood of all those who concealed it. Smith believes that, for a moment, he glimpsed in his own antique shop a portion of the treasure so long entangled in the spider web.

Walter Urion and Andy Moss, who first went to the diggings with Jones in 1924, concluded their own search years ago.[26] In November 1949 they and A. M. "Buck" Morgan sold the fifty-eight and a half acres encompassing those earlier discoveries to John Behringer, but, still harboring the dream that one day the treasure might yet be found, they reserved all mineral rights. In 1954 Behringer sold his land of 104 acres to Roy and James Butler, the present owners of the Spider diggings.[27]

Today the scars of a century of digging testify to the dreams seekers have brought to the banks of the Salt Fork. The red clay hill on which Arnold and the Mexican sheepherder unearthed the Spider Rock is pockmarked with the holes of those digging blindly. Deep trenches have been bulldozed on its east and west flanks by pursuers searching without any knowledge of how to decipher the clues to the age-old mystery. Otherwise, much of the Spider Rock hill remains much as it was when Arnold unearthed the first of his hieroglyphic stone maps there.

The Salt Fork of the Brazos. About three hundred yards to the south, Dave Arnold unearthed the Spider Rock. (Photo by the author)

Down the hill to the west and across the canyon from which the sheepherder retrieved the Spanish saber and silver epaulets, the huge excavation that Arnold and his followers dug with teams and scrapers lies virtually untouched since Jones and Dock sunk their drill bits through its bedrock three quarters of a century ago. Today those diggings are overgrown with a thicket of mesquite eight to ten feet high.

As Dock has said so often, not even he would have believed the myriad evidence had he not seen the proof scattered up and down the rivers, or listened to the accounts of those who had known and watched Arnold. But no one ever doubted the human skeletons, copper daggers, hand-hammered plates, ornate silver epaulets, or mysterious stone maps. No one ever doubted the charcoal and slag of the smelters, the silver crosses, the arrows and statuettes.

Incredible as it may seem, clues are still found. As late as one March day in 1976, Dock, his friend Don Smith, Duane Hale, and I were again examining the barely visible remains of the smelter a quarter-mile east of the Spider diggings.[28] From that hillside, Kiowa Peak lies in plain view, fifteen degrees west of north. It was a strange place for a smelter, but the bits of charcoal and slag revealed by clearing the surface covered an area seven or eight feet across. A cow trail led down the hill past the south side of the smelter, and lying beside it a small flat stone no larger than a man's hand caught Smith's eye.

Its surface was incised with the familiar markings of the Spider Rock: the letter N, the arrow of the same design so often found, what appeared to be a human eye, and other indiscernible symbols now too faint to determine. It was incredible that the stone had gone undetected all those years, despite the many searchers before us who must have passed that primitive hearth. The erosion of the cow trail had now exposed the stone. What message had its carver left us?

The Spaniards left that bizarre story etched in stone, even though the documents that might reveal their names, their purpose, and their story have not yet come to light. No one can deny that the trail of coded stones and cryptic maps laid down to lead them back has defied the imagination of scholar and treasure seeker alike. The Spider Rock today, as it did perhaps two centuries ago when implanted over the bodies of those chosen to guard it, harbors the key to this Spanish mystery code. That code remains unbroken to this day.

10

A Golden Obsession: Trapped in the Spider's Web

High on a bluff overlooking the Salt Fork of the Brazos is a dugout of sticks and stones, made by a man who became entangled in the web of the Spider Rock. Appearing more like a wilderness dwelling of the past century than one of recent times, the mud-chinked structure is all that remains of the broken dreams of a man who lived his life in quest of Spanish treasure always just beyond his grasp.

No one knows just how or when Frank Olmstead became intrigued with the Spanish legend. It has been said that he was living in Lawton, Oklahoma, when he came upon the story.[1] Olmstead was both well educated and once well to do. It is known that he was a college professor, dealt heavily in the stock market, traded in real estate and oil, and even conducted business in California and Florida. When he went to Texas in quest of lost gold in 1920, he owned a large farm in La Salle County, Illinois, with a good home and large barns.

A short, portly fellow, Olmstead loved everyone and everything. What he had learned about the Spider Rock entranced him, entrapping him in its enigmatic web like nothing he had known before. Such an entrapment is not difficult to understand, for the legend of the Spider Rock grips men's minds, begging for answers to the secret ciphers chiseled into stone. It may have been the curse the Spaniards knew would always follow those who dared to reveal those secrets. Olmstead gave up everything he owned in his attempt to unveil the mystery.

Olmstead first began his search at Double Mountain, on Jim McDonald's ranch. McDonald's daughter, Mrs. Lannie McMahon of Aspermont, even though only nine years old then, vividly recalls Olmstead's visits and the tunnel he dug into the northeast side of Double Mountain.[2] Olmstead may have been pursuing the trail left by Dave Arnold. Not long afterward, he learned that Arnold had lived for a time at the John Metcalf farm on the Salt Fork, twelve miles northeast of Aspermont, and dug east of the Metcalf house, where he found a concretelike formation bearing drill holes.

When Olmstead discovered that Jim McDonald had owned the land bordering Metcalf's, and had dug a cistern near Arnold's former diggings and found a similar formation also bearing drill holes filled with red sediment, he associated that discovery with the Spider Rock, which had also shown similar holes filled with red clay. Somehow Olmstead believed he had found the site that Arnold surely had missed, even though he had been a mere few feet away.

On January 17, 1921, Olmstead's wife, Mabel, purchased 329 acres on the Salt Fork from G. S. Hester. Later she deeded 239 acres to her husband. By 1925 the land had been reduced to 133 acres. Olmstead had begun a search that he could never free himself from. He questioned the Metcalf family, his neighbors on the west, about Dave Arnold's every move. Arnold had last visited the Metcalfs only about ten years before, sometime in 1910, and left them a copy of the Spider Rock he had made on oilcloth, along with copper replicas of the three copper objects found lying atop the stone.[3]

The oilcloth copy which Arnold left the Metcalfs is strangely not a duplicate of the old blueprint made of the Spider Rock. A comparison of the two shows some obvious differences, even a change of some symbols and numbers. The reason for those discrepancies perhaps only Arnold knew.

Olmstead learned, too, that Gurney Ward had visited the Metcalfs only months after Arnold, almost as if he were tracking him. Ward had continued the search at the Sembritzki farm near Clyde shortly after Arnold abandoned it. He gave no hint about why he followed Arnold's trail now. He was interested in the holes Arnold had dug on the Metcalf farm, and Ward even dug holes of his own on two separate occasions. Ward told the elder Metcalf that he had evidence that Arnold had murdered two Mexicans near the border to acquire the sheepskin map that led him to the hieroglyphic stones he had found. Ward, too, made a copy of the Spider Rock that Arnold had drawn on oilcloth and left with the Metcalfs, and then he disappeared, just as Arnold had only a few months before. It appears that Ward soon gave up following Arnold's trail and moved his search to the Sacramento Mountains of New Mexico.

At first, Olmstead did not move onto the land on which he came to believe the Spanish treasure would be found. He visited periodically, searching for months at a time, until finally, in 1933, he returned permanently. He announced to his closest neighbor and good friend, John Metcalf, that he had sold his rich Illinois farm for $500 an acre to finance his search. In the beginning, Olmstead's wife came with him. She soon returned home, but occasionally she would drive to Rule, where Olmstead would meet her. Finally, she divorced him, later remarried, and on one other occasion returned with her new husband to visit Olmstead at his diggings.

In frontier style, Olmstead had built his dugout into the side of a rock bluff overlooking the Salt Fork to the south. Hand-hewn cedar poles and corrugated iron served as his roof and mud-chinked stone as his walls.

"Olmstead once told me that he didn't understand why people had housing problems," John Metcalf remembered. "He said he solved the problem with only forty-five cents. That was the amount he paid for the windshield from an old car that served as his dugout window. He was really a wonderful man and highly educated. He would pick black-eyed peas from my garden, insisting that I take half of what he gathered. I would tell him just to take what he wanted, but he always insisted on doing it on the halves."[4]

Olmstead had to walk a mile to get his water. Once a week he would walk twice that distance to his mailbox, where he picked up the many magazines and newspapers he subscribed to. His only modern convenience was a radio, and he erected a tall antenna for it

Above and top of next page: Frank Olmstead was a college professor when he became enraptured by the Spider Rock treasure in 1920. He built his dugout high on a bluff overlooking the Salt Fork of the Brazos in Stonewall County. His primitive dwelling, with rock collection outside, remains much as it was when he died in 1948. (Photos by the author)

at one side of his primitive home. Over the years, Olmstead dug myriad holes and trenches. Many of those trenches were a hundred yards long by as much as fifteen feet deep. After completing one such excavation, he would move over and dig another.

In the beginning he hired out part of the work, but later he did it all himself. He would sink a shaft as deep as thirty feet, climb down on a rope ladder, dig enough rock and soil to fill a bucket, then climb back out and pull up the filled bucket. He dug scores of similar holes around his dugout, seemingly without rhyme or reason, always believing he would one day find the elusive gold. Once, recalls Metcalf, Olmstead found a rabbit trapped in one of the holes. He freed the rabbit and then covered up the pit. "He told me he didn't want rabbits or any other animals dying because of the holes he made," Metcalf said.

Everyone in the country knew about Olmstead's golden obsession. He picked up what little money he needed by working on neighboring farms, sometimes picking cotton, sometimes just taking care of a nearby farm while its owners were away. Olmstead once showed Mrs. George Pumphrey, whose ranch was across the Salt Fork, a picture of the Illinois farm he once owned. It featured a nice home and large barns, she remembered.[5]

Mrs. Pumphrey knew that Olmstead had made trips to California to consult a Catholic priest in his search, perhaps believing he could help solve the puzzle. He always believed

Olmstead was buried near his dugout in a trench he hoped would yield the Spanish treasure. In mining tradition, his digging tools were placed at the head of his grave. (Photo by the author)

that if he fully understood Catholicism, he would be able to find the treasure, Mrs. Pumphrey recalled. Metcalf knew that Olmstead once made a trip to Cuba, as shown by his passport, which Metcalf now possessed. No one ever knew just what he hoped to find. Like Arnold, he may not have known himself. There were legends of twenty jack-loads of Spanish gold, still later ones of forty. The stories of hidden Aztec gold, even Inca treasure, still hovered over the region.

There was also a story of a Spanish priest buried in a silver casket with a rare book and priceless ring. Olmstead once wrote the Vatican for information about such a book and ring that had been the property of a priest in Mexico. Olmstead may or may not have known that Arnold had found the grave of a presumed priest. Surely he knew that Arnold had sought that lost tomb. He may have even known about the rare book that Gurney Ward sought at the diggings on the Sembritzki farm after Arnold abandoned the site, a book wrapped in many layers of hides, Ward believed.

It has been said that Olmstead came into the possession of a map of his own, but if this is so, Metcalf never glimpsed it. The only map he possessed was the copy of the Spider Rock that Arnold had drawn on oilcloth years before, which he later left, along with reproductions of the copper artifacts found with it. While Olmstead sought the elusive treasure where Arnold had once dug ten miles or so upstream from the old Spider diggings, Pauline Tabor and her brother, Burt Edwards, conducted their own search, attempting to

In 1910 Dave Arnold left this oilcloth copy of the Spider Rock with the Metcalf family northeast of Aspermont. With the oilcloth were copper replicas of the plate, dagger, and key found with the stone. Ten years later, the legend attracted Frank Olmstead to the region. (Courtesy John Metcalf)

unravel the mysterious letter of instructions the Mexican sheepherder had left the Stuart family late one night before he vanished.

Pauline and her brother began their search in 1938, and during the trips that followed, they met Olmstead at his dugout close to his diggings. Pauline vividly recalls her impressions of Olmstead, how immaculate he was, how gentlemanly, how intelligent, and how out of place he seemed in the crude dugout atop the sandstone cliffs overlooking the river.[6] Yet he survived on the legend, on the quest, on the dream of finding the Spanish treasure.

On November 17, 1948, at the age of sixty-three, Olmstead died at his dugout beside his diggings of almost three decades. He never lost faith in the Spanish treasure he believed would be found. Ten years before, he had dug his own grave only a few feet away from his home on the Salt Fork. For his tomb he used a hole he had hoped would yield the lost gold. Metcalf buried Olmstead just as he had requested, in the grave he had dug for himself. He asked only that his shovels and picks be placed at the head of his grave, a custom of the West. Olmstead thought it fitting that he follow that tradition.[7]

Olmstead's dugout remains just as he left it, untouched except by the elements and by rodents and rattlesnakes that have claimed it for their own. Among a few clothes hangs a tuxedo. A kerosene lamp stands on the iron cookstove. Pots and pans hang from the walls. A radio stands on a nearby table. A long-outdated calendar hangs on a stone wall. Jars of sugar, flour, and black-eyed peas repose on a shelf near the blackened stove and iron bedstead and mattress.

Outside, a wooden door swings randomly on its rusted hinges as a howling wind sweeps through the canyon brakes. On a long table made of cut cedar poles lies Olmstead's collection of rocks gathered over the years that he sought the Spider Rock gold. The towering aerial he erected for his radio stands as a lonely sentinel overlooking Olmstead's diggings and dreams of nearly three decades.

Gurney Ward and Archie Frame had their own golden obsession, and it was no less intense than Olmstead's. It is known that Ward's story of lost Spanish treasure was so good that when he sold stock on the streets of Abilene in April 1911, Frame could not resist and was hooked for most of his life. When Ward divorced his wife in that year, he moved to Lampasas and opened a photography studio. Considering that Ward had been extremely interested in the wanderings of Dave Arnold, and probably knew more about Arnold than anyone else around, one wonders why Ward resettled in Lampasas. It is known he spent the remainder of 1911 and 1912 there. Frame recalled that he assisted Ward at the Sembritzki farm, but once he was again in need of funds, he again sold stock "and hit for the Sacramentos."[8]

Actually, it was several years before Ward migrated to the Sacramentos. He opened a photography studio in Alamagordo and ran an ad in the April 8, 1915, *Otero County News*.[9] That date coincides with Frame's memory of working with Ward for the next twenty-eight years at Ward's money pit in Alamo Canyon in the Sacramento Mountains, only a few miles northeast of Alamagordo. However, the way into the site is by way of High Rolls, between Alamagordo and Cloudcroft, about eleven miles southwestward near the confluence of Alamo and Good canyons. One might wonder if Ward followed Dave Arnold to this location, but no evidence survives of it. It is probable that Arnold eluded Ward just as he did everyone else who had known him in West Texas.

Frame remembered that when he had first asked Ward where all the gold had come from, Ward said, "the Sacramentos of New Mexico," where they had five mines, a smelter, and *arrastras*. No one knows exactly when Ward picked his site in Alamo Canyon, but Frame soon joined him and paid $2,700 for a half-interest in the search. "I joined Mr. Ward at Alamo Canyon," Frame said. "We found a cave with the opening sealed with masonry, or with an earthen fill. We got picks, shovels, and dynamite and blew down this enclosure. Inside, on the north wall of the cave, about six feet above our heads, we saw a familiar object—a copy of the chart stone." Ward said there were forty burro loads of gold and thirty-three bars of silver hidden there, Frame remembered.[10]

Carroll Wood of Alamagordo believed he remembered when Ward and Frame first came into the country. He did not remember the year, other than that it was early in the century. Carroll's father was made foreman of laying a pipeline from La Luz Canyon to Alamagordo via Alamo Spring, located in the mouth of Alamo Canyon. While on the project, Carroll and his brother Bill observed two white men and two Mexicans guiding about a dozen burros as they passed up the canyon through the crew of workers. They went to what was locally known as Indian Cave, at the top of the bluff. Carroll knew, or perhaps learned later, that two of the men were Frame and Ward. When they left, instead of coming back down the canyon, the foursome and their train of burros went over the hill and down into Caballero Canyon, which led into Alamo Canyon a mile below where the pipeline crew was working.

Several months later, one of the Mexicans who had been with them joined the pipeline crew. When a dynamite blast injured him severely, and he believed he was dying, he revealed that Frame and Ward and he and his companion had removed eleven bars of silver from the cave. The Mexican recovered and returned to Sonora. Carroll soon checked out his story. "Those bars of silver were buried in a shallow hole just inside the opening of the cave," Carroll remembered. "Five were laid side by side, like fingers," the Mexican told Carroll, "and five on top of them at right angles to the first layer. The eleventh was placed on top. Each bar was about eighteen inches long and three or more thick. The prints in the clay were plainly visible, confirming the Mexican's story of the arrangement of them."[11]

Frame confirmed that Ward and his three workmen had found eleven bars of silver but said they were found in a small creek in the mountains. For Ward to legally hold his "mine," he had to file a claim, and he did so in 1920. Frame tells a convoluted tale of finding more chart stones, and using colors, either soil or stone, to proceed in various directions. They dug two shafts into the mountain, one outside the entrance of the cave, the other just inside, which Ward said was indicated on the chart stones. Ward created a virtual money pit at Indian Cave, working it during the summer months, then going back to work in the winter to build a grubstake for the next season.

In 1927 Frame said they had a steam shovel digging for a while. But most of their work was with hammer and chisel and dynamite. During their search, several Spanish artifacts were found, among them a silver stirrup and bridle bit. Ward made use of them to generate publicity. Interestingly, Carroll Wood contributed to that story, even though he never believed Ward or Frame had anything of value. "More Relics of the Conquistadores in the Sacramento Mountains," appeared on page one of the *Alamagordo News* on June 20, 1929:

> With regard to the ox wagon mentioned a few days ago, other interesting relics were shown in Alamagordo this week—a hand-forged Spanish stirrup and a silver bit of a very early design. We are informed that Matt Massey, an old pioneer and mining man, found these within 500 yards of each other in the Alamo section and near where

> Mr. G. E. Ward has done considerable Spanish research work. Carroll Woods found in the same vicinity a piece of plate steel beautifully carved, pronounced by an expert in such lore to have been of Spanish or Moorish origin. Mr. Woods also found the handle of an old sword of brass construction. (While he is familiar with every noke and cranny, he never ran across the ox wagon found by Brown and Taylor.) Mr. Woods found an old piece of carved plate in a hole he presumed to be an old mine; this was in 1920, and he planned to go back but never did.

Ward said he took the artifacts to a museum in Los Angeles to have them identified, and "the scientists know of no workmanship corresponding to the design on them," he reported. The Spanish artifacts, the chart stones which only Frame and his wife were ever allowed to view, ruins of *arrastras*—stone troughs for crushing the ore—convinced Ward and Frame they were on to something just as wondrous as the one that must have been missed at the Sembritzki farm early in the century. Ward found financial backers in California for his venture and followed a cavern that descended 138 feet into the mountain.

Carroll Wood was sure the eleven ingots of silver were found by Ward, but he never had any faith that anything else of value would be found there. Carroll believed the Indian pictographs in the cave were authentic. They included painted zigzag symbols on the walls and ceiling, and footprints on the floor. Wood said the symbols outside the cave had been made by himself and his brother. They amused themselves by cutting designs with their rock drills. Some of the holes they drilled were triangular-shaped.

"Mr. Ward came in with a map calling for different marks," Wood said. "It gave the location of the treasure he sought, and he used many of the carvings Bill and I had made and the three-corned drill holes to find the clues left by the Spaniards. He had them on his map! One at the mouth of the cave on a hunk of gad almighty hard limestone was about ten inches deep. It was the final mark he was seeking, and right there he began to taken down into that wholly undisturbed limestone seeking this buried Spanish treasure. He would find 'kidneys' of flint of different colors embedded in that limestone which he claimed to have been left by the early Spanish—black, white, yellow I saw. Invariably when he found one he would turn a different direction, making a corkscrew-shaped tunnel. It started at the rimrock and went down below the bottom of the canyon. It is true that they pumped air to the men working in it.

"One day I was standing on a rock and Mr. Ward was reading this so-called map. I looked over his shoulder and saw that the paper had a watermark. He and Jim Shultz got into some trouble, of which they were exonerated, and Ward left for California. Jim died here. Later Mr. O'Conner, of the Crystal Beverage Company, and his son took over the operation and continued to dig down into the limestone. They ran out of funds and quit. Then Arch Frame and a man named Burkheimer came back. I think it was just a scheme to fleece people. I never thought Mr. Ward's map authentic."[12]

Gurney Ward had devoted twenty-eight years to his treasure cave when he died on March 31, 1943. His obituary is short, considering his many years of effort:

> Friends have just received word of the death of Gurney E. Ward, Sr., who died March 31st. He is survived by a wife, a son, and a daughter in Los Angeles, California. Mr. Ward has been estranged from his wife for many years.
>
> He lived here 23 years and operated a commercial photograph studio for 23 years

> and until 1940. Ward was about 86 years of age. He was born in New York City and at one time a fine photographer. He came to Texas when in middle life. After he came to Alamagordo he became obsessed with the idea that there were valuable "Spanish treasures" cached in Alamo Canyon. He spent a small fortune. He produced enough evidence in relics of old cavalry equipment, etc., to convince many persons that he was warranted in his "Spanish Research Work." For the past several years he had been interested in mining over near Silver City.[13]

Archie Frame told Eve Ball that he and Ward had reached 138 feet in their "ever-spiraling corridor," when Ward became ill and "we got him home before he died of a heart attack." Frame said he bought Ward's interest from his widow. "I had to borrow to make a down payment to Mrs. Ward." Frame tried to connect Ward's treasure cave to the treasure pit on the Sembritzki farm, which he had first bought into in 1911. He told Ball that "of the men who worked there, not one knew of my experience at Clyde, but one of these men drew exactly the same symbols I had seen at Clyde." Frame did not explain his story, or explain which symbols were the same.

Archie Frame had given up his quest by the time he told his story to Ball. "A year or so after Mr. Frame's death, a man from Seattle came here looking for Mr. Frame, or seeking information about him," states Ball. "He told me that he had invested over $20,000 in the search for the buried treasure, and believed it to be still buried near the shaft into which they tunneled. I was always curious about the chart stone and wanted to see it. If he had it, which I doubt, he never offered to let me do so; and I never asked to see it. Mr. Frame was a fine honest person, but rather a mystic, and there were many things I aked that he could not explain."[14]

Cabe Terrell died in June 1970 at eighty-seven years of age. Sometime afterward, the papers and artifacts he had guarded for more than six decades were passed on to his younger brother Charles. The mystery of the Terrell drug store fire spawned speculation from the moment of its destruction. Family heartache, financial loss, and defeated dreams persuaded then twenty-six-year-old Cabe to put aside the quest for phantom gold.

No doubt certain papers and contracts drawn up among the participants were also destroyed. Tracings of the Spider Rock and its sister stone from the Sembritzki farm, along with a handful of letters and contracts, were not in the drug store vault, but among Cabe's personal papers. Otherwise, not even those would now exist. Because of Cabe's silence, rumors began and were told over the years that the drug store was set on fire to destroy the evidence once the vault was broken into and its contents stolen. No one ever knew just how the fire began, but Charles remembers there was a large quantity of paint supplies in the store, and it was always believed those caught fire.

It was a sad time in the lives of the Terrell family. Cabe moved his family to Snyder, then later to Post City, and in 1913 to Baird, where he had worked in 1905 while Arnold carried out his search at the Sembritzki farm. The next year he went to Corpus Christi, and then in 1920 to Waco, where Jones visited him, hoping to learn something about Arnold's search that he had not learned firsthand.

Cabe had known Jones for many years. When Cabe was seventeen in 1900, he had recuperated at Jones's farm on the Salt Fork after being stricken with scarlet fever. However, it is doubtful that Cabe told Jones that any of the artifacts survived the fire. If Jones knew, he never passed that knowledge on. Over the years, Cabe would occasionally bring the artifacts and map tracings out from hiding, spread them over the table, and ponder them—and perhaps the curse that seemingly always hovered over them.

How ironic it was that in another part of Waco the James Roberts family possessed a stone bearing many of the same markings and concentric circles as appeared on the Spider Rock and the stone from the Sembritzki farm. It is doubtful Cabe ever had knowledge of it. However, he may have known the Mexican sheepherder who carried the stone to Waco prior to 1914 and died at the county farm, whispering about a treasure to be found.

Cabe never saw the Spider Rock again after he moved from Haskell. It remained concealed at the Terrell home over the years until one day in 1916, when Dr. Terrell's widow, Frances Caroline, and her children moved to Tulsa, Oklahoma. Mrs. Terrell's son, Barnie, was seventeen that year and had a job waiting at Standard Oil, where Charles now worked in Tulsa. The Spider Rock carried few good memories for the Terrell family. Barnie was ten when his father died. Barnie took the two pieces of stone and buried them where they would haunt no one again. He died in 1936 without attempting to recover them.[15]

Charles was gone from Texas for thirty years and returned only after he retired. Occasionally when visiting Cabe, they would discuss the Spider Rock and Arnold's quest, and their father's belief that the Spanish treasure would soon be found. Had the drug store not burned, the doctor not died, and Arnold not vanished, how might have the West Texas quest ended?

As Charles sat in his living room reflecting about the search almost three-quarters of a century before, he excused himself, saying he wanted to retrieve something in his office. Up to that time he had said nothing about anything surviving the drug store fire, and like everyone, I had no idea that anything had. He returned after what seemed like ten or fifteen minutes carrying a small coffee can and white cardboard box.

The contents of the coffee can and cardboard box were all that remained from the turn-of-the-century quest. Cabe had kept them, along with the papers and letters. When he died, those items were given to Charles. His first thought, Charles said, was to throw them into the nearest river, but he decided against it because he knew the artifacts were historically important—too valuable to destroy, and too real to ignore. Yes, the memories they spawned were not good ones.

One by one he pulled the Spanish artifacts from the coffee can and cardboard box: first the small silver crucifix, then the copper key, dagger, and strange irregular plate that had reposed for a century or more atop the Spider Rock. As far as I knew, I was the first person outside the immediate family to be shown those tantalizing objects in almost seven decades—since they had been reported destroyed in the drug store fire in 1909. Then there was the elongated plate that had been found at the bluff on Jones's farm—something that no one now living had any knowledge about.

Terrell pulled out the two small rising and setting sunbursts cut from thin copper that Arnold had unearthed on the Sembritski farm, along with the three strangely shaped daggers and much larger copper plate called "the crown"—all clues the Sembritzki family long believed were lost. He pulled the ornately engraved silver epaulets from the coffee can, those items unearthed with the Spanish sword. When first found, gold tassels hung from the epaulets.[16] Now only a handful of burned, silvery tassels remained.

I looked over the yellowed and brittle drawings—one a tracing of the Spider Rock that Cabe had made himself. Yet another was of the stone map from the Sembritzki farm. Another tracing bore symbols I had never seen, but which an 1897 letter described. Still another drawing of the Spider diggings showed where the clues had all been found, verifying what had been told over the years.

Does Charles Terrell believe the Spider Rock treasure to be authentic? Yes, and his reason for believing so might surprise most people. It was really quite simple, he explained. Charles did not think Dave Arnold had the ingenuity to create such a tale with all the complexity of the Spider Rock. Arnold's knowledge and ability never impressed Charles, even as a kid. His last memory of Arnold was sitting in a chair on the sidewalk in front of the family drug store talking with his father. His family always believed his father would be successful in the search, and several times they thought the treasure would be found the next day.[17]

For most of this century, perhaps even longer, men have puzzled over the enigmatic Spider Rock—its meaning, its purpose, its complexity, its secrets. Dock Henderson pondered it longer than most men. Many explanations have been offered, some logical, and some fanciful. Many have long believed the Spider Rock story to be one of two things: a fantastic Spanish hoax or something totally incredible from Spanish colonial times. More have believed the latter.

When I first became intrigued with the Spider Rock over forty years ago, I did not realize then that it was the mystery that I came to uncover over the next two decades, piecing together the many threads of evidence. Many seekers have tossed in their sleep while theorizing about the Spider Rock. There are many unanswered questions about Arnold,

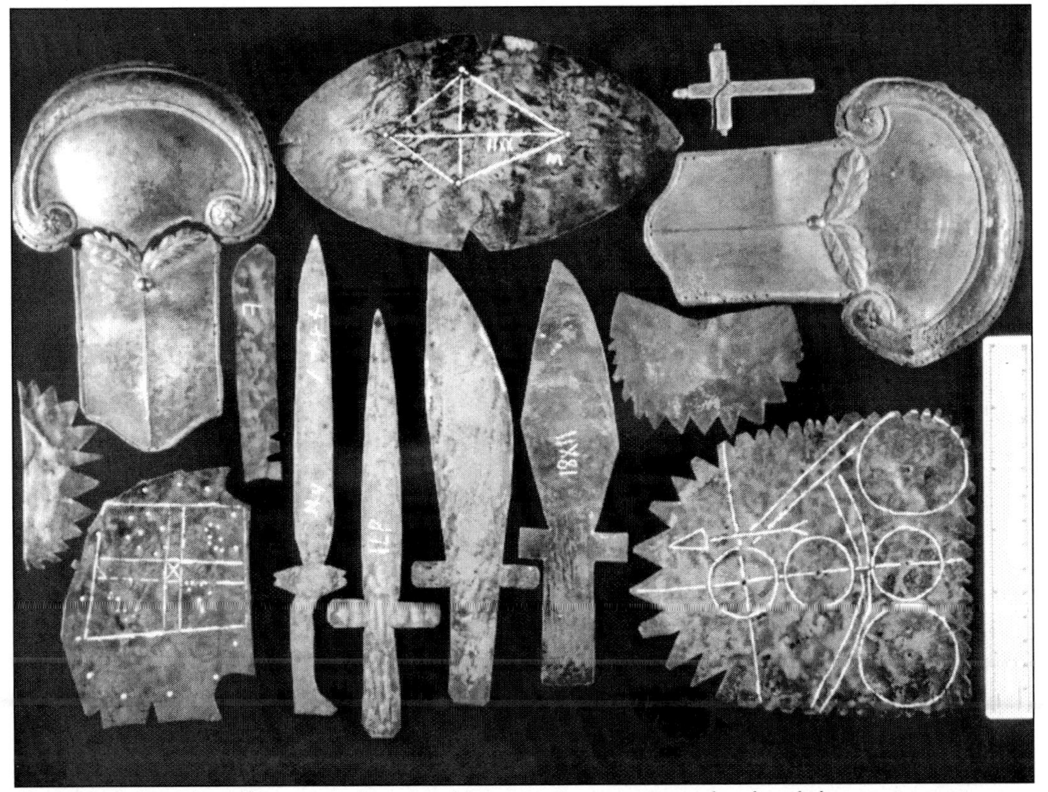

The various Spanish artifacts made from hand-hammered copper, some bearing their own strange tracery, along with the silver epaulets and crucifix found on the Salt Fork of the Brazos, and sixty miles away on the Sembritzki farm, are pondered today as much as they were when found a century ago. (Photo by the author)

his sojourn in Mexico, the sheepskin map he always carried, the conflicting stories he told, what he failed to tell, and even his own ultimate disappearance. With all three of the stones he is known to have found, Arnold actually divulged little of their story.

Strangely, none of the original hunters ever knew just what they were seeking, just as no one knew who had put it there, when, or why. Perhaps Arnold knew none of those answers. He obviously lacked the keys or knowledge to fully understand the complexity of his own search, or did a magnificent job of misleading everyone.

When I first reported Dock Henderson's story of his quest, many readers wrote offering ideas and possible ways of deciphering and reading the stone maps. More importantly, however, long-missing clues began to turn up—a story here, an artifact there, someone who had known Arnold, someone who had worked for him, even the third stone map found on Gyp Creek that had miraculously served as a doorstop for more than sixty years. A last-ditch effort to find a clue, an answer, or a detail resulted in the discovery of the copper daggers, symbolic figures, silver epaulets, crucifix, and letters and documents all long reported to have been destroyed.

The final chapter to this story cannot yet be written. The Spider Rock has not yet been deciphered. Its cryptic symbols remain unread, as do those of the other stone maps and copper plates and daggers. Many have attempted a translation, but none has yet succeeded. Where does the answer lie to that Spanish cryptopuzzle? Perhaps in the stars? Seventeenth- and eighteenth-century explorers navigated by the stars. Latitude determination depended on the North Star, and longitude by measuring from one place to another east or west. Astronomy was part of cartography. Mapmaking went hand in hand with celestial navigation. By the late 1600s, topographical surveying came into being. By the eighteenth century, a box compass with an alidade for measuring degrees was available.[18]

Such instruments would have been necessary in creating the Spider Rock and its sister stones. Why else the symbols, the numerals, the mixture of Roman and Arabic numbers, the angles, if not for degrees, distances, and landmarks? All would have been known to the educated eighteenth-century mind. Symbols of ancient astronomy, cartography, surveying, and mining must all interplay. Links or *varas*, leagues, or degrees must all be relevant to the symbol-ridden stones.

It appears that Arnold's sheepskin led him to the stone maps, but finding those stones was necessary to continuing the trail. How else but by degrees, distances, and landmarks could he have found the Spider Rock, then almost sixty miles southeastward, found the stone near Clyde, then sixty miles west-northwestward found the stone near Rotan? Interesting that the connecting lines from those three sites form an acute triangle created by the mind of a mapmaker who surely had a well-conceived, well-executed plan.

But what plan? Certainly nothing less than one worthy of the complex cartography, cryptic symbols, and tantalizing clues that all make up the story of the Spider Rock. What stories did the Spaniards intend to leave? Why would they have gone to such painstaking efforts? These are questions that remain unanswered. That is not to say they will never be answered. But beware, oh hunter. Do not forget that men have lost their fortunes, their wives, and their possessions. At least one has been murdered for his secrets!

Even today men dig blindly, ripping into the Spider Rock hill or some other location with bulldozers in a helter-skelter fashion, without rhyme or reason. The treasure, if there yet be one, will never be found by accident or chance. Everything Arnold found was with the aid of a map, a chart of which no copy is known to exist. Better than anyone, he could interpret the signs and follow them. He left over much of West Texas a trail that is now only a memory among many oldsters who remember him from their youth, or from stories others told about him.

What became of Arnold? Was he the victim of the curse he pursued? We know he did not find *all* that he believed was to be found, just as we do not know *all* that he found. We know that after Arnold's first wife died and he remarried, his three surviving children had little or no contact with him. The Johnson families of Munday last remember seeing him in 1914.

Duane Hale scans the vast, forbidding country from atop Kiowa Peak, the center of Spanish treasure quests for more than a century. (Photo by the author)

When Arnold's wife Martha died on March 9, 1906, she was fifty-six. The couple had been married for forty years. She was a Georgian by birth. They married when she was sixteen and he twenty, the year after the Civil War, perhaps in his native state of Missouri. Martha purchased their 320-acre farm on the North Concho River near Water Valley from Martin and Ella Davis of Hamilton County in September 1897. Two years later, Arnold and his wife made an agreement with Mrs. Susan Williams, a widow, who leased and owned land directly to their east. An irrigation ditch ran across all the farms adjacent to that part of the river, and in exchange for the right of way, Mrs. Williams granted them limited use of the ditch.[19]

Court records show that in December 1905, Martha Arnold sold a small tract of land to J. S. Robison, the father-in-law of her daughter, Maude. In September 1906, D. F. and Maude Robison sold land on Adams Creek, a tributary of the Concho River, to P. H. Gallagher. Arnold's son, Nathan, sold his interest in the farm to his sister Minnie Lee Motley in November 1906. Then on January 11, 1907, Dave Arnold, Minnie Lee, and her husband, Benjamin Reese Motley, sold 312 and 12/25 acres of the farm to Arnold's son-in-law, D. F. Robison, and his father, J. S. Robison. The sale did not include the acre of land donated for the Water Valley Cemetery, or the small tract sold to J. S. Robison.[20]

The following day, on January 12, Benjamin and Minnie Motley and D. F. and Maude Robison sold the remaining 6 and 13/25 acres to J. S. Robinson. Two days later, Dave

Arnold signed an affidavit stating that he was the husband of Mrs. M. A. Arnold, that she died at Water Valley on March 18, 1906, and left two surviving daughters, Minnie Motley and Maude Robison, and one son, N. B. Arnold, and they were the only heirs. Strangely, Arnold was wrong about the date of his wife's death; in fact, it was March 9. Nathan Arnold gave his sister Minnie Motley a release on April 21, 1908, that he had received "complete and final payment" due him from his inheritance.[21]

It's not known when D. F. and Maude Robison left Water Valley, but by August 1912 they were living in Hillsboro County, Florida. That month they were paid by the Concho, San Saba, and Llano Valley Railroad Company to build across their land. Two years later, the Robisons were living in Pinella County, Florida, when they sold P. H. Gallagher 640 acres, in September 1914. Finally, the Robisons sold the remainder of their interest in a town lot in Water Valley in July 1923.[22]

The Water Valley cemetery today holds but one member of Arnold's family, his first wife, Martha. In a lonely fenced gravesite, the marble tombstone with a fading inscription reads simply: "M. A. / Wife of D. M. Arnold / Born August 26, 1849 / Died March 9, 1906."

No record has been found showing when Arnold married Susan, although on one last visit to the Sembritzki farm in late 1906 or early 1907, he told the family he had remarried. Where he and Susan may have gone when they vanished perhaps will never be known. The death records of Texas, New Mexico, Kansas, and Oklahoma do not list him. His name does not appear on either the 1910 or 1920 U.S. Census.[23] By 1914 Arnold was nearing seventy. Where he spent his final days is but another mystery he must have wanted to keep.

Minnie Lee Arnold Motley died February 25, 1939, in Eastland, Texas, at age sixty-four. Her brother, Nathan B. Arnold, died March 27, 1947, in Abilene at age sixty-nine.[24] If either knew what had become of their father, that information was not passed on to family members. Minnie's daughter was born in San Angelo in 1906, a few weeks after her grandmother died. She recalled virtually nothing ever being said about her grandfather. Her son recalls only one incident relating to his great-grandfather. One day when he was ten or eleven years old, in 1935 or 1936, he was at his grandmother's home in Eastland. Two strangers had picked up the trail of Dave Arnold and traced it to his daughter Minnie.

Visiting his grandmother that day, the grandson recalls her selling an old map to the two men, a map that she had kept in a trunk where it had been stored since the family lived in San Angelo. There was talk of many Spanish artifacts being found with the map, but no gold. The men had found the shafts Arnold had dug years before near Clyde. The map was all Minnie still had from her father's wanderings.[25] Because the map pertained to the site on the Sembritzki farm, it was probably a tracing of the stone map Arnold had unearthed there in early 1905. The two strangers might well have been Joe Woods and Joe Cauble, who were digging at the Sembritzki farm during that time.

No one knew what became of Arnold and the sheepskin map he guarded with his life. It stands to reason that when he died, his wife inherited it. But no one has ever found a trace of his second wife.[26] The legend that Arnold was later murdered in Kansas remains the only clue to his disappearance. However, the evidence may be stronger for the belief that Arnold and his wife simply lived out their days in California.

Various participants in the quest have noted when they last saw Arnold. Two participants of recent years, father-and-son team James and Larry Armour of Wolfforth, Texas, offer yet another fascinating story. Bud Jones and his father Albert lived in a dugout about a mile north of the Salt Fork, across the river from the Spider diggings and almost due east of the stone ruins that Jones, and perhaps Arnold himself, believed to have been the Spanish mission. Of course, Arnold had found a copper plate not far from the Jones place, and he no doubt saw the various symbols carved nearby that Dock Henderson also later found, even though Dock knew nothing about the discovery of the plate.

In 1916 Albert Jones sold his farm to Skinner Pittock, who moved there from New Mexico. Pittock told Armour that Arnold first came to his ranch that year, driving a Model T Ford with California license plates.[27] Arnold wanted to look around and offered to pay them for his meals if he could stay with them. Pittock let him stay in an old shed behind the house and eat with them, but he never paid for his meals, Pittock remembered. The Pittocks raised mules, and while they would be out hunting for their animals, they would come across Arnold's Model T. Always he would be seen between the old mission ruins and Kiowa Peak.

The Pittocks never knew him to go over to the south side of the Salt Fork, where he had found the Spider Rock. He'd stay for a couple of weeks, then leave. Pittock remembered that Arnold returned every year through 1924, then came no more. It is ironic to think that the last season he came, Bud Jones, Dock Henderson, and others might well have been across the river at the old diggings, where that year Jones tried to recall everything Arnold had found and said, perhaps two decades before. If the year was correct, Arnold would have been seventy-nine by then.[28]

It is not difficult to understand how the mystery has enraptured so many of its seekers, causing them to grasp blindly through its web of entanglement. Many wild and illogical theories have sprung forth. Among those theories are underground tunnels, rooms with trap doors, deadly gases, and a host of intangibles.

Unfortunately, there were no historians or archaeologists to guide that incredible search as it occurred, to measure, to restore, to preserve all the clues, artifacts, and symbols—and perhaps even the treasure of a former people from a forgotten time. There may yet be those who bear clues to the mystery, who harbor missing artifacts found during Arnold's quest. Someone may still possess the silver statuettes, crosses, and arrows found thirty years later. Perhaps someone today guards the sheepskin map that led Arnold over that trail. Perhaps even more stone maps will come to light.

Allen J. McDaniel Jr., of Abilene, who has studied the Spider Rock and its sister stones, believes that "there have been at least eight Spider Rocks," or stone maps, which Arnold found. "To set a standard, the carved rock must have the compass circles and the directional lines," McDaniel believes. "Of course, the CXF, the F, the DLN, and other marks can help. The Rotan Spider Rock has traveled many miles in my car. It has been on my office desk for many hours, and beside my bed at night. I identifed a different Spider Rock about two years ago, another about a year ago, and already have one for this year. This last one should fit in a box about two inches deep, eight inches wide, and twenty-one inches long. It is dated, has the circles and the CXF, and more information."[29]

McDaniel states that he saw his "first Spider Rock gold about 1950, when my brother, Hal McDaniel, and Dr. Cyrus N. Ray brought it in." McDaniel believes the Mexican sheepherder was right and Arnold was wrong about the date on the stone found on the Sembritzki farm, believing that date to be just as the Mexican scrawled on the brown paper sack late one night. "Dave Arnold was wrong about the date. That Spaniard made part of his 6 small, then curled the tail around to make it look like a backward 3. That date is 1671."

McDaniel has other theories about the various artifacts, charcoal, and strange discoveries at the Sembritzki farm. "Dave Arnold was looking for a buried city, with rooms filled with gold. He went directly to the place following the old Mexican's map and instructions." But we know Arnold was successful only to a point. McDaniel believes Arnold misconstrued what the Mexican told him. "The Spaniards had trouble with the Indians, so for defense, they dug something on the order of an underground cavern. We take the Spanish word *defensa* and add *subterrania* and even *cueva* for 'cave.' We figure what the Mexican tried to tell him. Then we get *Appleton's New Spanish Dictionary*, 1940 edition, and look up the English word *dugout*. We find '*defensa subterania cueva.*'"

McDaniel interprets all the evidence Arnold's workmen found as indicating a fortified area, or a stockade, and the abundance of charcoal found there indicated "it could have been torched by departing Spaniards or vengeful Indians." Blue glass beads were plentiful, showing past trading activities, and McDaniel believes all the copper artifacts and trimmings were found by happenstance. And then there was the discovery of the perfectly arched doorway of yellow clay, about two feet wide and five feet high, "as smooth as glass," remembered Verne Sems.

McDaniel is sure the "ceramic doorway" was in fact a Spanish bathtub that had fallen upright into a dugout or underground fortification, accounting for its depth of five or more feet, and filled with pure white sand. Arnold interpreted it as a secret doorway, "smashed into it to go to the buried city, and found nothing." Unfortunately, McDaniel concluded, "those crazy treasure hunters destroyed much in their search," probably discarding all kinds of things of no value to them. "I enjoy solving puzzles," McDaniel explained, "and that is probably one of the biggest in the country."

Such a theory may in part be corrrect. Certainly, other Spanish artifacts found in the region in later years would indicate considerable activity. But if the stone map Arnold found at the Sembritzki farm explains the Spanish fortification at that site, what do the other stone maps indicate? Only time will tell if more clues will come to light, but time has a way of corrupting the facts and dimming memories. A change of hands and time erased much of the story of the third stone map Arnold found on Gyp Creek, probably discovered sometime after the drug store fire.

Of all the possibilities offered over the years for deciphering the Spider Rock and its sister stones, one idea presented by a civil engineer always appeared the most logically sound and applicable. Others have expressed similar theories, thinking much like a surveyor-engineer-mathematician of the 1700s might have. His belief is so fascinating, it warrants quoting in part:

> I do not believe that this particular map will offer any really insurmountable problem, but it is going to take one hell of a lot of trigonometry and logarithms. The trouble being that this mapmaker shifts back and forth in his use of numerals, etc. Thus one figure might be a logarithm, while another a function of an angle, and still another an antilog, etc.
>
> By assuming that one azimuth is a log, or I should say a mantissa, and assuming further that it is a measurement of distance along that particular azimuth, and converting it into kilometers, the total azimuth ends in the approximate area of the ... if I orient the map in two ways, and in the third orientation of the map the distance ends in the near vicinity of the ... I have obtained two triangles, using assumed azimuths (congruent triangles) that include approximately the ... in one, and approximately

the . . . in the other. Of course, these cannot be pinned down to anything more than gross approximations at this time.

From the apparent exactitude in which the Spider Rock is drawn, and the figures detailed, I am confident that the mapmaker used a transit, or else a good compass for surveying. This presents us with a further problem in allowing for the error in his instrument as well as the magnetic declination of the area. By making these allowances, what we will undoubtedly end up with is a very close approximation of the area in which something will be found. From this, we will have to narrow it down further by manual and electronic exploration in very great detail.

The science of engineering and surveying was well advanced in those days, and today we still use basically the same math, etc., as they did. Thus, I believe that whoever drew up the maps was essentially either an engineer or a surveyor. By use of algebra, trigonometry, logarithms, and geometry, some of the "mysterious symbols" translate out into something that is more than coincidence. The only difficulty will be in determining just when he is shifting from, say the mantissa of an ungiven number to that number itself, from algebra to trig, etc.

What will be necessary is to take each individual fact of the many he has given us and to apply all the operations possible to that particular fact, and then to plot them on the topographical maps using acetate or onion skin overlays. This might require several thousand indiviudal computations and plottings. Of the various alternatives that we get, we must then select the most acceptable ones and proceed on that basis.

The mapmaker is definitely making use of logarithms and trigonometery (heavy use) and is working by triangulation, azimuths, angles, and distances in his computations. All we have to do is to decide which, which is primarily a matter of patience and mechancis of problem solutions, not to mention a lot of research into the probable background of such a man as he might have been in those days.

I believe that only by plotting all the logical interpretations (mathematical interpretations) on a topographical map, and then systematically searching those locations, will the treasure be located. I think the Spider Rock map is the key map, and that anything else is merely reference material which supports the map, but which is not necessarily a part of that map. Some of the additional maps, I believe, are not necessarily even related to the Spider Rock map, and an effort to tie them into the Spider map would be to cast additional mystery which would result in what has apparently occurred—that is, everyone is so busy trying to tie everything together into one neat package with a sudden, inspirational, location of the treasure that they are making it impossible to comprehend anything intelligible from the map. I feel quite certain that this is not an uncipherable map, but is capable of solution once the facts have been gathered, analyzed, interpreted, and plotted.

To attempt to ferret out the meaning of each and every one of the symbols on the map would be to chase yourself around for centuries, and this is apparently just what has been happening. It seems inconceivable to me that a party returning at a later date, under possibly adverse conditions, would be expected to run around the countryside, digging up all sorts of clues, etc. This would not only take a lot of time, but would surely reveal the presence of the recovery party to any hostile Indians, Texans, or whoever might be around. A quick, unnoticed recovery would be, militarily, the only one to make sense.[30]

Computing the numbers. Plotting the azimuths. Finding the distance and azimuth relationships. Comparing those relationships with the known discovery sites at the various distances and degrees from where the Spider Rock was found. That is the scientific method, surely the method applied by the ingenious creator of the stone maps, who must have been well versed in the ancient arts. Therein lies the final chapter to the Spider Rock story, the mystery of a road map carved into stone centuries ago by persons unknown. Perhaps someday, somewhere, yellowed Spanish documents will come to light, telling about the bizarre stone maps buried on the banks of Los Brazos de Dios, revealing who, when, why—and what.

The complete story of the Spanish mystery entangled in its web of perplexing clues, an incredible network of cryptographic diagrams and symbols carved into stone, hidden almost as if to preserve them through the ages—yet obviously meant to be read and followed—perhaps one day will be told. Whoever the mystery Spaniards were, whatever they buried for whatever purpose, they devised a system that no one yet has fully understood. What is known is that those travelers of a forgotten time were ingenious in creating maps to guide them back to something which warranted an incredible mastery of signs and symbols.[31]

It is with those thoughts in mind that this story has been written. But remember, oh hunter, those who have been trapped in the spider's web. For the one who is willing to risk that entrapment, the mystery lies beckoning, daring its secrets to be revealed. Only when they come to light can the final chapter be written to the Spider Rock mystery.[32]

Notes

Chapter 1. The Mysterious Dave Arnold and His Sheepskin Map

1. Verne Sems, who first met Dave Arnold in 1905, provided the best descriptions of him and his activities to the author in a long correspondence that began on June 7, 1965. In addition, Charles Terrell met him in 1902 and recalled those meetings in interviews on May 31 and December 28, 1976. Finally, Dock Henderson, who was drawn into the quest in 1924 when a young man, worked with many who had known and observed Arnold. The author's correspondence and interviews with Henderson began on August 7, 1960, and continued over the next twenty-five years.

2. U.S. Population Census, 1900, Tom Green County, Texas. David M. Arnold, Record Group 29, vol. 101, p. 2A, National Archives, Washington, D.C.; D. F. Robinson and M. M. [Mary Maude] Arnold, January 14, 1900, Marriage Record, vol. C, p. 323; and Benjamin R. Motley and Minnie Arnold, June 1, 1902, Marriage Record, vol. C, p. 401, County Clerk, Tom Green County, San Angelo, Texas. Although recorded as Robinson, the name was actually Robison.

3. Deed Record, September 2, 1897, vol. 15, p. 207, County Clerk, Tom Green County, San Angelo, Texas. Dave Arnold is not listed in the 1880 Texas census. A check of the Hamilton County, Texas, deed records between 1866 and 1917 shows he never owned land in that county. On the other hand, Arnold purchased his land from longtime residents Martin S. and Ella C. Davis, who obtained their first 160 acres in November 1876, reared five sons and a daughter, and bought and sold land for many years to come. For a record of Davis's land transactions, see Deed Record, vol. G, p. 304; vol. U, p. 117; vol. Q, p. 549; vol. P, pp. 497-98, 576; vol. 25, p. 546; vol. 33, p. 388; vol. 35, p. 181; vol. 36, p. 438; vol. 52, p. 206; vol. 53, p. 543; vol. 55, p. 326; vol. 58, pp. 295-97; vol. 59, p. 268; vol. 60, pp. 9 and 167; and vol. 63, pp. 278-80, County Clerk, Hamilton County, Hamilton, Texas.

4. Charles E. Terrell, interview by author, Eastland, Texas, May 31 and December 28, 1976; and Terrell, letter to author, June 18 and August 30, 1976.

5. Miguel Anhubta to M. Dillon, March 7, 1897, Charles E. Terrell personal collection.

6. Charles E. Terrell, interview by author, May 31 and December 28, 1976.

7. See the *Haskell Free Press* of April 25, November 21, 1903; October 29, 1904; January 25, 1907; and January 11, July 18, and October 10, 1908.

8. J. K. "Kelly" Johnson, a participant in Arnold's quest for the Spider Rock, recalled that search in a story by Jim Koethe, "Lost Diamond Mine Object of Intense Treasure Hunt," *Wichita Falls Record News,* December 6, 1956, p. 2B. Other stories reviving interest in the legend were Jim Koethe, "Brazos Area Waste Land is Searched for Lost Gold," ibid., October 11, 1956, p. 5A; and Lon Pate, "Legendary 'Spider Rock' Treasure Story is Revived in Haskell County," ibid., October 24, 1956, p. 1.

9. Herbert Eugene Bolton, ed., *Spanish Exploration in the Southwest, 1542-1706* (1908; reprint, New York: Barnes & Noble, 1959), p. 313; Herbert E. Bolton, "The Jumano Indians in Texas, 1650-1771," *Texas Historical Association Quarterly* 15 (July 1911), pp. 66-74; Herbert E. Bolton, "The Spanish Occupation of Texas, 1519-1690," *Southwestern Historical Quarterly* 16 (July 1912), pp. 8-10, 19-24; Carlos E. Castañeda, *Our Catholic Heritage in Texas, 1519-1936,* vol. I (Austin: Von Boeckmann-Jones Co., 1936), pp. 200-204; George P. Hammond, ed., *Fray Alonso de Benavides' Revised Memorial of 1634,* vol. IV (Albuquerque: University of New Mexico Press, 1945), pp. 92, 94, 312-13, 315, 318; and Charles Wilson Hackett, trans. and ed., *Pichardo's Treatise on the Limits of Louisiana and Texas,* vol. II (Austin: University of Texas Press, 1934), pp. 327, 358-62.

10. Bolton, *Spanish Exploration in the Southwest,* pp. 314-15; Bolton, "The Jumano Indians in Texas," pp. 68-

74; Bolton, "The Spanish Occupation of Texas," pp. 9-11, 20-24; Castannda, *Our Catholic Heritage in Texas,* vol. I, pp. 204-7; Hammond, *Fray Alonso de Benavides,* p. 312; and Hackett, *Pichardo's Treatise,* pp. 143, 361-62, 368.

11. Castañeda, *Our Catholic Heritage in Texas,* vol. VIII, p. 255.

12. For the story of Colonel Parrilla's battle at Spanish Fort, see Henry Easton Allen, "The Parrilla Expedition to the Red River in 1759," *Southwestern Historical Quarterly* 43 (July 1939), pp. 53-71; Castañeda, *Our Catholic Heritage in Texas,* vol. IV, pp. 125-32; Robert S. Weddle, *The San Sabá Mission: Spanish Pivot in Texas* (Austin: University of Texas Press, 1964), pp. 118-43; and Steve Wilson, "The Secrets Spanish Fort Tells," in *Oklahoma Treasures and Treasure Tales* (Norman: University of Oklahoma Press, 1976), pp. 39-67.

13. Herbert Eugene Bolton, trans. and ed., *Athanase de Mézières and the Louisiana-Texas Frontier, 1768-1780,* vol. I (Cleveland: Arthur H. Clark Co., 1914), pp. 294, 296.

14. Ibid., vol. I, p. 104, and vol. II, p. 38.

15. Elizabeth A. H. John, *Storms Brewed in Other Men's Worlds: The Confrontation of Indians, Spanish, and French in the Southwest, 1540-1795* (College Station: Texas A&M University Press, 1975), p. 650; and Adán Benavides, Jr., comp. and ed., *The Béxar Archives (1717-1836): A Name Guide* (Austin: University of Texas Press and San Antonio: University of Texas Institute of Texas Cultures, 1989), pp. 122 and 1066.

16. John, *Storms Brewed in Other Men's Worlds,* p. 655.

17. Ibid., pp. 657-58; see also Noel M. Loomis and Abraham P. Nasatir, *Pedro Vial and the Roads to Santa Fe* (Norman: University of Oklahoma Press, 1967), pp. 262-368; Castañeda, *Our Catholic Heritage in Texas,* vol. III, pp. 150-70; and Herbert Eugene Bolton, *Texas in the Middle Eighteenth Century* (Berkeley: University of California Press, 1915), pp. 129-32.

18. Loomis and Nasatir, *Pedro Vial,* pp. 171, 265-67, 285-87, 297, 315, 351, 388; and Castañeda, *Our Catholic Heritage in Texas,* III, pp. 155-57, 164.

19. John, *Storms Brewed in Other Men's Worlds,* pp. 746-47; Texas State Archives Ms., labled as Hawkins, "The Adventures in Texas and Louisiana of Alexander Dupont"; Benavides, *The Béxar Archives,* pp. 278, 734; and Shelly Morrison, ed., *Alexander Dupont: Adventures in Spanish Texas* (Austin: W. M. Morrison Books, 1985), 29 pp.

20. Roderick B. Patten, trans. and ed., "Miranda's Inspection of Los Almagres: His Journal, Report, and Petition," *Southwestern Historical Quarterly* 74 (October 1970), pp. 223-54.

21. John, *Storms Brewed in Other Men's Worlds,* pp. 746-47; and Patten, "Miranda's Inspection of Los Almagares: His Journal, Report, and Petition," pp. 233-34.

22. Benavides, *The Béxar Archives,* p. 278. Dupont obviously spent considerable time among the Taovayas (Wichitas) and Comanches in the Red River country. One wonders if his interest in mines in the "Taovayas Mountains" might have been the Wichita Mountains forty miles north of Red River in southwestern Oklahoma, an area not that far north of the Spider Rock country and that has also spawned more than its fair share of legends of lost Spanish treasure. See the author's "Ghosts of Devil's Canyon and Their Gold" in *Oklahoma Treasures and Treasure Tales* (Norman: University of Oklahoma Press, 1976), pp. 111-28.

23. Loomis and Nasatir, *Pedro Vial,* pp. 459-534.

24. Ibid., p. 492.

25 Ibid., pp. 508-9. Loomis states the league was 2.6 miles, p. 294.

26. Assistant state geologist for Texas, W. F. Cummins, stated that "as indicated by the meridian, the crossing of the latitude—lines of latitude or longitude—the mine would be in Young county." However, the distance south of Red River as shown by the map placed it in Wilbarger County. See *The United States, Complainant, v. The State of Texas in Equity,* vol. II (Washington, D.C.: Judd & Detweiler, 1894), pp. 977-78. Interestingly, historic copper mines have been found in both regions. When a shaft was dug on Gold Mountain at Graham in 1891, the *Leader* reported on October 7 that the rusted tools of previous miners were found, left there "probably over a hundred years ago." See Carrie J. Crouch, *A History of Young County, Texas* (Austin: Texas State Historical Association, 1956), p. 158.

27. See "Jacob Snively" and "Snively Expedition" in *The New Handbook of Texas,* vol. V (Austin: Texas State Historical Association, 1996), pp. 1126-28; and Stephen B. Oates, *Visions of Glory: Texans on the Southwestern Frontier* (Norman: University of Oklahoma Press, 1970), pp. 3-24.

28. E. W. Winkler, *Manuscript Letters and Documents of Early Texians, 1821-1845* (Austin: Steck Co., 1937), p. 277; and Jacob Snively to James H. Starr, James Harper Starr Papers, Center for American History, University of Texas, Austin.

29. Other early frontiersmen also came across the mysterious copper mine on the Brazos. "Mr. Johnson, who was for some time engaged as a trader with the Comanches, informed Judge Burnet while in the Comanche country about fifteen years ago [1828], that he had visited a very vauable copper mine on the Brazos about 150 miles above the mouth of the Bosque," stated the *Telegraph and Texas Register,* October 18, 1843. "Mr. Reynolds, who aided the Hon. Wm. Wharton in effecting his escape from Matamoras, informed us that he discovered several copper mines while trapping on the Brazos about the Salt Lake."

30. Snively to Starr, James Harper Starr Papers, Center for American History, University of Texas, Austin.

31. "Ruins on the Leona."

32. Snively to Starr, James Harper Starr Papers, Center for American History, University of Texas, Austin.

33. Ibid.

34. Jake Snively returned to Texas in late 1866 for yet another lost mine expedition. For that adventure, see the author's "Colonel Snively's Lost Ledge of Gold," *True Frontier* (September 1968), pp. 14-17, 50-53; "Indians and Treasure Don't Mix," *Frontier Times* (December-January 1974), pp. 8-13, 40-41; "In Search of the Lost Ledge of Gold," *Texas Highways* (January 1982), pp. 28-33; and "Colonel Snively's Lost Ledge of Gold," *Great Plains Journal* 24-25 (1985-86), pp. 2-20.

35. Carl Coke Rister, *Land Hunger: David L. Payne and the Oklahoma Boomers* (Norman: University of Oklahoma Press, 1942), p. 140.

36. Henry Ray, interview by author, Vernon, Texas, June 1963. For other Spanish artifacts found to the northwest in the Texas Panhandle, see the author's *Oklahoma Treasures and Treasure Tales* (Norman: University of Oklahoma Press, 1976), pp. 106-9.

37. R. E. Sherrill of Haskell recorded many of the early details of Arnold's quest in his "Lost Copper Mines and Spanish Gold, Haskell County," in *Legends of Texas* (1924; reprint, Hatboro, Penn.: Folklore Associates, 1964), pp. 72-77. Strangely, Sherrill had forgotten Arnold's name, perhaps indicative of the impression he made if one did not know him. J. Frank Dobie added to the chronicle in his *Coronado's Children: Tales of Lost Mines and Buried Treasures of the Southwest* (New York: Grosset & Dunlap, 1930), pp. 280-84.

38. Charles Terrell, interview by author, May 31 and December 28, 1976; and Charles Terrell, letter to author, June 18 and August 30, 1976.

39. Dr. C. L. Terrell to Saul Rodriguese, October 19, 1902, Charles Terrell collection.

40. R. H. McKee to G. W. Matthews, November 10, November 16, and December 3, 1902, Charles Terrell collection.

41. Dock Henderson, letter to author, August 7, October 25, 1960, July 28, 1962, June 30, August 18, December 19, 1963; Dock Henderson, interview by author, Rule, Texas, July 1963, and numerous occasions over the following years; Edwin K. Johnson, interview by author, Munday, Texas, October 3, 1976, and April 24, 1977; Ed and Mary Johnson, interview by author, Munday, Texas, April 24, 1977; and Jim Koethe, "Lost Diamond Mine Object of Intense Treasure Hunt," *Wichita Falls Record News,* December 6, 1956, p. 2B.

42. Dock Henderson, interview by author, July 1963; Rhoda Allen Epply, interview by author, Haskell, Texas, August 1960 and December 1969; and Bertha Allen Worley, interview by author, Haskell, Texas, August 1960.

43. Mrs. R. D. Gray, *Early Days in Knox County* (New York: Carlton Press, 1963), pp. 14-15.

44. Sherrill, "Lost Copper Mines and Spanish Gold," pp. 72-77; and Dobie, *Coronado's Children,* pp. 280-84.

Chapter 2. The Spider Rock and Its Ingenious Clues

1. Reconstructing the discovery of the Spider Rock has been possible only with the knowledge and memory of Dock Henderson, who knew many of the original participants and was drawn into the search in 1924. The author first visited the old diggings with Henderson in July 1963 and reported the story in "Four Decades of Searching Yields Clues, Little Treasure," *Wichita Falls Times Features Magazine,* July 28, 1963, pp. 12-13. This was enlarged to "Mystery of the Spider Rock Treasure," *True West* (May-June 1964), pp. 20-22, 56-57; and "Strange Maps to the Spider Rock Treasure," *Argosy* (May 1965), pp. 40-43, 114-18. Many subsequent trips followed over the years.

Other articles on the region by the author are: "Inca Treasure Believed Buried in Stonewall County on Brazos," *Wichita Falls Times Features Magazine,* August 18, 1963, p. 4; "Two Maps May Hold Key to 'Spider Rock' Gold," *Wichita Falls Times Features Magazine,* October 13, 1963, p. 12; "Spider Rock—Will O' the Wisp of Treasure Hunters," *True West* (July-August 1965), pp. 30-31; "Missing Spanish Treasure Near Double Mountain," *True Treasure* (March-April 1972), pp. 34-38, 43; "Endless Quest for the Spider Rock Treasure," parts 1-2, *True Treasure* (July-August 1972), pp. 38-42, 47; and *Treasure World* (August-September 1972), pp. 40-42, 47, 50-52.

2. While stories over the years differed as to the symbols etched into the copper artifacts, as well as one's relationship to the other, there is no present doubt about the etchings as clearly seen on the various pieces.

3. Some of the early details of the hunt are preserved in Sherrill, "Lost Copper Mines and Spanish Gold," pp. 72-77. Owner of the hardware store in Haskell, Sherrill personally knew the Terrell family.

4. Ibid.; and Dobie, *Coronado's Children*, pp. 280-84.

5. Dock Henderson found prehistoric mammoth bones and tusks in the area and knew of still others to be found. In 1965 he showed one such discovery to the author.

6. Many witnessed the artifacts as they were found. Unfortunately, no inventory was made of them, and no diagram or map exists of each artifact as it was found, as would be the case in a modern archaeological excavation. For a possible identification of the cavalry saber, see Sidney B. Brinckerhoff and Pierce A. Chamberlain, *Spanish Military Weapons in Colonial America, 1700-1821* (Harrisburg, Pa.: Stackpole Books, 1972), pp. 90-95, showing various cavalry and dragoon blades.

7. The copper plate would remain with Dr. Terrell and was virtually forgotten. Its discovery might have been completely forgotten except for a fragile envelope among the doctor's papers with an undated, typed message telling just where the plate was found, and a rough drawing showing its discovery in relation to the Spider Rock and other discoveries. Charles Terrell collection.

8. Jim Koethe, "Lost Diamond Mine Object of Intense Treasure Hunt," *Wichita Falls Record News*, December 6, 1956, p. 2B; and Edwin K. Johnson, interview by author, Munday, Texas, October 3, 1976, and April 24, 1977.

9. Bertha Allen Worley, interview by author, Haskell, Texas, August 1960.

10. Rhoda Allen Epply, interview by author, Haskell, Texas, August 1960, and December 1969. The Allen sisters directed the author to Dock Henderson in 1960.

11. Edwin K. Johnson, interview by author, Munday, Texas, October 3, 1976, and April 24, 1977.

12. The part Bud Jones played in the search, and what he believed, is all based on the memory of Dock Henderson and the knowledge Jones shared with him in later years. Dock Henderson, interview by author, Rule, Texas, July 1963, and numerous other occasions over the next twenty years.

13. Sherrill, "Lost Copper Mines and Spanish Gold," p. 76; Dobie, *Coronado's Children*, p. 83; and Dock Henderson, interview by author, July 1963, and many other occasions.

14. Bud Jones remembered this, and perhaps even others, who in turn later told Dock Henderson.

15. Dock Henderson did not observe the copper vessels but discussed them with Crawford Allen on various occasions.

16. The fragile envelope bears no date, but its diagram shows the canyons, prominent hills, location of the Spanish saber, and major excavation on the Salt Fork, all of which dovetail with the details told to Dock Henderson by many of the participants. Charles Terrell collection.

17. The writing on the back of the envelope, in pencil, is extremely faint. It obviously was folded on numerous occasions, as if carried in a shirt pocket.

18. Lon Pate, "Legendary 'Spider Rock' Treasure Story Is Revived in Haskell County," *Wichita Falls Record News*, October 24, 1956, p. 1; Koethe, "Lost Diamond Mine Object of Intense Treasure Hunt," *Wichita Falls Record News*, December 6, 1956, p. 2B; and Edwin K. Johnson, interview by author, Munday, Texas, October 3, 1976, and April 24, 1977.

19. Frank X. Tolbert used Marvin Post's story in his column in the *Dallas Morning News* on February 6, 1957. Prompted to write when Tolbert mentioned the Spanish artifacts found by a Haskell doctor, Post said: "Your druggist was C. L. Terrell. We called him Dr. Terrell. When I was a small boy we lived across the street from him. Doc Terrell spent as much time and money as he was able to looking for buried Spanish treasure in Stonewall County." The newspaper clipping was sent to Charles Terrell the same day by longtime friend Henry S. Livingstone of Fort Worth. Livingstone asked Charles, then living in Birmingham, Alabama, "Were all of the relics destroyed in the fire?"

Charles wrote Livingstone back on February 26, explaining, perhaps for the first time, what artifacts were found that he remembered, and that after the drug store burned, "as I recall, only the sword hilt was destroyed, while the epaulets were recovered minus the gold fringe." Charles Terrell collection.

20. Frank Tolbert had written two previous stories about Spanish artifacts being found in Stonewall County, first in "Spaniards Buried On Baugh Ranch?", *Dallas Morning News*, January 18, 1957, and in his column,

"Tolbert's Texas," on January 29. In the former he mentioned a Comanche legend that told of horsemen buried in their armor at Double Mountain, and according to George Willis Evans of Mexia, the site was excavated in the 1930s, resulting in much rusted armor and weapons.

That prompted an Austin man, Tolbert stated January 29, 1957, "who doesn't want his name used here," to write "that a Haskell, Texas, druggist in January 1906 showed him some relics he had taken from a grave near Copper Mountain. These relics were a copper plate, with some tracery on it like a map but not lettering; the hilt of a sword; some gold fringe, evidently from an officer's uniform, and a small ebony and silver crucifix.

"The crucifix was dated either 1767 or 1778, the letter writer has forgotten which. The Austin man believes that was from the grave of an officer in a Spanish expedition which was sent out some time between 1813 and 1821 from San Antonio to try to find the headwaters of either the Colorado or Brazos River. And the expedition came to grief in what is now Stonewall County. And, sad to report, a Haskell drug store is supposed to have burned up and the old relics were lost in the fire."

21. *Taylor County News* (Abilene, Texas), June 29, 1888, p. 5.

Chapter 3. Cryptic Symbols to a Lost City

1. John Sembritzki paid $1,400 to W. E. and Annie Mayes for his 320 acres located in the SE 1/4 of Section 73, and SW 1/4 of Section 82 of the Buffalo Bayou, Brazos & Colorado Railroad Survey. Purchased on October 7, 1899, and filed on December 16, the land was part of Abstract Nos. 38 and 837. Deed Record, October 7, 1899, vol. V, p. 612, County Clerk, Callahan County, Baird, Texas.

2. Verne Sems of Redwood Valley, California, wrote the author June 7, 1965, after reading "Mystery of the Spider Rock Treasure," *True West* (May-June 1964). She had never known about the Spider Rock hunt but knew plenty about Arnold's quest at her homeplace near Clyde. She recalled that search in great detail in a series of letters. Sems, letters to author, June 7, 20, July 8, and November 18, 1965; and January 21, 26, February 8, 23, March 1, 7, 30, May 18, 25, June 8, July 4, September 29, and November 14, 1976.

Verne also wrote an article of her own about Arnold's search on the Sembritzki farm. See "Mexican Bullion on the Flying H Bar Ranch," *True West* (July-August 1966), pp. 38-39, 66-68. Although unrelated to Arnold's search, Verne also recorded the story of a friendly ghost in their home, in "Close Quarters with the Supernatural," *Frontier Times* (December-January 1971), pp. 20-21,73-74.

No one knew who the ghost was, but Verne elaborated: "When I lived near Clyde years ago, there were all kinds of rumors of hidden treasures. There was supposed to be another hidden treasure on our place too, Hubbard's treasure. This Mr. Hubbard, according to tradition, was afraid of an Indian attack, and buried his money when he and a number of cowboys camped for the night. That night the Indians did attack, and all were killed except one man. When my dad first bought the place, some of the posts from Hubbard's cattle corral were still there." Verne Sems, letter to author, July 8, 1965.

Verne's niece, Claire Walker, also wrote about Arnold's quest, based on Verne's knowledge, in "Has Coronado's Treasure Been Found?" *Treasure World,* August-September 1969, pp. 9-11, 40-44.

3. Sems, letters to author, June 7, June 20, July 8, November 18, 1965; and Ann Sembritzki Fuqua, interview by author, Abilene, Texas, July 1967 and March 11, 1976.

4. Sems, letter to author, February 23, 1976.

5. Sems, "Mexican Bullion on the Flying H Bar Ranch," *True West* (July-August 1966), p. 38.

6. Ibid., p. 39.

7. Sems, letters to author, February 23 and March 1, 1976.

8. Sems, "Mexican Bullion," *True West* (July-August 1966), p. 39; and Sems, letters to author, July 8, November 18, 1965, and July 4, 1976.

9. Sems, letter to author, June 8, 1976.

10. Sems, letter to author, June 20 and February 23, 1976.

11. Sems, letter to author, February 23 and May 18, 1976.

Chapter 4. A Company to Dig $60 Million in Gold

1. Perhaps neither John Hart nor Arnold ever told what fate had brought them together. Hart's farm was just north of Putnum about fifteen miles east of Clyde. Some years before, he had observed the arrows carved into the trunks of the older trees on his land, and near Hart's double-log cabin he had found a charcoal cross that stretched ten feet over the surface. How Arnold knew to renew his search fifteen miles westward is a puzzle, but young Sam Hart drove him to the Sembritzki farm, where Lucretia could show him what he sought, early in 1905.

Duane Kendall Hale records this in his "Evidence of Early Spanish Mining in the Big Country of West Texas," (master's thesis, Abilene Christian College, 1972), p. 148, and "Riddle of the Big Country's Stone Maps Remains Unsolved," *West Texas Historical Association Year Book* 74 (1998), p. 20. One wonders if other discoveries in the area helped lead Arnold to this site. Hale chronicles others in his article (pp. 15-33).

Perhaps the earliest known discovery in the region was reported in the local newspaper on November 15, 1879, telling of several graves discovered about eight miles south of Belle Plain, which was six miles southeast of Baird. Found on Rough Creek near Langford's Ranch, various items consisted of a human skeleton, "a solid silver medal about the size of a Mexican dollar," a battle axe, a tomahawk, a brass camp kettle, a badly corroded Mexican gun, and other articles.

Around the left-hand side of the medallion appeared the words "CARLOS III REY DE ESP," and on the right hand side, "EMP DELAS INDIAS." In the center appeared the image of a female with a crown on her head, and below her the word "Prieto." On the opposite side of the medal in the center appeared the word "AL," and immediately beneath it the word "MERITO." Dr. Largen, who examined the skeleton, believed it "to have been a man about six feet, six inches high." See "Archaeological," *Callahan County Clarendon* (Belle Plain), November 15, 1879, p. 2, and Hale, "Riddle of the Stone Maps," p. 25.

Later stories centered on the hills near Cisco, twenty-five miles east of Clyde. In November 1890 a brief newspaper story told that three geologists were hunting the hills near Cisco "with a map and a Mexican as a guide trying to locate a lost mine that was once worked by the Mexicans." Stories of similar quests persisted, and in March 1892 it was reported that "three old Mexican smelters" had been discovered on the land of Charlie Daniels three miles southwest of Cisco. See "That Lost Mexican Mine Again," *Dallas Morning News*, November 4, 1890, p. l, part II; and "Silver, Iron and Coal," ibid., March 2, 1892, p. 5.

2. Indenture forming Sembritzki Mineral Company, May 20, 1905; minutes of Sembritzki Mineral Company, May 20, 1905, Charles Terrell collection; and Deed Record, vol. 36, pp. 373-74, November 15, 1905, County Clerk, Calllahan County, Baird, Texas.

3. Lease of John and Lucretia Sembritzki, May 20, 1905, Terrell collection.

4. Deed Record, vol. 36, pp. 373-74, November 15, 1905, County Clerk, Callahan County, Baird, Texas.

5. Account records kept on various pieces of paper in Terrell collection.

6. Verne Sems, letter to author, November 18, 1965. Without Sems' photographic memory, much of the detail of this search would have been lost. Her memory was unique, but as she once wrote: "I have an uncanny memory for numbers—telephone numbers, addresses, etc. I can still remember my address and telephone numbers during World War I, in 1918. I lived in Dallas at that time." Sems, letter to author, February 8, 1976.

7. Account records kept by Dr. Terrell, in Terrell collection.

8. The invoice for twenty sticks of dynamite purchased on August 31, 1905, and eight sticks on September 2, from Cason, Cox & Co. Hardware in Haskell, was marked paid on January 18, 1906, in ibid.

9. Account Statements of Lester Smith, R. R. Davis, W. J. Carouth, J. K. Johnson, J. L. Johnson, and W. J. Jones, all from "Lama Vista," August 14, 1905, in ibid.

10. Alberta Epllis to Dr. C. L. Terrell, September 6, 1905, in ibid.

11. Statement of Labor, W. W. Crume, J. A. Hodges, C. L. Terrell, J. S. Hart, and John Sembritzki, August 17 to September 21, 1905, in Terrell collection. Even though Arnold had returned to the Sembritzki diggings, it would appear that work continued into the fall at the Spider Rock diggings. A checking account stub in Dr. Terrell's collection shows that on October 20, 1905, he paid "To Kelly Camp S.F." (perhaps Kelly Johnson at camp on the Salt Fork) $10.55. The stub showed a credit of $107.10, less the $10.55, leaving $96.55 carried forward.

12. Minutes of the Executive Committee, August 10, 1905, by C. L. Terrell, secretary and treasurer, in Terrell collection.

13. Hicks A. Turner, ed., *I Remember Callahan: History of Callahan County, Texas* (Dallas: Taylor Publishing Co., 1986), p. 96.

14. Verne Sems, letter to author, February 23, 1976.

15. John Sembritzki and J. F. Hart to C. L. Terrell, October 16, 1905; and Sembritzki and Hart to W. M. Crume, October 16, 1905, in Terrell collection.

16. W. M. Crume, M.D., to Dr. C. L. Terrell, October 19, 1905, in ibid.

17. Cabe Terrell to Dr. C. L. Terrell, October 28, 1905, in ibid.

18. Contract of Sembritzki Mineral Company, J. F. Hart and John Sembritzki with Lester S. Smith, November 20, 1905, in ibid.

19. D. M. Arnold to Dr. C. L. Terrell, November 23, 1905, in ibid.

20. Lester S. Smith to Dr. C. L. Terrell, January 1, 1906, in ibid.

21. Lester S. Smith to Dr. C. L. Terrell, February 1, 1906, in ibid.

22. Dr. Terrell's checking account stub shows that he credited or paid Cabe $20 on January 22, 1906, "for expenses to Baird for CFT"; and as late as August 30, 1906, R. R. Davis was paid $10 "for sand and gravel."

23. Verne Sems, letter to author, November 18, 1965.

24. "Death at Water Valley," *San Angelo Standard,* March 17, 1906, p. 7. The lonely tombstone inscription in the Water Valley Cemetery northwest of San Angelo gives the birth and death dates of M. A., wife of D. M. Arnold, in a fenced-in, one-grave space. Mary N. Speakman, letter to author, August 13, 1977.

25. Verne Sems, "Mexican Bullion on the Flying H Bar Ranch," *True West* (July-August 1966), pp. 66-67; and Sems, letter to author, February 23 and July 4, 1976.

26. "Aztec Mine Near Abilene," *Fort Worth Telegram,* October 27, 1907, p. 2.

27. The lease to Ward and Ely was signed by Ward on October 8, 1907, and recorded November 3, 1908. See Deed Record, vol. 40, pp. 99-101, May 27, 1907, County Clerk, Callahan County, Baird, Texas.

28. In 1907 Gurney E. Ward lived at 317 Cedar Street in Abilene. His photography studio was at 211 1/2 Pine. *Directory of Abilene, Texas, 1907-08* (Fort Worth: Fort Worth Directory Co., 1908).

29. The author is grateful to Duane Hale for a copy of this story. Hale, letter to author, February 26, 1973.

30. Allen J. McDaniel, Jr., of Abilene, a founder of the Central Texas Gem and Mineral Society and historian of the region, who has long studied the Spider Rock and its sister stones, believes that Verne Sems was wrong in her memory of the stone found on her family's farm. He believes what Verne rememberd as *puente* was in fact *poniente,* the Spanish word for "west." "Actually, those rocks should have been called Compass Rocks," McDaniel believes. Communication with author, December 29, 2000. If that is so, then Ward's word *orient* for the eastern stone may well be correct, since *oriental* also means "east," as does *este.*

31. Verne Sems, letter to author, February 23, 1976.

32. "Philadelphia Man to Look at Ward Mine," *Abilene Daily Reporter,* November 26, 1909, p. 3.

33. "'Victory Is in Sight,' Gurney Ward's Message," *Abilene Semi-Weekly Farm Reporter,* September 6, 1910, p. 2.

34. John Metcalf, interview by author, Aspermont, July 1963.

35. Gurney E. Ward, "It Has Proven a Mammoth Proposition; The Old Spanish Diggins," *Abilene Daily Reporter,* April 14, 1911, p. 8.

36. Considerable legal records exist at the Taylor County Courthouse documenting Gurney Ward's whereabouts and the disposition of his property. In November 1911 Ward stated that he and his wife "are now living apart and have for several months and agree to remain separate." Their children, Gurney E. Ward, Jr., Otis M. Ward, and Jewel E. Ward, were residing with their mother, Margaret Ann. G. E. Ward, living in Lampasas, deeded his children his half of the home on Cedar Street, while Margaret released her right to a section of land in El Paso County and certain lots in Electra, Texas. See Deed Record, November 29, 1911, vols. 73-74, pp. 143-44, County Clerk, Taylor County, Abilene, Texas. For other references to the property, see Deed Record, January 21, 1911, vol. 71, p. 66; April 14, 1920, vol. 120, p. 457-60; November 23, 1920, vol. 122, pp. 288-89; and January 1, 1924, vol. 140, p. 445. In 1920 Ward was living in Otero County, New Mexico, and his former wife in Los Angeles.

37. Eve Ball, "The Treasure of Alamo Canyon," *Treasure World* (July-August 1968), pp. 14-15, 40-42; and Arch Frame as told to Eve Ball, "The Treasure of Alamo Canyon," *True West* (November-December 1973), pp. 34-36, 52-53, 56.

38. Ball, "The Treasure of Alamo Canyon," *Treasure World* (July-August 1968), p. 15. Frame may have confused his story here. Ward and his wife never lived in Clyde; however, they did have a boarder in Abilene, as shown by the story "Escaping Gas Overpowers High School Instructor," *Abilene Reporter,* November 26, 1909, p. 1.

Verne Sems also verified this: "Clyde had a small hotel as far back as I can remember," she explained. "Even before I started to school, it was owned and operated by a Mrs. Edwards. I went to school later with her daughter Dixie. Mrs. Edwards sold the hotel to Mr. and Mrs. Diltz, and they owned it until I left home during World War I. We literally knew everyone in Callahan County. When I was a kid we used to walk three miles in that terrific West Texas heat, carrying a pound of butter to the Diltz Hotel who paid us fifteen cents for it, and we felt like we were rich." Sems, letter to author, February 23, 1976.

39. Ball, "The Treasure of Alamo Canyon," *True West,* p. 36.

40. Ibid.

41. Deed Record, vol. 124, pp. 607-8, August 24, 1927, County Clerk, Callahan County, Baird, Texas. When the author interviewed Charles Terrell on two occasions in 1976, he never mentioned the lease, or his search on the Sembritzki farm.

42. Deed Record, vol. 144, p. 53, July 30, 1934, and vol. 146, p. 239, March 25, 1935, County Clerk, Callahan County, Baird, Texas.

43. Duane Hale tells this story, quoting John E. Smith of Abilene. See Hale, "Evidence of Early Spanish Mining in the Big Country of West Texas" (master's thesis, Abilene Christian College, 1972), p. 75; and Deed Record, vol. 146, p. 239, March 25, 1935, County Clerk, Callahan County, Baird, Texas.

44. Deed Record, vol. 171, pp. 174-76, November 10, 1942, County Clerk, Callahan County, Baird, Texas. J. M. Cauble and Joe G. Wood's lease was dated June 13, 1936. Also Joe Woods, interview by author, Abilene, March, July 1963, July 1967, June 1969; Joe Cauble, interview by author, Snyder, December 1969; and Joe Woods, letter to author, June 26, 1963.

45. On this subject, Verne Sems wrote: "You mentioned that it is strange that no historians were notified about all the discoveries on our place. In our present-day modern thinking world, yes, but take into consideration in those days the people were ignorant, illiterate, who did not think beyond their daily chores of clearing land, farming, having kids, trying to feed them and themselves. Telephones were almost a novelty, no one had them. We had heard of telephones, but had never seen one." Sems, letter to author, Feburary 23, 1976.

46. Verne further elaborated: "Dad wouldn't have thought of allowing anyone to dig in his field. It would have spoiled some of the crop." Sems, letter to author, March 7, 1976. Verne Sems died in June 1982, at age eighty-seven.

47. "Archaeological," *Callahan County Clarendon* (Belle Plain), p. 2; Hale, "Evidence of Early Spanish Mining in the Big Country of West Texas," p. 148; and Hale, "Riddle of the Big Country's Stone Maps Remains Unsolved," pp. 24-25. Louise Trammell, "Does Lake Cover Buried Treasure?" *Cisco Daily News,* September 15, 1929, p. 1, cites other tales of early Mexicans returning to the hills west of nearby Cisco in pursuit of gold hidden generations before. Various residents about Clyde and Baird tell of the Spanish armor they have seen found in the nearby hills.

Chapter 5. The Curse of Dave Arnold's Map

1. Checking account stubs for Dr. Terrell shows that he paid W. J. "Bud" Jones $15 on February 18, 1907, for work on the "vault"; $15 on March 21, 1907, "for work"; $35 to Jones on April 29, 1907, "to pay note at bank"; $12.50 to S. L. Robertson on August 1, 1907, "for act [account] Arnold"; and $5 to Bud Jones on September 21, 1907, for "act CLT," in Terrell collection; and Charles E. Terrell, interview by author, Eastland, Texas, May 31 and December 28, 1976; and Terrell, letter to author, June 18, July 12, and August 30, 1976.

2. R. E. Sherrill, "Lost Copper Mines and Spanish Gold, Haskell County," in *Legends of Texas,* p. 76; and J. Frank Dobie, *Coronado's Children: Tales of Lost Mines and Buried Treasures of the Southwest,* p. 284.

3. Dock Henderson, interview by author, Rule, Texas, July 1963, and numerous occasions over the following years.

4. Bud Jones related this to Dock Henderson when Jones returned to the old diggings in 1924 to renew his search, and Henderson and his father soon joined in. Dock Henderson, interview by author, July 1963.

5. Louise Terrell, daughter of Cabe Terrell, letter to author, August 10, 24, and September 7, 1976.

6. Bankruptcy File, October 2, 1908, vol. 44, p. 249, County Clerk, Haskell County, Haskell, Texas.

7. It appears that 1908-1909 was a pivotal period for the Terrell family. The *Haskell Free Press* noted on July 18, 1908, that "Dr. C. L. Terrell and son Caleb went to Abilene Wednesday on business." Was it really business perhaps at Clyde? Dr. Terrell owned Lots 1-3 and 5-8 in Block 39 of Haskell. On May 28, 1908, he sold Lot 1 to his son C. E. (Charles). Deed Record, vol. 39, p. 501, County Clerk, Haskell County, Haskell, Texas.

8. Louise Terrell, letter to author, August 24 and September 7, 1976; Louise Terrell, interview by author, El Paso, Texas, May 11, 1977; and Probate Record, Estate of C. L. Terrell, deceased, no. 152, July 1, 1909, County Clerk, Haskell County, Haskell, Texas.

9. Charles E. Terrell, interview by author, May 31 and December 28, 1976; and Louise Terrell, interview by author, May 11, 1977.

10. D. M. Arnold, by A. M. Johnson, to Cabe Terrell, June 21, 1909, in Charles E. Terrell collection.

11. R. R. Davis to Bud Jones, July 26, 1909, in ibid.

12. Bud Jones to Cabe Terrell, July [August] 1, 1909, in ibid.

13. Louise Terrell, daughter of Cabe, states, "There is a record of a prescription for Mrs. Post dated April 11, 1899. According to my father, his father treated Mr. Post for tuberculoisis. Together they worked on the formula for Postum." Louise Terrell, letter to author, August 24, 1976.

14. Walter Prescott Webb and H. Bailey Carroll, eds., *The Handbook of Texas,* vol. II (Austin: Texas State Historical Association, 1952), p. 397; and Dumas Malone, ed., *Dictionary of American Biography,* vol. XV (New York: Charles Scribner's Sons, 1935), pp. 112-13.

15. Louise Terrell, letter to author, August 10, 24, September 7, 1976, June 8, 1979; and Louise Terrell, interview by author, May 11, 1977.

Chapter 6. Inca Treasure, Aztec Gold: The Stone from Double Mountain

1. Bob Hayes, interview by author, Rotan, Texas, March 10, 1976.

2. Robert G. Ferguson, *Lost Treasure: The Search for Hidden Gold* (New York: Vantage Press, 1957), pp. 37-45.

3. J. Frank Dobie, "Don Español and the Four Skeletons," *Frontier Times* (Summer 1959), pp. 32-33.

4. Ibid., p. 33.

5. Marvin H. Sanders of Artesia, New Mexico, first wrote the editor of *Treasure World* about this discovery (October-November 1972), pp. 8 and 12, and the author in turn wrote Sanders. Marvin Sanders, letter to author, November 7, 1972.

6. Sanders, letter to author, November 7, 1972.

7. Bob Hayes, interview by author, Rotan, Texas, March 10, 1976.

8. George T. McBeth, interview by author, Rotan, Texas, March 10, 1976.

9. Jess Lee Kiker, interview by author, Rotan, Texas, March 10, 1976.

10. Walter W. Leach, interview by author, Rotan, Texas, June 1969.

11. Allen J. McDaniel, Jr., of Abilene, university librarian, a founder of the Central Texas Gem and Mineral Society, and aficionado of the Spider Rock, has studied Arnold's Rotan stone carving many an hour. "That rock has been on the desk in this office, and has traveled many a mile in my car." For example, he does not believe the VROE are as they appear. "That is not a V," he believes. "Look at it carefully. It's a sombrero, and represents a dead man. Also, that is not an R. It looks like one at first glance, but the Spaniard connected his mark to the bottom of the semicircle where it connects to the bar of the R. The mark that makes it look like an R is really an accidental scratch on the rock. I looked at that carefully. That makes it POE, actually standing for *poniente,* colloquial Spanish for west." His deduction seems reasonable. Communication with author, December 29, 2000, May 18, 2001.

12. Dock Henderson possessed Dave Arnold's third stone map for several years between 1964 and 1969, allowing the author to photograph and study it.

13. Bob Hayes, interview by author, Rotan, Texas, March 10, 1976.

14. Walter W. Leach, interview by author, Rotan, Texas, June 1969.

15. John E. Smith, interview by author, Abilene, Texas, October 28, 1972.

16. George Willis Evans of Mexia, Texas, was familiar with this legend, and the knowledge that in the 1930s many human and horse bones were found, along with considerable rusted Spanish armor and weapons. See Frank X. Tolbert, "Spaniards Buried on Baugh Ranch?" *Dallas Morning News,* January 18, 1957.

17. Edwin K. Johnson, interview by author, Munday, Texas, October 3, 1976, and April 24, 1977.

18. Ibid.

19. Blanche Nelson, interview by author, Munday, Texas, April 24, 1977.

20. Ed and Mary Johnson, interview by author, Munday, Texas, April 24, 1977.

21. Ibid.

22. Jim Koethe, "Lost Diamond Mine Object of Intense Treasure Hunt," *Wichita Falls Record News,* December 6, 1956, p. 2B.

23. Amos Sheppard, interview by author, Gatesville, Texas, June 1969.

24. Joe Woods, interview by author, Abilene, Texas, March and July 1963, July 1967, and June 1969.

25. John E. Smith, interview by author, Abilene, Texas, October 28, 1972.

26. Walter W. Leach, interview by author, Rotan, Texas, June 1969. Dock Henderson, too, had always heard that Arnold met his demise in Kansas. Henderson, interview by author, Rule, Texas, July 1963, and numerous occasions over the years.

27. Louise Terrell, interview by author, El Paso, Texas, May 11, 1977. The author attempted to contact

Cabe Terrell in Waco in June 1969. He phoned a Terrell listed in the phone directory, and a "Mrs. Arnold" answered—a rather bizarre occurrence in itself. Cabe's name was no longer listed in the directory, and he died within a year.

28. Uda Roberts, interview by author, Waco, Texas, March 14, 1976.

29. Naomi Roberts Cleghorn, interview by author, Waco, Texas, March 13 and September 13, 1976.

30. The author's "Mystery of the Spider Rock Treasure," *True West* (May-June 1964), pp. 20-24, 56-57, launched a renewed search for the Spanish legend, bringing back many seekers who had first come years before or were associated with those who had. Even Bud Jones's son, Henry, and Stanley Carouth, son of Jones's father-in-law, W. J. Carouth, visited Dock in the mid-1960s from California. Charles Terrell also read the story and was impressed with its accuracy, as he later told the author.

Chapter 7. The Mexican Sheepherder's Letter

1. Burt Edwards, interview by author, Pauls Valley, Oklahoma, January 16, 1970, and November 3, 1976; and Pauline Edwards Tabor, interview by author, Pauls Valley, November 3, 1976.

2. R. E. Sherrill, "Lost Copper Mines and Spanish Gold, Haskell County," in *Legends of Texas*, pp. 72-77, gave the best account of this. J. Frank Dobie, *Coronado's Children*, p. 278, quoted Sherrill. Crawford Allen kept the copper vessels for many years.

3. Several copies of the sheepherder's letter have circulated since 1964, when the author's "Mystery of the Spider Rock Treasure" also prompted Burt Edwards and his sister Pauline Tabor to return to the old Spider diggings. This version was read and corrected by Pauline, who believed it to be correct. Burt and Pauline contacted Dock Henderson, who in turn was contacted by mining promoter Alpheus Bruton of Las Vegas, Nevada. For a time, all worked together on the mysterious letter. Bruton, too, had committed it to memory, and he scrawled a copy for the author in October 1964. He shared various translations with Dock, Burt, and Pauline. Al Bruton to Dock and Burt, September 23, 1964, and Bruton to Dock, November 26, 1964; copies given to the author. Bruton tried to mine nearby copper deposits, but he was no more successful at unraveling the sheepherder's letter than those before him.

4. Dr. E. Michael Gerli, Georgetown University, to Vance Tiede, March 8, 1976. Vance Tiede, letter to author, November 22, December 1, 1975, March 14 and March 24, 1976. The author is grateful to Vance Tiede for obtaining this translation from Dr. Gerli, and his pinpointing the dialect of the original Spanish-Portuguese writer.

5. Dr. Clevy Strout, University of Tulsa, letter to author, December 13, 1976, and January 19, 1977. Dr. Strout added: "I'm afraid this may not help you much, for the copyist, truly, has done an atrocious job of transcription—purposely or not."

6. Burt Edwards, interview by author, January 16, 1970, and November 3, 1976; and Pauline Edwards Tabor, interview by author, November 3, 1976. The author first wrote about Stuart and his map in "Two Maps May Hold Key to 'Spider Rock' Gold," *Wichita Falls Times Features Magazine*, October 13, 1963, p. 12. A photograph of the blueprint was published with the story. Bud Jones had kept blueprints of both the Spider Rock and the Sembritizki stone. But the same carving was always believed copied, then destroyed by Stuart only a mile and a half from the discovery of the Spider Rock.

Chapter 8. The Treasure Dave Arnold Missed: Dock Henderson's Fifty-Year Search

1. Four decades have passed since the author first corrresponded with and met Dock Henderson, led to him in part by two of Jim Koethe's stories that highlighted Henderson: "Brazos Area Waste Land is Searched for Lost Gold," *Wichita Falls Record News*, October 11, 1956, p. 5A, and "Outlaw Treasure Supposed to be Buried in Burk Area," October 25, 1956, p. 7B. Koethe chronicled other pieces of the Spanish legend in "Is There Lost Gold Mine in Knox or Baylor County?" August 23, 1956, p. 5A; "Old Prospector Finds Lost Mine, September 13, 1956, p. 8A; "Tales of Lost Treasures in Area Lure Many Men," September 20, 1956, p. 8A; "Two Lads from Knox City and Haskell Hunt Treasure," October 4, 1956, p. 4A; and "Lost Diamond Mine Object of Intense Treasure Hunt," December 6, 1956, p. 2B. The articles were part of a series of nineteen which Koethe wrote for the *Record News*. Lon Pate wrote "Legendary 'Spider Rock' Treasure Story is Revived in Haskell County," October 24, 1956, p. 1. Interestingly, at that time Crawford Allen questioned whether the Spanish artifacts were really destroyed in the drug store fire.

Dock Henderson, letter to author, August 7, October 25, 1960; July 28, 1962; and Henderson, interview by author, Rule, Texas, July 1963, and numerous occasions over the years while visiting the old diggings and surrounding sites.

2. Dock Henderson, interview by author, July 1963, October 1964, June 1965, August 1967, December 1969, February 1972, October 28, 1972, October 6-7, 1973, December 13-14, 1975, March 5-6, May 28-30, October 1-3, 1976, and April 22-24, 1977, and other occasions.

3. Interestingly, R. E. Sherrill, who stated, "Nearly every man of that searching party of seventeen years ago was a friend of mine," did not name Dave Arnold. He wrote in 1924 that "a man in Haskell now is trying to organize an expedition to seek the remaining part of the treasure and to gather more relics." No doubt he was referring to none other than Bud Jones. See Sherrill, "Lost Copper Mines and Spanish Gold, Haskell County," in *Legends of Texas,* pp. 72-77.

4. Charles E. Terrell, interview by author, Eastland, Texas, May 31 and December 28, 1976.

5. Dock Henderson, interview by author, July 1963, and many other occasions. Dock remembered that Jones told him Cabe had revealed, or perhaps did not deny, that the Spider Rock in fact had survived the drug store fire. But he could not, or would not, show it to him. Or, did Jones just suspect that the Spider Rock survived and hope that if it had, he would see it once again?

6. Louise Terrell, interview by author, El Paso, Texas, May 11, 1977.

7. Dock Henderson, interview by author, December 13-14, 1975.

8. Dock Henderson and the author first visited the ruins in July 1963.

9. Bill Males, interview by author, Rule, Texas, December 14, 1975.

10. Dock Henderson, interview by author, December 13-14, 1975.

11. Floyd E. Ewing, Jr., "Copper Mining in West Texas: Early Interest and Development," *West Texas Historical Asssociation Year Book* 30 (1954), pp. 17-29. For other sources on the copper mining in this region, see Llerena Friend, ed., *M. K. Kellogg's Texas Journal 1872* (Austin: University of Texas Press, 1967); Mrs. R. D. Gray, *Early Days in Knox County* (New York: Carlton Press, 1963), pp. 13-15; Jerome R. Whitmire, "The History of Stonewall County, Texas" (master's thesis, Texas Technological College, 1936), pp. 34-36; G. D. Railsback, "History of Stonewall County" (master's thesis, Hardin-Simmons University, 1940), pp. 61-63; and Willard L. Dent, "History of Stonewall County" (master's thesis, East Texas State Teachers College, 1949), pp. 63-66.

Duane Kendall Hale covers the subject most thoroughly, in addition to the Spanish legends, in his "Evidence of Early Spanish Mining in the Big Country of West Texas" (master's thesis, Abilene Christian College, 1972), pp. 57-58, 62-63, 180-81; and his "Prospecting and Mining on the Texas Frontier" (Ph.D. diss., Oklahoma State University, 1977), pp. 157-60, 171-72, 186-89. In Hale's thesis, he examined what he believed were thirty-three "Spanish smelting devices" scattered over fourteen Central and West Texas counties known as the Big Country. Hale does a good job of explaining the procedure of smelting, and the difference between a smelter and a more common lime kiln, used for burning broken limestone into lime, necessary in the construction of all the frontier forts. See pp. 100-142.

It becomes more tricky, however, if not impossible, when one tries to distinguish a smelter constructed in Spanish colonial times—up to the early 1820s—with one used in the Mexican period to the mid-1830s, or one made by early Anglo Americans from the latter period on. Smelters, often like old mines, appear ancient after fifty years or more, as can be observed in almost any mining region.

12. For more on this fascinating subject, see Otis E Young, Jr., "The Spanish Tradition," in *Western Mining: An Informal Account of Precious-Metals Prospecting, Placering, Lode Mining, and Milling on the American Frontier from Spanish Times to 1893* (Norman: University of Oklahoma Press, 1970), pp. 55-101. Also related to this subject is Robert Raymond, *Out of the Fiery Furnace: The Impact of Metals on the History of Mankind* (University Park and London: Pennsylvania State University Press, 1984); and Beth and Bill Sagstetter, *The Mining Camps Speak: A New Way to Explore the Ghost Towns of the American West* (Denver: BenchMark Publishing of Colorado, 1998).

13. Dock Henderson showed the author the stone carving in July 1963 and on other occasions over the years. Dock kept it covered by another stone, which long protected the glyphs, precariously on the edge of the cliff.

14. Chunks of slag and charcoal were still easily found at the site when Henderson first showed it to the author in July 1963.

Chapter 9. Silver Arrows, Crosses, and Statuettes: The Uncanny Luck of Bill Reid

1. Dock Henderson, interview by author, Rule, Texas, July 1963, October 1964, June 1965, August 1967, December 1969, February 1972, October 6-7, 1973, December 12-14, 1975, and numerous other occasions over the years.

2. Dock Henderson, interview by author, February 1972.

3. Henderson believed he once spied Bill Reid suddenly go out the back door of a barber shop in Abilene a few years after he disappeared from the cedar brakes of Stonewall County. He later heard that Reid had a band in Oklahoma. Henderson, letter to author, August 7, 1960.

4. Joe Cauble, interview by author, Snyder, Texas, December 1969. Like Gurney Ward, Cauble and Joe Woods followed in the footsteps of Dave Arnold, but they never found the evidence Arnold always managed to reveal. The stone he said he found near the confluence of the Salt Fork and Double Mountain Fork, perhaps no more than a mile or so from the site of the Spider Rock, is obviously related to the mystery. He did not say where the stone itself was. In 1969 Cauble gave the author photographs of the stone and asked him to pass them on to Dock Henderson. Others, however, believe the stone was found elsewhere, perhaps on Gyp Creek.

5. Allen McDaniel, communication to author, May 2, 2001.

6. Dock Henderson, interview by author, December 14, 1975. Jack Childress's discovery, like Bill Reid's, remains a mystery, at least to the participants in their quests.

7. Dock Henderson, interview by author, December 13-14, 1975.

8. Ibid. Crawford Allen, who with his father was among the first to join in Arnold's search in 1902, and continued searching periodically over much of his life, died in 1967.

9. Jim Koethe, "Is There Lost Gold Mine in Knox or Baylor County?" *Wichita Falls Record News,* August 23, 1956, p. 5A.

10. Koethe, "Tales of Lost Treasures in Area Lure Many Men," ibid., September 20, 1956, p. 4A; and Mrs. W. B. Gillentine, Benjamin, Texas, interview by author, October 29, 1960. Among Noah Gillentine's possessions were a tracing of the Spider Rock blueprint, a drawing of the cryptic symbols he had found somewhere in the Narrows, and a rough drawing of the Indian's map Riddle had brought from Albuquerque.

11. Koethe, "Old Prospector Finds Lost Mine," *Wichita Falls Record News,* September 13, 1956, p. 8A.

12. In 1969 the A. B. Sams Ranch three miles east of Benjamin began charging visitors a $1 "prospector's pass" to search the 1,750-acre expanse of the rough canyon country. Mrs. Sams knew about Gillentine's search for the ninety-foot shaft that Riddle first sought, and when Gillentine died and others attempted to find it, she decided to charge a fee. Larry Grauerholz, "The Gold at Benjamin Lies South of the Star . . . Maybe!" *Prospector* (August 1969), p. 1.

13. Dock Henderson and the author visited the old workings in February 1972.

14. Jack Gore, interview by author, Rule, Texas, March 7, 1976.

15. Burt Cochran, interview by author, Aspermont, Texas, October 1960 and July 1963; Joe Cauble, interview by author, Snyder, Texas, December 1969; and Dock Henderson, various interviews. Henderson, who for well over a half-century was a walking encyclopedia on the Spider Rock story, died in May 1985.

16. Joe S. McCombs, "On the Cattle Trail and Buffalo Range," *West Texas Historical Association Year Book* 11 (1935), p. 96.

17. Duane Hale, letter to author, November 8, 1972; and C. O. Duke, interview by author, Rotan, Texas, March 10, 1976.

18. The discovery of this copper disc seems almost too convenient. With an extremely rough Spider Rock on one side, and the stone from the Sembritzki farm on the other, it would appear to lend no purpose, considering the incomplete etchings. Bill Townsley bought the disc from the Duke family in 1997, and the reader can view it on the web site http://www.texfiles.com/features/spiderrock.htm.

19. Duane Kendall Hale, "Evidence of Early Spanish Mining in the Big Country of West Texas" (master's thesis, Abilene Christian College, 1972), pp. 168-69.

20. L. D. Bertillion, "Lost Lead Mine on the Brazos, King County," in *Legends of Texas* (1924; reprint, Hatboro, Penn.: Folklore Associates, 1964), pp. 77-78.

21. Fred Arrington, *A History of Dickens County Ranches and Rolling Plains* (Quanah, Texas: Nortex, 1971), pp. 193-94.

22. Eldon C. Wade, "The Terrapin Map and an Old Man's Gold," *Dallas Morning News,* March 12, 1933, section IV, p. 1; Joe Cauble, interview by author, Snyder, Texas, December 1969; and Hale, "Evidence of Early

Spanish Mining," pp. 95-97, 167-68. Wade's story obviously concerned Joe Cauble, although unnamed, who was still working at the site in the fall of 1932.

23. Apparently when Eldon Wade wrote his story for the *Dallas Morning News* in 1933, he did not have a copy of the Cartwheel stone found near Treasure Butte. Interestingly, Joe Woods had kept a tracing of the stone, which Duane Hale obtained after Woods' death. Unknowingly, the author published a copy of the stone map in his own *Oklahoma Treasures and Treasure Tales* (Norman: University of Oklahoma Press, 1976), p. 127. Jack Brown or his father had obtained an early copy of the stone etching in the 1930s, supposedly from a native of Mexico, who wanted to hunt the treasure with Brown but could not, due to age. Brown believed it was to a site in the Wichita Mountains to the north and apparently never knew it was a copy of the Cartwheel stone from Kent County—and part of the Spider Rock mystery. Jack Brown, interview by author, Sunset, Texas, June 1963; and Duane Hale, interview by author, Cisco, Texas, May 31, 2001.

24. Wade, "The Terrapin Map," *Dallas Morning News*, March 12, 1933.

25. John E. Smith, interview by author, Abilene, Texas, October 28, 1972.

26. Andy Moss returned to his home in Hamilton City, California, convinced that one day the treasure would be found.

27. Deed Record, vol. 2, p. 591, April 19, 1950; vol. 4, p. 96; vol. 15-B, Patent no. 64, Abstract no. 1931, April 19, 1950; vol. 101, p. 345, November 2, 1949; vol. 109, p. 245, February 1951, County Clerk, Stonewall County, Aspermont, Texas.

28. On March 6, 1976, the lone stone was just one more clue waiting to be found exposed in the cow trail.

Chapter 10. A Golden Obsession: Trapped in the Spider's Web

1. It has not been found where Olmstead served as a professor, but if he was living in Lawton, Oklahoma, when he was drawn into the Spanish legend—only 150 miles or so away—he might well have been teaching at the then junior college there.

2. Xanthus Carson covered this with his story of the lost Spanish-Inca treasure. See "The $63 Million Inca Loot that Landed in West Texas," parts 1-3, *Lost Treasure* (December 1976), pp. 15-20; (January 1977), pp. 28-33, 37-38; and (February 1977), pp. 30-33, 36, 38, 40-41.

3. John Metcalf, interview by author, northeast of Aspermont, Texas, July 1963. The author has long believed that the unnamed seeker for the golden Inca sun-god which Robert G. Ferguson discussed in his *Lost Treasure: The Search for Hidden Gold* (New York: Vantage Press, 1957), p. 45, was in fact Frank Olmstead.

4. Metcalf, interview by author, July 1963.

5. Mrs. George Pumphrey, interview by author, Old Glory, Texas, October 29, 1960.

6. Pauline Edwards Tabor, interview by author, Pauls Valley, Oklahoma, November 3, 1976.

7. John Metcalf, interview by author, July 1963.

8. Eve Ball wrote "The Treasure of Alamo Canyon," for *Treasure World* (July-August 1968), pp. 14-15, 40-42, and *True West* (November-December 1973), pp. 34-36, 52-53, 56. The latter contains the most details.

9. Duane Hale and Bob Kyker have pursued Gurney Ward's quest in the Sacramentos. Hale read the Lampasas and Alamagordo newspapers to follow Ward's trail and kindly supplied the dates to the author. Hale, communication with author, July 23-24, 2001.

10. Ball, "The Treasure of Alamo Canyon," *True West*, p. 52.

11. Carroll Wood to Eve Ball, April 16, 1958, copy in possession of author.

12. Ibid. Wood wrote Ball seven pages on his recollections of Ward's treasure cave. Carroll Wood was a youngster in 1896 when his father was made foreman of the water improvements at Alamagordo. Not long afterward, the Wood family homesteaded at the head of Alamo Canyon. Such proximity allowed Carroll Wood to observe Ward and Frame working nearby at their treasure cave over many years.

13. "Death of G. E. Ward, Sr., a Former Resident," *Alamagordo News*, May 13, 1943, p. 1.

14. Eve Ball, letter to author, Ruidoso, New Mexico, September 28, 1969, February 21, 1974, and January 3 and 5, 1976. Ball added: "I promised Mr. Frame that so long as he was living, the article would not be published, and of course, kept my promise." Duane Hale and Bob Kyker have investigated Ward and Frame's treasure cave. There are two shafts: one 45 feet deep inside the Indian Cave, and the other outside, which corkscrews downward 168 feet. Hale, communication with author, August 9, 2001.

15. Charles E. Terrell, interview by author, Eastland, Texas, May 31 and December 28, 1976.

16. For a photograph of the same type of Mexican officer's epaulets as those found near the Spider Rock, see David Nevin, *The Mexican War* (Alexandria, Virginia: Time-Life Books, 1978), p. 52. The design of the sil-

ver epaulet is the same, with the exception being the insignia on the center of the epaulets, these representing an engineer officer. Those found by Arnold were plain, perhaps representing a cavalry officer. Today the Terrell collection of artifacts can be seen at the Lela Latch Lloyd Memorial Museum in Cisco, where the viewer can also see the third stone map, found by Arnold on Gyp Creek, in addition to murals of all the stone maps in the Spider Rock mystery.

17. Charles Terrell died in November 1978. Every letter, document, tracing, and artifact in the Terrell collection has been copied and quoted, explained, or shown in this book.

18. Lloyd A. Brown, *The Story of Maps* (New York: Bonanza Books, 1949). See especially "The Latitude," pp. 180-207, and "The Longitude," pp. 208-40.

19. Arnold's oldest daughter, Mary Maude, married D. F. Robison on January 14, 1900. Arnold's second daughter, Minnie Lee, married Benjamin Reese Motley on June 1, 1902. Marriage Record, vol. C, p. 323, January 14, 1900, and vol. C, p. 401, June 1, 1902; Deed Record, vol. 15, p. 207, September 2, 1897; and vol. 18, pp. 71-73, August 21, 1899, County Clerk, Tom Green County, San Angelo, Texas.

20. Deed Record, vol. 31, p. 240, December 7, 1905; vol. 35, p. 621-22, September 18, 1906; vol. 39, p. 121, November 19, 1906; and vol. 38, p. 403, January 11, 1907, in ibid.

21. Deed Record, vol. 38, p. 424, January 12, 1907; vol. 105, p. 535, January 14, 1907 [Arnold's affidavit was filed for record on November 15, 1922]; and vol. 52, pp. 21-22, April 21, 1908, in ibid.

22. Deed Record, vol. 69, p. 533, August 29, 1912; vol. 83, p. 39, April 29, 1914; vol. 95, p. 91, September 23, 1914; vol. 108, p. 187, July 18, 1923; vol. 118, p. 165, November 28, 1925, in ibid. Apparently J. S. Robison and his wife, Sarah, moved to Florida with their son D. F. and Maude. Sarah E. Robison died in Pinellas County on April 13, 1912. No probate records exist for Mary Maude (Arnold) Robison or her husband in Clearwater, Pinellas County, Florida. Paul Cloninger, chief deputy clerk, Probate Division, Pinellas County, letter to author, April 19, 1977.

23. The Texas Department of Health Resources, Austin, Texas, checked its Index to Texas Deaths from 1903 to 1940; the Division of Vital Statistics, Oklahoma State Department of Health, Oklahoma City, Oklahoma, seached death records from 1908 to 1938; and the Department of Health and Environment, Topeka, Kansas, checked death records from 1911 to 1923. The author is grateful to Ms. Rita Bryan of Fort Worth, Texas, for checking census records (September 18, 1992).

24. Arnold's daughter, Minnie Lee Motley, was born July 15, 1874. Her husband, Benjamin Reese Motley, born February 9, 1860, died on October 13, 1936. See Shirley Brittain Cawyer and Weldon I. Hudson, comps., *Cemetery Inscriptions, Eastland County, Texas* (Eastland: n.p.), vol. II, p. 46; Mrs. Robert H. Vann, Centennial Memorial Library, Eastland, Texas, letter to author, April 24, 1977; and Laurie Miller, Texas State Library, Austin, Texas, letter to author, April 11, 1977. Arnold's son, Nathan, apparently had never married when he died in Abilene on March 27, 1947.

25. Telephone interviews by the author were conducted with Dave Arnold's granddaughter (Minnie's daughter), and her son, on May 2, 1977. Because they wished to remain anonymous, their names are not listed here.

26. Dave Arnold's second wife, Susan, appears to have vanished along with her husband. While there were five Susan or Susie Arnolds who died in Texas between 1915 and 1938, after checking their death certificates, none match the right Susan Arnold.

27. Larry Armour, letter to author, Wolfforth, Texas, December 16, 1989.

28. Armour states that he and his father met Skinner Pittock in 1968, and Pittock claimed he knew Dave Arnold very well. It is difficult to imagine someone accustomed to a gypsy-style life in a wagon pulled by two horses in 1914 changing his method to an automobile in 1916, at seventy-one years old. It doesn't seem to fit Arnold, but it certainly wouldn't be impossible. If he had been on the old Jones place in 1924, surely Bud Jones would have found out about it. Yet nothing was ever said concerning it.

29. Allen J. McDaniel, Jr., letter to author, Abilene, Texas, February 4, 1995; and McDaniel, communication with author, December 14, 18, 29, 2000, January 3, May 18, 25, 31, June 4, 14, 25, July 6, and August 6, 2001.

30. Charles B. Waits, letter to author, Corvallis, Oregon, July 14, 1965, and January 1, 1966.

31. The Spider Rock story will never grow old, so long as so much of it remains a mystery. New writers continue to breathe life into the legend, such as Jerry M. Eckhart, "Spider Rock Revisited: Update on Elusive Texas Treasure," *Treasure Search* (September-October 1989), pp. 46-50. Duane Hale, Robert Kyker, and Johnny Terrell joined forces to write a four-part series, "Mystery of the 3 Spider Rocks," *Treasure* (December 1989), pp.

12-16; (January 1990), pp. 39-41, 43-46, 48, 67; (February 1990), pp. 52-60, 76; and (March 1990), pp. 58-62, 67-70.

The cover of the January 1990 issue carried a color photograph of the stone map Arnold unearthed east of Rotan, which an unknown Mexican carried to Waco soon afterward. It was the first time the stone was made public. Hale published a photo of it again in his "A Spidery Mystery: Riddle of Three Strange Big Country Rocks Remains Unsolved," *Abilene Reporter-News,* November 1, 1992, p. 13A. Johnny Terrell, who fell heir to the stone, placed it on exhibit in the museum in Cisco. In July 1997, Jerry Eckhart of Cisco and Duane Hale offered a four-day workshop devoted to the Spider Rock enigma. It is not likely the legend will remain silent long.

32. The author would like to see a scientific archaeological cadre take an interest in the Spider Rock story and properly excavate a number of sites that would yield interesting and revealing information, perhaps even helping solve the mystery of the Spanish miners—and curious mapmakers—of so long ago.

Bibliography

Archival Sources

Callahan County, Texas. Deed Record, vol. V, p. 612, October 7, 1899; vol. 36, p. 373-74, May 20, 1905; vol. 40, pp. 99-101, May 27, 1907; vol. 124, pp. 607-8, August 24, 1927; vol. 144, p. 53, April 2, 1934; vol. 146, p. 239, March 25, 1935; and vol. 171, pp. 174-76, November 10, 1942. County Clerk, Baird.

Hamilton County, Texas. Deed Record, vol. G, p. 304, November 20, 1876; vol. U, p. 117, November 22, 1887; vol. Q, p. 549, October 2, 1886; vol. P, pp. 497-98, November 8, 1884, p. 576, August 9, 1884; vol. 25, p. 546, November 9, 1906; vol. 33, p. 388, November 1, 1906; vol. 52, p. 206, January 28, 1907; vol. 53, p. 543, November 14, 1913; vol. 55, p. 326, November 14, 1913; vol. 58, pp. 295-97, September 10, 1915; vol. 59, p. 268, January 1, 1916; vol. 60, p. 9, November 26, 1915, p. 167, April 27, 1917; and vol. 63, pp. 278-80, November 25, 1916. County Clerk, Hamilton.

Haskell County, Texas. Deed Record, vol. 31, p. 417; vol. 39, p. 501, May 28, 1908; vol. 44, p. 249, October 2, 1908; vol. 68, p. 401, January 24, 1919; Probate Record, no. 152, estate of C. L. Terrell, July 1, 1909. County Clerk, Haskell.

Hawkins, ———, comp. "The Adventures in Texas and Louisiana of Alexander Dupont." Typescript made from Dupont's diary found in Mexico City, in Biographical and Historical file, Texas State Archives, Austin.

Snively, Jacob, to James H. Starr, May 20, 1844, December 20, 1845, December 15, 1846. James Harper Starr Papers. The Center for American History, University of Texas, Austin.

Stonewall County, Texas. Deed Record, vol. 2, p. 591, April 19, 1950; vol. 4, p. 96; vol. 15-B, no. 1931, April 19, 1950; vol. 101, p. 345, November 2, 1949; vol. 109, p. 245, February 1951. County Clerk, Aspermont.

Taylor County, Texas. Deed Record, vols. 73-74, pp. 143-44, November 29, 1911; vol. 71, p. 66, January 21, 1912; vol. 120, pp. 457-60, April 14, 1920; vol. 122, pp. 288-89, November 23, 1920; and vol. 140, p. 445, January 1, 1924. County Clerk, Abilene.

Terrell, Charles E., Papers. Private collection of Charles E. Terrell. Copy in possession of the author. Miguel Anhubta to M. Dillon, March 7, 1897; Dr. C. L. Terrell to Saul Rodriguese, October 19, 1902; R. H. McKee to G. W. Matthews, November 10, 16, and December 3, 1902; Alberta Epllis to Dr. C. L. Terrell, September 6, 1905; John Sembritzki and J. F. Hart to Dr. C. L. Terrell and Dr. W. M. Crume, October 16, 1905; Cabe Terrell to Dr. C. L. Terrell, October 28, 1905; Lester Smith to Dr. C. L. Terrell, November 21, 1905, January 1, February 1, 1906; D. M. Arnold to Cabe Terrell, June 21, 1909; Bud Jones to Cabe Terrell, July 1, 1909; R. R. Davis to Bud Jones, July 26, 1909. Indenture forming Sembritzki Mineral Co., May 20, 1905; Lease of John and Lucretia Sembritzki, May 20 (filed for record November 15, 1905); Minutes of Sembritzki Mineral Co., May 20, 1905; Transfer and Contract of Executive Committee to Dr. John Collier, August 10, 1905; Minutes of Executive Committee, Sembritzki Mineral Co., August 10, 1905; Indenture between Executive Committee of Sembritzki Mineral Co. and Lester Smith, November 20, 1905.

Tom Green County, Texas. Deed Record, vol. 15, p. 207, September 2, 1897; vol. 18, pp. 71-73, August 21, 1899; vol. 31, p. 210, December 7, 1905; vol. 35, pp. 621-22, September 18, 1906; vol. 38, p. 103, January 11, 1907, and p. 424, January 12, 1907; vol. 39, p. 121, November 19, 1906; vol. 52, pp. 21-22, April 21, 1908; vol. 69, p. 533, August 29, 1912; vol. 83, p. 39, April 29, 1914; vol. 95, p. 91, September 23, 1914; vol. 105, p. 535, January 14, 1907 [filed for record November 15, 1922]; vol. 108, p. 187, July 18, 1923; vol. 118, p. 165, November 28, 1925; Marriage Record, vol. C, p. 323, January 14, 1900; and vol. C, p. 401, June 1, 1902. County Clerk, San Angelo.

U.S. Population Census, 1880, Hamilton County, Texas. M. S. Davis, vol. 15, p. 14. Federal Archives and Records Center, Fort Worth, Texas.

U.S. Population Census, 1900, Tom Green County, Texas. David M. Arnold, Record Group 29, vol. 101, p. 2. National Archives, Washington, D.C.

Wood, Carroll, to Eve Ball, April 16, 1958. Copy in possession of the author.

Books

Arrington, Fred. *A History of Dickens County Ranches and Rolling Plains*. Quanah, Texas: Nortex, 1971.

Benavides, Adán, Jr., comp. and ed. *The Béxar Archives (1717-1836): A Name Guide*. Austin: University of Texas Press, and San Antonio: University of Texas Institute of Texas Cultures, 1989.

Bolton, Herbert Eugene, trans. and ed. *Athanase de Mézières and the Louisiana-Texas Frontier, 1768-1780*. 2 vols. Cleveland: Arthur H. Clark Co., 1914.

———, ed. *Spanish Exploration in the Southwest 1542-1706*. 1908. Reprint. New York: Barnes & Noble, 1959.

———. *Texas in the Middle Eighteenth Century*. Berkeley: University of California Press, 1915.

Brinckerhoff, Sidney B., and Pierce A. Chamberlain. *Spanish Military Weapons in Colonial America, 1700-1821*. Harrisburg, Pa.: Stackpole Books, 1972.

Brown, Lloyd A. *The Story of Maps*. New York: Bonanza Books, 1949.

Castañeda, Carlos E. *Our Catholic Heritage in Texas, 1519-1936*. 7 vols. Austin: Von Boeckmann-Jones Co., 1936-58.

Cawyer, Shirley Brittain, and Weldon I. Hudson, comps. *Cemetery Inscriptions, Eastland County, Texas*. Stephenville: N.p., 1976.

Crouch, Carrie J. *A History of Young County, Texas*. Austin: Texas State Historical Association, 1956.

Directory of Abilene, Texas 1907-8. Fort Worth: Fort Worth Directory Co., 1908.

Dobie, J. Frank. *Coronado's Children: Tales of Lost Mines and Buried Treasures of the Southwest*. New York: Grosset & Dunlap, 1930.

Felker, Rex A. *Haskell: Haskell County and Its Pioneers*. Quanah, Texas: Nortex Press, 1975.

Ferguson, Robert G. *Lost Treasure: The Search for Hidden Gold*. New York: Vantage Press, 1957

Friend, Llerena, ed. *M. K. Kellogg's Texas Journal 1872*. Austin: University of Texas Press, 1967.

Gray, Mrs. R. D. *Early Days in Knox County*. New York: Carlton Press, 1963.

Hackett, Charles Wilson, trans. and ed. *Pichardo's Treatise on the Limits of Louisiana and Texas*. 1934. Reprint, vol. II. Freeport, New York: Books for Libraries Press, 1971.

Hammond, George P., ed. *Fray Alonso de Benavides' Revised Memorial of 1634*. Coronado Cuarto Centennial Publications, 1540-1940, vol. IV. Albuquerque: University of New Mexico Press, 1945.

John, Elizabeth A. H. *Storms Brewed in Other Men's Worlds: The Confrontation of Indians, Spanish, and French in the Southwest, 1540-1795*. College Station: Texas A&M University Press, 1975.

Loomis, Noel M., and Abraham P. Nasatir. *Pedro Vial and the Roads to Santa Fe*. Norman: University of Oklahoma Press, 1967.

Morrison, Shelldy, ed. *Alexander Dupont: Adventures in Spanish Texas*. Austin: W. M. Morrison Books, 1985.

Nevin, David. *The Mexican War*. Alexandria, Virginia: Time-Life Books, 1978.

Raymond, Robert. *Out of the Fiery Furnance: The Impact of Metals on the History of Mankind*. University Park and London: Pennsylvania State University Press, 1984.

Rister, Carl Cole. *Land Hunger: David L. Payne and the Oklahoma Boomers*. Norman: University of Oklahoma Press, 1942.

Sagstetter, Beth and Bill. *The Mining Camps Speak: A New Way to Explore the Ghost Towns of the American West*. Denver: BenchMark Publishing of Colorado, 1998.

Turner, Hicks A., ed. *I Remember Callahan: History of Callahan County, Texas*. Baird: Callahan County Historical Commission, 1986.

The United States, Complainant, v. The State of Texas in Equity. 2 vols. Supreme Court of the United States, October Term, 1894, No. 4, Original. Washington, D.C.: Judd & Detweiler, 1894.

Weddle, Robert S. *The San Sabá Mission: Spanish Pivot in Texas*. Austin: University of Texas Press, 1964.

Wilson, Steve. *Oklahoma Treasures and Treasure Tales*. Norman: University of Oklahoma Press, 1976.

Winkler, E. W. *Manuscript Letters and Documents of Early Texians, 1821-1845*. Austin: Steck Co., 1937.

Young, Otis E., Jr. *Western Mining: An Informal Account of Precious-Metals Prospecting, Placering, Lode Mining, and Milling on the American Frontier from Spanish Times to 1893*. Norman: University of Oklahoma Press, 1970.

Articles and Newspapers

"Archaeological," *Callahan County Clarendon* (Belle Plain), November 15, 1879.

"Aztec Mine Near Abilene," *Fort Worth Telegram*, October 27, 1907.

Ball, Eve. "The Treasure of Alamo Canyon." *Treasure World* (July-August 1968).
——. "The Treasure of Alamo Canyon." *True West* (November-December 1973).
Bertillion, L. D. "Lost Lead Mine on the Brazos, King County." In *Legends of Texas*. Publications of the Texas Folklore Society, no. III. 1924. Reprint. Hatboro, Penn.: Folklore Associates, 1964.
Carson, Xanthus. "The $63 Million Inca Loot that Landed in West Texas." *Lost Treasure*, part 1 (December 1976); part 2 (January 1977); part 3 (February 1977).
"Death at Water Valley," *San Angelo Standard*, March 17, 1906.
"Death of G. E. Ward, Sr., A Former Resident," *Alamagordo News*, May 13, 1943.
"Death to Those Who Enter Without Right Was Evidently the Theory on Which the Ancient Spaniards Planned the Works Found by Ward." *Abilene Daily Reporter*, May 13, 1909.
Dobie, J. Frank. "Don Español and the Four Skeletons." *Frontier Times* (Summer 1959).
———. "His Favorite Phantom Pursue." In *A Good Tale and a Bonnie Tune*. Publications of the Texas Folklore Society, no. 32. Dallas: Southern Methodist University Press, 1964.
Eckhart, Jerry M. "Spider Rock Revisited: Update on Elusive Texas Treasure." *Treasure Search* (September-October 1989).
"Escaping Gas Overpowers High School Instructor," *Abilene Reporter*, November 26, 1909.
Ewing, Floyd E., Jr. "Copper Mining in West Texas: Early Interest and Development." *West Texas Historical Association Year Book* 30 (1954).
Grant, A. W. "Lost Mines of Spain Found in Texas Hills," *Fort Worth Telegram*, February 6, 1906.
Grauerholz, Larry. "The Gold at Benjamin Lies South of the Star . . . Maybe!" *Prospector* (August 1969).
Hale, Duane K. "Riddle of the Big Country's Stone Maps Remains Unsolved." *West Texas Historical Association Year Book* 74 (1998).
———. "A Spidery Mystery: Riddle of Three Strange Big Country Rocks Remains Unsolved," *Abilene Reporter-News*, November 1, 1992.
Hale, Duane K., Robert Kyker, and Johnny Terrell. "Mystery of the 3 Spider Rocks." *Treasure*, part 1 (December 1989); part 2 (January 1990); part 3 (February 1990); part 4 (March 1990).
Haskell Free Press, April 25, November 21, 1903; October 29, 1904; January 25, 1907; January 11, July 18, October 10, 1908.
Koethe, Jim. "Brazos Area Waste Land Is Searched for Lost Gold." *Wichita Falls Record News*, October 11, 1956.
———. "Is There Lost Gold Mine in Knox or Baylor County?" *Wichita Falls Record News*, August 23, 1956.
———. "Lost Diamond Mine Object of Intense Treasure Hunt." *Wichita Falls Record News*, December 6, 1956.
———. "Old Prospector Finds Lost Mine." *Wichita Falls Record News*, September 13, 1956.
———. "Outlaw Treasure Supposed to be Buried in Burk Area." *Wichita Falls Record News*, October 25, 1956.
———. "Tales of Lost Treasures in Area Lure Many Men." *Wichita Falls Record News*, September 20, 1956.
———. "Two Lads from Knox City and Haskell Hunt Treasure." *Wichita Falls Record News*, October 4, 1956.
"Mine Hunting." *Northern Standard* (Clarksville, Texas), reprinted from *Houston Telegraph and Texas Register*, May 1, 1844.
"More Relics of the Conquistadores in the Sacramento Mountains," *Alamagordo News*, June 20, 1929.
Otero County News (Alamagordo, New Mexico), April 8, 1915.
"Overcome By Gas in the Old Spanish Mine. G. E. Ward Carried Out Unconscious but Recovers." *Abilene Daily Reporter*, June 12, 1909.
Pate, Lon. "Legendary 'Spider Rock' Treasure Story is Revived in Haskell County." *Wichita Falls Record News*, October 24, 1956.
"Philadelphia Man to Look at Ward Mine." *Abilene Daily Reporter*, November 26, 1909.
"Ruins on the Leona." *Northern Standard* (Clarksville, Texas), October 29, 1845.
Sanders, Marvin H. "Treasure Leads," *Treasure World* (October-November 1972).
Somo, Verne. "Close Quarters with the Supernatural," *Frontier Times* (December-January 1971).
———. "Mexican Bullion on the Flying H Bar Ranch." *True West* (July-August 1966).
Sherrill, R. E. "Lost Copper Mines and Spanish Gold, Haskell County." In *Legends of Texas*. Publications of the Texas Folklore Society, no. III (1924). Reprint. Hatboro, Penn.: Folklore Associates, 1964.
"Silver, Iron and Coal." *Dallas Morning News*, March 2, 1892.
"Silver Mine." *Northern Standard* (Clarksville, Texas), May 1, 1844.
Taylor County News (Abilene, Texas), June 29, 1888, reprinted from *Comanche Chief*.
"That Lost Mexican Mine Again." *Dallas Morning News*, November 4, 1890.
Tolbert, Frank X. "Spaniards Buried on Baugh Ranch." *Dallas Morning News*, January 18 and 29, 1957.

Trammell, Louise. "Does Lake Cover Buried Treasure?" *Cisco Daily News,* September 15, 1929.
"'Victory Is in Sight,' Gurney Ward's Message." *Abilene Semi-Weekly Farm Reporter,* September 6, 1910.
Walker, Claire. "Has Coronado's Treasure Been Found?" *Treasure World,* September 1969.
Wade, Eldon C. "The Terrapin Map and an Old Man's Gold." *Dallas Morning News,* March 12, 1933.
Ward, Gurney E. "It Has Proven a Mammoth Proposition, the Old Spanish Diggins." *Abilene Daily Reporter,* April 14, 1911.
———. "The Old Spanish ILP Mine." *Taylor County News* (Abilene, Texas), January 13, 1908.
Wilson, Steve. "Colonel Snively's Lost Ledge of Gold." *Great Plains Journal* 24-25 (1985-1986).
———. "Colonel Snively's Lost Ledge of Gold." *True Frontier* (September 1968).
———. "Endless Quest for the Spider Rock Treasure." *True Treasure,* part 1 (July-August 1972); *Treasure World,* part 2 (August-September 1972).
———. "Four Decades of Searching Yields Clues, Little Treasure." *Wichita Falls Times Features Magazine,* July 28, 1963.
———. "Inca Treasure Believed Buried in Stonewall County on Brazos." *Wichita Falls Times Features Magazine,* August 18, 1963.
———. "Indians and Treasure Don't Mix." *Frontier Times* (December-January 1974).
———. "Missing Spanish Treasure Near Double Mountain." *True Treasure* (March-April 1972).
———. "Mystery of the Spider Rock Treasure." *True West* (May-June 1964).
———. "In Search of the Lost Ledge of Gold." *Texas Highways* (January 1982).
———. "The Spider Rock Treasure: Bizarre Quest for Lost Spanish Gold." *Great Plains Journal,* part 1, 28-29 (1989-1990); part 2, 30-31 (1991-1992).
———. "Spider Rock—Will O' the Wisp of Treasure Hunters." *True West* (July-August 1965).
———. "Strange Maps to the Spider Rock Treasure." *Argosy* (May 1965).
———. "Two Maps May Hold Key to 'Spider Rock' Gold." *Wichita Falls Times Features Magazine,* October 13, 1963.

Theses and Dissertations

Dent, Willard L. "History of Stonewall County." Master's thesis, East Texas State Teachers College, 1949.
Hale, Duane Kendall. "Evidence of Early Spanish Mining in the Big Country of West Texas." Master's thesis, Abilene Christian College, 1972.
———. "Prospecting and Mining on the Texas Frontier." Ph.D. diss., Oklahoma State University, 1977.
Railsback, G. D. "History of Stonewall County." Master's thesis, Hardin-Simmons University, 1940.
Whitmire, Jerome R. "The History of Stonewall County, Texas." Master's thesis, Texas Technological College, 1936.

Personal Interviews

Brown, Jack. Sunset, Texas, June 1963.
Cauble, Joe. Snyder, Texas, December 1969.
Cleghorn, Naomi Roberts. Waco, Texas, March 13, September 13, 1976.
Cochran, B. J. Aspermont, Texas, October 1960; July 1963.
Duke, C. O. Rotan, Texas, March 10, 1976.
Edwards, Burt. Pauls Valley, Oklahoma, January 16, 1970; November 3, 1976.
Epply, Rhoda Allen. Haskell, Texas, August 1960; December 1969.
Fuqua, Ann Sembritzki. Abilene, Texas, July 1967; March 11, 1976.
Gillentine, Mrs. W. B. Benjamin, Texas, October 29, 1960.
Gore, Jack. Rule, Texas, March 7, 1976.
Henderson, Dock. Rule, Texas, July 1963; October 1964; June 1965; August 1967; December 1969, February 1972, October 28, 1972; October 6-7, 1973; December 13-14, 1975; March 5-6, May 28-30, October 1-3, 1976; April 22-24, 1977; and other occasions over the years.
Johnson, Ed and Mary. Munday, Texas, April 24, 1977.
Johnson, Edwin K. Munday, Texas, October 3, 1976; April 24, 1977.
Kiker, Jess Lee. Rotan, Texas, March 10, 1976.
Leach, Walter W. Rotan, Texas, June 1969.
McBeth, George T. Rotan, Texas, March 10, 1976.
Males, Bill. Rule, Texas, December 14, 1975.
Metcalf, John. Aspermont, Texas, July 1963.

Nelson, Blanche. Munday, Texas, April 24, 1977.
Pumphrey, Mrs. George. Old Glory, Texas, October 29, 1960.
Roberts, Uda. Waco, Texas, March 14, 1976.
Sheppard, Amos. Gatesville, Texas, June 1969.
Smith, John E. Abilene, Texas, October 28, 1972.
Tabor, Pauline Edwards. Pauls Valley, Oklahoma, November 3, 1976.
Terrell, Charles E. Eastland, Texas, May 31, December 28, 1976.
Terrell, Louise. El Paso, Texas. May 11, 1977.
Woods, Joe. Abilene, Texas, March, July 1963; July 1967; June 1969; October 1972.
Worley, Bertha Allen. Haskell, Texas, August 1960.

Personal Correspondence

Armour, Larry. Wolfforth, Texas, March 22, December 16, 17, 1989; February 14, 1990; February 13, 1993; February 26, March 2, March 13, April 3, 2001.
Ball, Eve. Ruidoso, New Mexico, September 28, 1969; February 21, 1974; January 3, 5, 1976.
Cochran, B. J. Aspermont, Texas, April 19, 1961.
Gerli, Dr. E. Michael. Washington, D.C., March 8, 1976.
Hale, Duane. Cisco, Texas, October 29, 1970; January 29, 1971; January 20, October 12, November 8, 1972; February 21, 26, April 30, July 3, September 3, October 4, 1973; April 30, 1974; April 1, 1975; January 24, October 27, 1977; July 28, November 1, 1978; July 23, 24, August 9, 2001.
Henderson, Dock. Rule, Texas, August 7, October 25, 1960; July 28, 1962; June 30, August 18, December 19, 1963; January 26, March 18, April 18, April 26, May 16, August 21, December 17, 1964; January 19, March 14, May 2, July 18, 1965; July 2, 1966; June 21, 1967; January 1, June 8, August 19, 1969; January 1, March 23, April 5, 1970; June 16, July 10, 1973.
Kyker, Robert. Sand Springs, Oklahoma, March 20, 1972; February 3, 1973; February 25, 1993.
McDaniel, Allen J., Jr. Abilene, Texas, February 4, 1995; December 14, 18, 29, 2000; January 3, May 18, 25, 31, June 4, 14, 25, July 6, August 6, 2001.
Sanders, Marvin H. Artesia, New Mexico, November 7, 1972.
Sems, Verne. Redwood Valley, California, June 7, 20, July 8, November 18, 1965; January 21, 26, February 8, 23, March 1, 7, 30, May 18, 25, June 8, July 4, September 29, November 14, 1976; July 27, 1977; June 9, 1978; January 25, February 21, July 15, 1979; June 2, December 29, 1981.
Strout, Dr. Clevy L. Tulsa, Oklahoma, December 13, 1976; January 19, 1977.
Terrell, Charles E. Eastland, Texas, June 18, July 12, August 30, December 30, 1976.
Terrell, Louise. El Paso, Texas, August 10, 24, September 7, October 26, 1976; June 8, 1979.
Speakman, Mary N. Wichita Falls, Texas, August 13, 1977.
Tiede, Vance. Arlington, Virginia, December 1, 15, 1975; February 11, March 14, 24, 1976; July 14, October 17, 26, 1984; August 8, 1985.
Waits, Charles B. Corvallis, Oregon, July 14, 1965; January 1, 1966.

Index